W9-DGC-876

ADMINISTERING WELFARE REFORM

International transformations in welfare governance

Edited by Paul Henman and Menno Fenger

First published in Great Britain in March 2006 by

The Policy Press
University of Bristol
Fourth Floor
Beacon House
Queen's Road
Bristol BS8 1QU
UK

Tel +44 (0)117 331 4054
Fax +44 (0)117 331 4093
e-mail tpp-info@bristol.ac.uk
www.policypress.org.uk

British Library Cataloguing in Publication Data
A catalogue record for this book is available from the British Library.

Library of Congress Cataloging-in-Publication Data
A catalog record for this book has been requested.

ISBN-10 1 86134 652 2 hardcover
ISBN-13 978 1 86134 652 0

Cover design by Qube Design Associates, Bristol
Printed and bound in Great Britain by MPG Books, Bodmin

Contents

List of tables

Preface

Just as major social and economic changes – the effects of market liberalism in the late 19th century, the 1930s' Depression and the two World Wars – precipitated the development and expansion of the welfare state project, the 1970s' oil crisis and the consequent project of economic readjustment has led to an ongoing programme of reforming welfare policy. Since the mid-1980s, activation and workfare policies have featured particularly heavily in the policy transformations that have occurred in advanced welfare states. Such policies have been widely studied both at national and international levels. Comparative social policy has concurrently grown in these last few decades and has stimulated many new insights about the various manifestations of social protection and their ongoing transformations.

Despite this intense research interest in analysing, evaluating and theorising welfare reform, the domain of the implementation and administration of welfare policy has received somewhat less research attention. This, however, is changing. This book represents a fourfold effort: to understand the transformations in welfare administration concomitant to welfare reform; to identify the particular effects of public sector reform in the nature of welfare state provision; to provide some international comparative data on such transformations; and to draw greater attention to the importance of welfare administration in providing a deeper understanding of its role in the nature, practices and effects of the welfare state.

This book draws on our long-standing interests in welfare governance. Paul Henman has been particularly interested in the role of technology in shaping the nature and substance of both welfare administration and welfare policy, whereas Menno Fenger's research focuses on processes of long-term policy change in the field of social policies.

This book has its origin in two themed sessions on 'Welfare reform in international perspective' held at the 'International Sociological Congress 2002' in Brisbane, Australia organised by Paul Henman. Many of the papers presented at this conference examined the issues of welfare administration, which was then, and still remains, an under-examined topic. It was at this conference that we met and together determined the need to provide a concentrated outlet for such innovative work. In addition to some of the papers presented at the conference, new works were commissioned that fitted in the framework we had developed for this book. We are very pleased with the collection assembled in your hands for its breadth and depth. But we are also very aware of the book's limitations. In particular, like many studies of the welfare state the various studies reported in this book involve only Organisation for Economic Co-operation and Development (OECD) countries. The emerging welfare states of Eastern Europe and Asia are not examined; let alone the welfare policies of Africa and the Middle East. Nevertheless, we hope that this collection stimulates a broader and more coordinated programme of study of welfare state administration that both draws upon and contributes to the established comparative studies of welfare state policies.

Paul Henman and Menno Fenger
February 2006

Acknowledgements

As with all intellectual projects, this one has been made possible by the resources of people, time, money and technology. First, we gratefully acknowledge the contributions of the various authors included in this collection, for without them this book would remain a dream. We are most grateful to Angela Sutherland and Anthea Rogers for their editorial assistance. We thank the various staff of The Policy Press – Dawn Rushen, Laura Greaves, Emily Watt and Natasha Ferguson – who have supported this venture. They have provided us with invaluable guidance and a realistic timeframe within which to produce the typescript. Our current and former employers (Macquarie University, Erasmus University Rotterdam, University of Queensland) have also supported the production of this book through conference travel grants, sabbatical leave and, of course, the time to work on this project. The Centre for European Studies, Harvard University, has further facilitated the completion of this book by hosting Menno Fenger as a visiting scholar. Last, we acknowledge the critical importance of advanced information and communication technologies to the fruition of this project. The wonders of e-mail and the World Wide Web enabled the international collaboration processes required to bring about this project. For all these actors, both human and non-human, we are most grateful.

List of abbreviations

AFDC	Aid to Families with Dependent Children Programme (US)
ANAO	Australian National Audit Office
BA	Bundesanstalt für Arbeit (Employment Agency) (Germany)
CPCA	Conférence Permanente des Coordinations Associative (France)
CSO	customer service officer (Australia)
CWI	Centre for Work and Income (the Netherlands)
DAC	Development Assistance Committee (of the OECD)
DWP	Department for Work and Pensions (UK)
EES	European Employment Strategy
EITC	Earned Income Tax Credit (US)
ES	Employment Service (UK)
ESF	European Social Fund
EU	European Union
FDI	foreign direct investment
ICT	information and communication technology
IGO	intergovernmental organisation
ILO	International Labour Organisation
IMF	International Monetary Fund
INGO	international non-governmental organisation
INPS	Istituto Nazionale della Previdenza Sociale (Italy)
LIVEAS	Livelli assistenziali essenziali (Italy)
MNC	multinational corporation
NCVO	National Council of Voluntary Organisations (UK)
NGO	non-governmental organisation
NPM	New Public Management
OECD	Organisation for Economic Co-operation and Development
OMC	Open Method of Coordination (EU)
PA	personal advisor
PRWORA	Personal Responsibility and Work Opportunity Reconciliation Act (US)
QOL	Quality On-Line
RMI	Reddito Minimo di Inserimento (Italy)
RMI	revenu minimum d'insertion (France)

RUI	Reddito di Ultima Istanza (Italy)
TANF	Temporary Assistance for Needy Families (US)
TEP	Territorial Employment Pact (EU)
UK	United Kingdom
UN	United Nations
UNHCR	United Nations High Commission for Refugees
US	United States
VSI	Voluntary Sector Initiative (Canada)
WTO	World Trade Organisation

Notes on contributors

Jo Barnes is a Senior Lecturer in the Department of Societies and Cultures at the University of Waikato, New Zealand. Her research interests include the role of the third sector in welfare, poverty and women and retirement and she is currently developing a study on the role of personal coaching in work–life balance. Her ongoing research focuses on measuring the impact and effect of philanthropic institutions in New Zealand.

Menno Fenger is Assistant Professor in Public Administration at Erasmus University Rotterdam, the Netherlands. His research focuses on processes of long-term policy change, particularly in the field of social policy. He is currently working on a comparative study of welfare reform in Central and Eastern Europe. In 2005 he was a visiting scholar at the Centre for European Studies, Harvard University.

Angela Genova is a freelance Researcher in Sociology at the University of Urbino, Italy. Her main research interests are in welfare policies and modes of governance in comparative perspective. In her PhD studies she addressed public health policies. She is part of a European research network working on welfare policies and urban governance (RTN Urban Europe), in which she is evaluating local welfare service projects.

Joel F. Handler is the Richard C. Maxwell Professor of Law in the Law School at University of California, Los Angeles (UCLA) and Professor in the Policy Studies Department. He has recently published *Social Citizenship and Workfare in the United States and Western Europe: The Paradox of Inclusion* (Cambridge University Press, 2004) and *We the Poor People: Work, Poverty, and Welfare Reform* with Yeheskel Hasenfeld (Yale University Press, 1997).

Paul Henman is Lecturer in Social Policy at the University of Queensland, Australia. His main research interest is in the nexus between social policy, public administration and information technology, where he is an international expert on e-government. He is currently completing a book entitled *E-government: Reconfigurations in Public Administration, Policy and Power.*

Cosmo Howard is an Assistant Professor in the Department of Political Science and School of Public Administration at the University of Victoria, British Columbia, Canada. His research interests include the role of bureaucratic identity in public sector reform, governance challenges for autonomous public agencies, social policy implications of individualisation and the street-level implementation of welfare reform. He is co-author of *Social Policy, Public Policy: From Problem to Practice* (Allen and Unwin, 2001).

Yuri Kazepov is Professor of Urban Sociology and Comparative Welfare Systems at the University of Urbino, Italy. His main research interest is the territorial reorganisation of social policies. He has recently been coordinating national and international projects on poverty, social exclusion and social policies funded both by the Italian Ministry for Higher Education and by the European Union. His last book is *Cities of Europe: Changing Contexts, Local Arrangements and the Challenge to Urban Cohesion* edited for Blackwell (2004).

Gaby Ramia is Senior Lecturer in International Business at Monash University, Australia. His research has spanned comparative and international aspects of the welfare and social protection roles of civil society, industrial relations/labour markets and governments. More specifically he has current interests in: global governance, social policy and international non-governmental organisation management strategy; international education markets and the protection of cross-border students; and social security in China. He is the author (with Terry Carney) of *From Rights to Management: Contract, New Public Management and Employment Services* (Kluwer, 2002).

Carla Valadas is a Lecturer in the Faculty of Humanities at the University of Oporto, Portugal. She is preparing her PhD in Sociology at the University of Coimbra. Her thesis studies the effects of European social policy on Portuguese unemployment policies. She has been participating in research projects at the Centre for Social Studies, School of Economics, University of Coimbra. Her research interests lie in issues of social policies, globalisation and unemployment.

Deena White is a sociologist and Professor of Social Policy at the University of Montreal, Canada. Her ongoing research focuses on shifting state–civil society relations in liberal welfare states, including cross-sectoral policies, government–third sector partnerships and the socio-political role of the third sector. She is currently working with colleagues on a book entitled *The Policies and Politics of the Social Investment State.*

Sharon Wright is Lecturer in Social Policy at the University of Stirling, UK. Her research interests are in the processes of making and implementing social policy at street level, unemployment, welfare-to-work, social security and poverty. Her most substantial research has been an ethnographic case study of the implementation of unemployment policy in one Jobcentre office. She has also contributed to cross-national work on the role of employment services and active labour market policies.

ONE

Introduction: administering welfare reform

Menno Fenger and Paul Henman

After a century of relatively unchallenged growth of the welfare state, the last decade of the 20th century marked the start of the era of welfare reform. The Reagan and Thatcher administrations appeared to be among welfare reform's frontrunners in the 1980s, but throughout the remaining years of the 20th and the start of the 21st century, welfare reform has been a prominent item on the agenda of almost every government in the modern democratic capitalist world. Among the developments that are said to have triggered welfare reform processes are economic globalisation, the development of new (information and communication) technologies, changing household structures, population ageing and the position of women (see Taylor-Gooby, 2005). There seems to be a wide variation in the directions of welfare reform processes: decreasing the level of benefits; adjusting eligibility rules for programmes; reforming or ending programmes; changing the institutional setting of programmes; and increasing efforts to activate the unemployed are all examples of various governments' efforts to cut back on welfare expenditures that can be united under the 'welfare reform' label.

Causes and consequences of welfare reform and the policy details of welfare reforms have been dealt with quite extensively by a large amount of scholars from all over the world, especially within European and North American contexts (see, for instance, Esping-Andersen, 1996; Pierson, 2001a; Taylor-Gooby, 2005). However, the *practical* side of welfare reform – namely transformations in the administration of welfare – seems to have received somewhat less attention. This book provides such a much-needed overview through comparative studies of the way welfare reform has been implemented in various countries and the participants that have been involved. The book focuses on the under-studied areas of the changing institutional participants of welfare administration and practices of administering and managing welfare delivery. It is these aspects of welfare reform that complement studies of welfare reform policies, causes and consequences, that is increasingly being recognised as important to understanding the full nature and effects of welfare reform. The goal of this book is to give greater prominence to the administration of welfare reform as a way in which to understand and assess the range of effects of welfare reform on welfare claimants, staff and agencies. In doing so, we advocate a more extensive understanding of policy than is often the focus of analysis, one that sees policy as practice.

By focusing on the impact of welfare reform on welfare administration, this book stresses the interconnectedness of two streams of welfare state research: the public administration discipline and the sociologically and economically inspired stream of welfare state research. Traditionally, these streams of research go hand in hand. In the early years of its development, the public administration discipline greatly benefited from the experience of implementing and managing the great social programmes like Roosevelt's New Deal, and the large-scale social programmes that started to develop in most western countries after World War II. But the cross-fertilisation also works the other way round; recent welfare reforms to some extent are inspired by New Public Management (NPM) ideas that have emerged in the academic discipline of public administration in the late 1980s and early 1990s (compare: Osborne and Gaebler, 1992; Pollitt, 1993). More recently, the concept of 'governance' that is highly popular in public administration also has found its way into welfare state practice and theory. Both the governance perspective and the NPM perspective focus on the practical, administrative side of policy processes, therefore offering a highly relevant perspective on the administration of welfare reform. This introductory chapter starts with a brief overview of the 'state of the art' in both welfare state research (section two) and public administration (section three). The remaining chapters of this book build upon these fundamentals. Section four introduces the theoretical framework. Section five outlines the structure of this book.

Analysing welfare reform: the state of the art

This book focuses on the practical side of welfare reform. It studies the political and policy *processes* through which welfare reforms are implemented, the transformations in the roles of *participants* in welfare governance, and the changing administrative *practices* in welfare agencies. However, we cannot bypass the extensive literature on the background of welfare reforms that has been published during the last few years. Therefore, this section provides a brief overview of the developments that are generally regarded as causes for welfare reform, and of the various types of welfare reform that might be distinguished.

Background to welfare reform

There is an extensive academic debate on the factors that might or might not have contributed to welfare reform processes in western countries. For instance, Pierson (2001a) and Schwartz (2001) argue that the impact of globalisation on national welfare states has been highly overestimated. Instead of taking a position in this debate, we follow the approach of Taylor-Gooby (2005, p 20), who identified a set of developments that possibly triggered welfare reform based on a broad literature review. Without claiming to be complete, we distinguish four groups of developments: demographic changes, globalisation, labour market changes and political and social changes.

Concerning *demography*, there are three developments that increase the demand for social benefits. First, in all western countries the proportion of older people in the population has increased significantly. For instance, the proportion of people aged 65 and above in the total population has increased from 11.4% in 1975 to 14.7% in 2000 in Europe, from 10.5% to 12.3% in the US in the same period, and from 7.9% to 17.2% in Japan (United Nations Population Division, 2002). Main causes for the ageing of the population are dropping fertility rates combined with increasing life expectancy. Population ageing leads to increasing demands for pensions, health services and social care services. Second, the traditional family is no longer the only possible household structure in most western countries. The number of single households and single parents has grown, thus increasing the number of independent people that may require social benefits. Third, since the 1960s there has been a greatly increased number of women in the labour market. In most countries, this stimulated reforms promoting gender equality not only in conditions of employment and pay, but also in social security programmes.

Globalisation is usually considered as a second important cause of welfare reform. It has at least two effects on the welfare state. First, the global integration of financial markets has enhanced international speculation. As a consequence, national governments are required to demonstrate financial probity, leading to policy convergence towards low deficits and monetarism (Pierson, 2001a, p 80; Taylor-Gooby, 2005, p 107). Second, the development of transnational and global corporations has led to the international transfer of labour-intensive production processes to the newly industrialised countries. Workers' wages in those countries are much lower, primarily because of much lower life standards, but also because of the absence of extensive social security programmes. As Pierson (2001a, p 81) states: 'there is a widespread sentiment that this new global environment threatens a "race to the bottom", or at least convergence on the much more modest level of social provision characteristics of "liberal" welfare states like the United States or the United Kingdom'. Moreover, the globalisation of the production process also undermines national governments' tax revenues as not only labour but also financial capital becomes footloose in the era of globalisation.

Labour market changes form a third broad category of factors affecting the welfare state. First, technological developments and de-industrialisation decreased the availability of jobs, especially low-skilled manual work in the manufacturing sector. This has led to high unemployment rates especially for vulnerable groups like poorly educated people. Second, in almost every western country working life has shortened. People enter the labour market in a later stage of their life, and leave it well before they reach the age of 65, whether voluntarily or involuntarily. Combined with ageing, this implies that fewer people need to earn the funds necessary to guarantee the social protection of more people. Finally, 'atypical' jobs, such as temporary jobs and part-time jobs, are becoming a common phenomenon in almost all industrialised countries:

> These jobs are usually relatively insecure, low paid, more weakly protected by employment rights, and are disproportionately occupied by women and migrant workers. The outcome is not only a cutback in protection for these groups from employment related benefits, but also a decline in revenues in social insurance systems. (Taylor-Gooby, 2005, p 107)

Political and social factors are the fourth group of factors underlying welfare reform. This label unites a diverse group of changing party politics and social attitudes, often associated with neo-liberalism and neo-conservatism, that might trigger welfare reform. The first element concerns changing attitudes towards the welfare state. Developed as a solution for social problems, increasingly the *welfare state* is considered as a *cause of social problems* as well. The welfare state is said to damage work incentives, undermine family ethics and pre-empt skilled labour. This changing attitude also reflects on partisan politics. As Kitschelt (2001, p 265) argues, since the 1980s it has become harder to assemble political coalitions that support further expansion of the welfare state, whereas on a number of occasions parties were elected into office that announced cutbacks in social policies ahead of elections. Whereas welfare retrenchment has been on the menu of most right and centre-right parties since the 1980s, since the mid-1990s it seems to be an item on the political agenda of most social-democratic parties, especially in Europe, as well. Third, Rosanvallon (2000) highlights how '*solidarity*', a basic principle of welfare states, is being eroded. He argues that the traditional 'insurance' model of social policy depends on ignorance concerning risk factors leading to conditions that require aid. Given the increasing knowledge of risk factors for, say, disease (including genetic factors), those who lack such factors begin to wonder why they should contribute to a scheme whose benefits will almost surely go disproportionately to some sub-group whose members can be identified in advance. Finally, the emergence and increasing impact of *multinational organisations* is considered as an important factor that might induce processes of welfare reform. The most obvious illustration of this is the growing importance of the European Union (EU) in fields beyond the traditional economic domain (see Chapter Ten of this book), but in second- and third-world countries also the World Bank and the International Monetary Fund (IMF) play an important role in welfare reform processes. Moreover, in Chapter Nine of this book, Ramia points our attention to the growing importance of international non-governmental organisations (INGOs) in welfare policy.

Although this overview is not complete, it does cover most of the dominant arguments in the discussion on causes for welfare reform. As the concept of 'welfare reform' is a key concept in this book, the next step in this chapter is to identify the various forms welfare reform might take.

Types of welfare reform

The previous section illustrated the wide variety of developments that affect modern welfare states and create pressures to reform these welfare states. In welfare state research, there seems to be somewhat more consensus on the shapes these reforms might take. Pierson (2001b) and Taylor-Gooby (2005) distinguish three types of reform: re-commodification, cost containment and recalibration. Following Cox (1998), we would like to add 'administrative reforms' to this typology.

De-commodification 'occurs when a service is rendered as a matter of right, and when a person can maintain a livelihood without reliance on the market' (Esping-Andersen, 1990, pp 21-2). According to Pierson (2001b, p 422), re-commodification 'essentially involves the effort to reverse that process – to restrict the alternatives to participation in the labour market, either by tightening eligibility or cutting benefits'. The (re)introduction of work incentives – for instance in the highly popular workfare programmes (see Lødemel and Trickey, 2000) – are a clear example of the importance of re-commodification in welfare reform.

Cost containment is a second reform strategy. Although successful re-commodification strategies decrease spending on social programmes as well, the strategy of cost containment refers to other means to control the costs of social policies. The label of 'cost containment' unites a wide variety of strategies including tightening of eligibility rules and reduction of benefit levels (Pierson, 2001b, pp 423-4, 434-5).

Recalibration refers to reforms 'which seek to make contemporary welfare states more consistent with contemporary goals and demands for social provision' (Pierson, 2001b, p 425). There are two different types of recalibration: rationalisation and updating. Rationalisation involves the reform of programmes to better achieve its targets, for instance by correcting elements that are obviously dysfunctional to, or incompatible with, the targets of the programme. Updating involves 'efforts to adapt to changing societal demands and norms' (Pierson, 2001b, p 425). For instance, social programmes have been adjusted now that the household model of a single male breadwinner is losing its dominance and gender equity has greatly increased in importance.

Although often overlooked in discussions of welfare reform, administrative reform is the final welfare reform strategy. It refers to reforms in the implementation and management structure of social programmes, without necessarily adjusting the contents of the programmes. This concept covers shifts like decentralisation, privatisation and restructuring administrative responsibilities.

Pierson argues that the reform strategies a country chooses depends on its welfare state type. 'The three worlds of welfare capitalism differ in critical respects, which generate quite different political dynamics of welfare restructuring' (Pierson, 2001b, pp 454-5). In the liberal welfare regimes, re-commodification and cost containment are the dominant strategies. In social democratic regimes, cost containment and rationalisation are the common strategies to cope with challenges. In conservative regimes, cost containment and updating are the dominant strategies (Pierson, 2001b, pp 454-5). Because Pierson did not consider administrative reform as an alternative strategy, his analysis fails to take into account the role of administrative reform in the welfare regimes. Differences between welfare regimes in their use of administrative reforms is not yet sufficiently researched nor understood.

Public administration: the state of the art

The administration of welfare reform is a topic that is situated on the crossroads of welfare state theory and the public administration discipline. In the previous section we very briefly outlined the state of the art in welfare state analysis. In this section we focus on recent developments in the science of public administration that are relevant for creating a framework to analyse the administration of welfare reform. In our perspective, at least three issues need to be taken into account: the evolution of the so-called NPM agenda; the more recent popularity of the concept of 'governance'; and the role of new information and communication technologies (ICTs) in the public sector.

New Public Management

Developed in the late 1980s, NPM has evolved into a highly popular label for a wide variety of reforms in the public sector that have two common features: 'lessening or removing differences between the public and the private sector and shifting the emphasis from process accountability towards a greater element of accountability in terms of results' (Hood, 1995, p 94). In greater detail, Pollitt (2003, pp 27-8) identifies the following eight key elements of NPM:

- a shift in the focus of management systems from inputs and processes towards outputs and outcomes;
- a shift towards measurement and quantification, especially through the development of performance indicators and benchmark systems;
- a preference for more specialised, 'lean', 'flat' and autonomous organisational structures;
- a substitution of formal, hierarchical relationships between or within organisations by contracts or contract-like relationships;
- a much wider deployment of markets or market-type mechanisms for the delivery of public services;
- an emphasis on service quality and a consumer orientation;
- a broadening and blurring of the frontiers between the public sector, the market sector and the so-called third or non-profit sector; and
- a shift in value priorities away from universalism, equity, security and resilience towards efficiency and individualism.

These elements of NPM have been applied in a wide variety of policy domains throughout the world, including the field of welfare policy that takes a central place in this book.[1]

Governance

'Whatever happened to public administration? Governance, governance everywhere', asks Frederickson (2005: forthcoming) rhetorically. Indeed, governance seems to have become a dominant theme in public administration since the late 1990s.[2] The general argument in the governance literature is that a wide variety of developments has undermined the capacity of governments to control events within the nation state. Trends such as the flow of power away from traditional government institutions upwards to transnational bodies and downwards to regions and sub-regions, the rise of global financial markets, the increasing importance of networks and social partnerships, greater access to information, and growing social complexity usually are held accountable for this. As a consequence, the state 'can no longer assume a monopoly of expertise or of the resources to govern, but must rely on a plurality of interdependent institutions and actors drawn from within and beyond government' (Newman, 2001, pp 11-12). The growth of governance is also seen as a response to both bureaucratic and market failure as models for the management and delivery of state welfare services. Van Kersbergen and van Waarden (2004) have identified numerous shifts that they connect to the concept of 'governance', including changes in the forms and mechanism of governance, in the location of governance, in governing capabilities and in styles of governance. The previous discussion illustrates the fuzziness that is connected with the governance concept. Frederickson (2005, p 1) therefore concludes that in some cases governance is 'substantively the same as already established perspectives in public administration, although in a different language'. Therefore, he proposes to reserve the governance concept in public administration for three primary forms of governance:

(1) vertical and horizontal interjurisdictional and interorganisational cooperation;
(2) the extension of the state or jurisdiction by contracts or grants to third parties, including sub-governments; and
(3) forms of public non-jurisdictional or non-governmental policy making and implementation (Frederickson, 2005, p 16).

The chapters in this book are greatly influenced by the focus and observations of both the governance and the NPM perspectives. By stressing the importance of transformations in state administration, these perspectives have highlighted the lack of attention given to these transformations as part of welfare reform.

Information and communication technologies

Due to the centrality of ICTs in the operation and delivery of welfare, it is no longer possible to administer welfare without it. Accordingly, a book on administering welfare reform is not complete without a consideration of these technologies.

Although electronic digital computers have been in widespread existence in government bureaucracies since the 1970s, if not earlier, the role of such technology in public administration in general, and welfare in particular, has only received sustained academic examination since the 1990s. The rapid deployment of the Internet (and other new networked ICTs) and its public promotion as a world-transforming technology, has generated a heightened interest in how such technologies can shape the nature, form and delivery of government services. Dovetailing nicely with the governance focus on partnerships and networks, 'e-government' is being heralded as a way in which to build seamless, customer-focused government services by breaking down the silos of government. The new technologies are said to enable more individualised and customised policy and service delivery, to make government accessible 24 hours a day, all year round, and to enhance participatory democracy.[3]

The deployment of the Internet for welfare services has grown rapidly. Initially, the Internet involved passive web usage, such as posting government information, brochures and forms on single-agency websites and inter-agency web portals. Increasingly, web usage has become interactive, through such tools as search engines, online applications, questions and feedback forms. Although still embryonic, the Internet (and other networked information technologies) are supporting greater networking between government agencies and other government, private and voluntary sector agencies to enhance government outcomes by 'joining up' fragmented and piecemeal government. Alongside these developments are experiments to enhance participatory democracy through online public participation in public consultations, policy discussions and electronic voting.

Although the Internet has received much of the attention, other ICTs that are now a growing part of the operation of welfare include electronic data networks, digital telephony, electronic kiosks, call centres, smart cards, expert systems/decision support systems, geographical information systems, computer modelling and data matching.

Against the (prospective) advantages of these new technologies must be weighed the negatives and difficulties. Data protection, privacy and data fraud are growing issues, particularly in an environment of inter-agency cooperation (Bellamy et al, 2005). Increased levels of surveillance and compliance checking of both welfare subjects and welfare staff are occurring as a result of such technology. Computerisation has also reduced the discretion of frontline workers and provided the means for the intensive control of welfare works and their clients (Bovens and Zouridis, 2002).

While ICTs are generally understood as an element of public administration, there is some evidence that its use has some impact on the shape and nature of welfare policy (Henman, 1999). In particular, ICTs are providing the means by which to think about and implement increasingly targeted welfare policies (Henman, 2004), and the capacity to link data between agencies is underpinning a widening use of conditionality.

How these technologies interplay with administrative and policy processes in the reform of welfare remains a key area for study.

Conceptual framework

This book is greatly indebted to the recent governance literature for giving prominence to the significant and ongoing transformations in government administration and service delivery. This literature has highlighted the shifting and blurring boundaries between the public, private and non-profit sectors resulting from the use of contracting, outsourcing and partnerships. In doing so it has given attention to the transformation and creation of new participants in government administration, and the changing state–citizen relationship. The governance literature and its NPM forerunner have also heightened an examination of new managerial techniques, including performance indicators, customer charters and framework agreements. This literature thus defines the substantive topics and the locus and focus of analysis of this book.

Governance defines the substance, but not the theoretical framework, for the book. In examining the administration of welfare reform, the book explicitly links welfare administration and governance with welfare policy. In doing so, this book seeks to augment the focus of governance literature on administration with a consideration of the substantive policy it implements. Indeed, our theoretical framework starts from policy, rather than administration or governance per se. In particular, we advance a more expansive understanding of policy than what is usually considered in examining welfare, one that embraces policy as practice. In so doing, we understand the administration and governance of policy as an element in the formation and production of policy. Accordingly, to analyse and understand the full effects of welfare reform, be it on welfare agencies, staff, claimants or the citizenry, requires an analysis and understanding not only of substantive policy, but of its very production in administration. It is ultimately to advance our knowledge of the effects of welfare reform, rather than an interest in welfare administration in and of itself, that we offer this book.

Outline of the book

In the following chapter, Paul Henman develops this conceptual framework by arguing for the use of the Foucault-inspired governmentality analytic as the means by which to draw together a critical analysis of substantive policy and policy rhetoric on the one hand, with policy administration and governance on the other. He argues that such a framework has several advantages over the governance perspective, particularly in its post-structuralist sensitivity to the formation of subjects and spaces, and its focus on regimes and practices of power.

The remainder of this book is structured in three parts: the participants, the practices and the processes of welfare reform. *Part One: Participants: reforming the agents of welfare delivery* – examines the way in which welfare reform is redefining the identities and nature of the participants of welfare. New agencies, new types of welfare workers and new coalitions for the delivery of welfare are brought into being as a result of welfare reform. In Chapter Three, Deena White gives an example of this in her discussion of state–third sector partnership frameworks in Britain, Canada, Québec and France. She argues that these very partnerships defined a unity and coherence of the third sector, and in doing so, created it as an actor in welfare reform. Apart from new participants, welfare reform involves the transformation of participants already within the welfare nexus. For example, workfare attempts to reconfigure welfare subjects from 'passive' to 'active' agents. In the same way, Jo Barnes (Chapter Five) examines how the enrolment of voluntary social service agencies by government in welfare delivery in the UK, the US and New Zealand has transformed those organisations from being based on voluntary work to more professionally and managerially organised. In doing so, their rationality of service provision shifts from those in need to the deserving poor. Welfare reform has also involved the reconfiguration of the relationships between participants. In Chapter Four, Menno Fenger examines the governance shifts between state, market and third sector in the delivery of employment services in the UK, Sweden, Germany and the Netherlands.

The focus of the three chapters in *Part Two: Practices: the welfare governance of street-level practices* is on the street-level operation of workfare. In these chapters, which each examine the experience in a single country, the focus is on the production of workfare at the local level and its implications for welfare workers and welfare recipients. Joel Handler (Chapter Six) summarises the varied experiences of workfare implementation in the US, Cosmo Howard (Chapter Seven) examines the Australian experience and Sharon Wright (Chapter Eight) presents a study of British workfare. The work is remarkable in the similarities of their observations, such as the management by welfare workers of tensions between assessing and ensuring client eligibility while supporting and maintaining job-search activities, the limited time and resources, which meant that the individualised services promised by policy was not feasible, and, in contrast to the policy intention, the 'creaming' of quality clients for jobs while neglecting hard-to-place clients as a result of the incentives and pressures constructed by performance indicators. For welfare clients, the chapters observe the greater application of sanctions for non-compliance on those already most disadvantaged (for example, those who are illiterate, have a mental illness, are suffering from domestic violence, or who lack childcare, thereby exacerbating their social deprivation, rather than working to enhance outcomes. They note that, contrary to the rhetoric of customer choice and contract, welfare clients had little choice and power, and were subject to considerable coercion. Jobs into which welfare clients moved tended to be low-paid and temporary with little chance for career advancement, contradicting the 'stepping-stone' thesis. Furthermore, clients in these jobs tended to remain in poverty. However, it is important to note the more limited target population of workfare in the US – unwed poor mothers. Howard (Chapter Seven) makes the interesting point that the transformations under workfare have not always been in the one direction, with many shifts in the locus of power and the key focus of welfare administration.

Part Three: Processes: the changing spaces of welfare governance examines the spatial shifts of welfare governance under welfare reform. Such spatial shifts are now recognised as a key element of the new governance. From an analytical and operational focus on the nation state, welfare policy and administration is increasingly caught within processes that are at the same time more internationalised, regionalised and localised. Taking a global scope, Gaby Ramia (Chapter Nine) examines the growing importance of international non-governmental organisations (INGOs) in global social policy, particularly as it relates to emergency relief and social development. He notes how the United Nations (UN) and government agencies are increasingly using INGOs as the mechanism for delivery of these services. This has occurred partly from a consolidation of the sector and its greater use of managerial, rather than traditional voluntary, forms of governance. The seemingly paradoxical international policy on localisation is discussed in Chapter Ten by Carla Valadas in her examination of European social policy on unemployment and the development of Territorial Employment Pacts. The impact of increasingly localised welfare governance is discussed by Yuri Kazepov and Angela Genova (Chapter Eleven). From their analysis of the Italian experience, they note that localised welfare governance has tended to reinforce regional inequalities, rather than ameliorate them.

The book concludes with a discussion on the lessons learnt from the various studies. Drawing on the earlier chapter by Paul Henman (Chapter Two), it uses these insights to progress a governmentality analysis of welfare reform. Some areas for future research are also outlined.

Notes

[1] Key accounts of NPM include: Osborne and Gaebler (1992), Pollitt (1993), Lane (2000), Pollitt and Bouckaert (2004). Useful analyses of NPM and welfare include: Taylor-Gooby and Lawson (1993), Clarke et al (1994, 2000), Bartlett et al (1998).

[2] For an introduction to the governance literature, see Kooiman (1993), Rhodes (1997), Minogue et al (1998), Newman (2001), Bovaird and Löffler (2003). For discussions on governance and welfare, see Butcher (1995), Geddes and Benington (2001), Glendinning et al (2002).

[3] For an introduction to ICTs in government and e-government, see Bellamy and Taylor (1998), Snellen and van de Donk (1998), Fountain (2001), Pavlichev and Garson (2004). For recent discussions on ICTs and welfare, see Henman and Adler (2001, 2003), Adler and Henman (2005).

References

Adler, M. and Henman, P. (2005) 'Computerising the welfare state: an international comparison of computerisation in social security', *Information, Communication and Society*, vol 8, no 3, pp 315-42.

Bartlett, W., Roberts, J. and Le Grand, J. (eds) (1998) *A revolution in social policy: Quasi-market reforms in the 1990s*, Bristol: The Policy Press.

Bellamy, C. and Taylor, J.A. (1998) *Governing in the information age*, Buckingham: Open University Press.

Bellamy, C., 6, P. and Raab, C. (2005) 'Joined-up government and privacy in the United Kingdom: managing tensions between data protection and social policy: Parts I & II', *Public Administration*, vol 83, no 1, pp 111-33; vol 83, no 3, pp 383-415.

Bovaird, T. and Löffler, E. (eds) (2003) *Public management and governance*, London: Routledge.

Bovens, M. and Zouridis, S. (2002) 'From street-level to system-level bureaucracies: how information and communication technology is transforming administrative discretion and constitutional control', *Public Administration Review*, vol 62, no 2, pp 174-84.

Butcher, T. (1995) *Delivering welfare: The governance of the social services in the 1990s*, Buckingham: Open University Press.

Clarke, J., Cochrane, A. and McLaughlin, E. (eds) (1994) *Managing social policy*, London: Sage Publications.

Clarke, J., Gewirtz, S. and McLaughlin, E. (eds) (2000) *New managerialism, new welfare?*, London: Sage Publications.

Cox, R.H. (1998) 'The consequences of welfare reform: how conceptions of social rights are changing', *Journal of Social Policy*, vol 27, no 1, pp 1-16.

Esping-Andersen, G. (1990) *The three worlds of welfare capitalism*, Cambridge: Polity Press.

Esping-Andersen, G. (1996) *Welfare states in transition: Social security in the new global economy*, London, Sage Publications.

Fountain, J. (2001) *Building the virtual state*, Washington, DC: Brookings Institution Press.

Frederickson, H.G. (2005) 'Whatever happened to public administration? Governance, governance everywhere', in E. Ferlie, L. Lynn Jr and C. Pollitt (eds) *The Oxford handbook of public management*, Oxford: Oxford University Press pp 282-302.

Geddes, M. and Benington, J. (ed) (2001) *Local partnerships and social exclusion in the European Union: New forms of local social governance?*, London: Routledge.

Glendinning, C., Powell, M. and Rummery, K. (ed) (2002) *Partnerships, New Labour and the governance of welfare*, Bristol: The Policy Press.

Henman, P. (1999) 'The bane and benefits of computers in Australia's Department of Social Security', *International Journal of Sociology and Social Policy*, vol 19, no 1-2, pp 101-29.

Henman, P. (2004) 'Targeted!: population segmentation, electronic surveillance and governing the unemployed in Australia', *International Sociology*, vol 19, no 2, pp 173-91.

Henman, P. and Adler, M. (2001) 'Information technology and transformations in social security policy and administration: a review', *International Social Security Review*, vol 54, no 4, pp 23-47.

Henman, P. and Adler, M. (2003) 'Information technology and the governance of social security', *Critical Social Policy*, vol 23, no 2, pp 139-64.

Hood, C. (1995) 'The "New Public Management" in the 1980s: variations on a theme', *Accounting, Organisation and Society*, vol 20, no 2-3, pp 93-109.

Kitschelt, H. (2001) 'Partisan competition and welfare state retrenchment: when do politicians choose unpopular policies?', in P. Pierson (ed) *The new politics of the welfare state*, Oxford: Oxford University Press, pp 265-302.

Kooiman, J. (ed) (1993) *Modern governance: New government–society interactions*, London: Sage Publications.

Lane, J.E. (2000) *New Public Management*, London: Routledge.

Lødemel, I. and Trickey, H. (2000) 'A new contract for social assistance', in I. Lødemel and H. Trickey (eds) *'An offer you can't refuse': Workfare in international perspective*, Bristol: The Policy Press, pp 1-39.

Minogue, M., Polidano, C. and Hulme, D. (eds) (1998) *Beyond the New Public Management: Changing ideas and practices of governance*, Cheltenham: Edward Elgar.

Newman, J. (2001) *Modernising governance: New Labour, policy and society*, London: Sage Publications.

Osborne, A. and Gaebler, T. (1992) *Reinventing government: How the entrepreneurial spirit is transforming the public sector*, Reading, MA: Addison-Wesley.

Pavlichev, A. and Garson, G.D. (eds) (2004) *Digital government: Principles and best practices*, Hershey: Idea.

Pierson, P. (2001a) 'Post-industrial pressures on the mature welfare states', in P. Pierson (ed) *The new politics of the welfare state*, Oxford: Oxford University Press, pp 80-104.

Pierson, P. (2001b) 'Coping with permanent austerity: welfare state restructuring in affluent democracies', in P. Pierson (ed) *The new politics of the welfare state*, Oxford: Oxford University Press, pp 410-56.

Pollitt, C. (1993) *Managerialism and the public services: The Anglo-American experience*, Oxford: Blackwell.

Pollitt, C. (2003) *The essential public manager*, Maidenhead: Open University Press.

Pollitt, C. and Bouckaert, G. (2004) *Public management reform: A comparative analysis* (2nd edn), Oxford: Oxford University Press.

Rhodes, R.A.W. (1997) *Understanding governance*, Buckingham: Open University Press.

Rosanvallon, P. (2000) *The new social question: Rethinking the welfare state*, Princeton, NJ: Princeton University Press.

Schwartz, P. (2001) 'Round up the usual suspect! Globalization, domestic politics, and welfare state change', in P. Pierson (ed) *The new politics of the welfare state*, Oxford: Oxford University Press, pp 17-44.

Snellen, I.Th.M. and van de Donk, W.B.J.J. (eds) (1998) *Public administration in an information age*, Amsterdam: IOS Press.

Taylor-Gooby, P. (2005) *Welfare reform and the management of societal change, Final Report*, Brussels: DG Research, European Commission.

Taylor-Gooby, P. and Lawson, R. (eds) (1993) *Markets and managers: New issues in the delivery of welfare*, Buckingham: Open University Press.

United Nations Population Division (2002) *World population ageing 1950-2050*, Washington, DC: United Nations.

van Kersbergen, K. and van Waarden, F. (2004) 'Governance as a bridge between disciplines: cross-disciplinary inspiration regarding shifts in governance and problems of governability, accountability and legitimacy', *European Journal of Political Research*, vol 43, pp 143-71.

TWO

Welfare reform as governance reform: the prospects of a governmentality perspective

Paul Henman

How might we think about the nature of welfare reform and its administration? This chapter, and this book more generally, argue that an understanding of welfare reform cannot be achieved without reference to its administration. Welfare administration is the very locus in which the operation and effect of policy is defined and governmental power relations flowing through welfare agencies, staff and claimants constituted. This chapter begins with this perspective, by arguing that welfare reform is governance reform. Such a perspective requires a coherent analytical framework to advance our critical understanding of this topic. To this end, this chapter advocates the Foucauldian governmentality analytic, which is summarised in section three. How the governmentality analytic can be applied to the domain of welfare reform is then discussed and demonstrated.

Welfare reform as governance reform

On the surface, an examination of the administration of welfare reform focuses on the implementation and the ongoing administration of a predefined policy. Such a view reflects the conventional account of public policy-making processes. Policy is made and defined by government – be it the executive or Parliament – and introduced and made real by public servants in government departments (or their outsourced delegates). While the classical account of policy as a decision-making process has now been broadened into studies of policy cycles (Bridgman and Davis, 2004, ch 3), policy networks (Marsh and Smith, 2000) and policy advocacy coalitions (Sabatier and Jenkins-Smith, 1993), the central imaginary of most policy studies is a formal policy determined by government.

This delineation between policy making and policy implementation is also reinforced by the disciplinary foci of 'public policy' and 'social policy', on the one hand, and 'public administration' and 'social administration', on the other. Saying both precedes and commands doing.

This conceptualisation of the distinction between a formal policy decision and its implementation is reflected in the policy studies literature, when it defines 'policy' in terms of government decisions. For example, Bridgman and Davis discuss policy as 'authoritative choice', as 'hypothesis' and as 'objective' (2004, pp 4-6). However, the policy studies literature also has a more encompassing understanding of policy. For example, Levin (1997, pp 15-18) examines policy as: a stated intention; a current or past practice; an organisational practice; and an indicator of the formal or claimed status of a past, present or proposed course of action. Such an articulation of policy displaces the priority given to the discursive (and rational intent in the) construction of policy, to recognise that policy is also constructed in actions and practice. Furthermore, Levin's account decentres 'policy' by recognising both the role of rational decision making by the powerful, but also the activities of subservient bureaucrats and other in co-producing and, therefore, co-constituting policy.

This account of policy, which is informed by post-structuralist thought, draws attention beyond political discourses (the spin, the formal statements and stated objectives) to the way in which policy is practised. In doing so, it opens a window onto domains often hidden from policy analysis, such as the treatment of citizens, effective (rather than formal) administrative justice, technologies of policy, and so on. It thereby provides a deeper and richer understanding of the dynamic of policy and its impact.

The examination of the administration and governance of welfare reform could tell two very different stories, based on these two different understandings of policy. The first story would be to account for the different ways in which formal reforms to welfare policies are put into place and managed on an ongoing basis. In this story, the substance of policy would be marginal or irrelevant, and the processes of implementation and governance would not impact on the substance of welfare reform policy in any way. Policy would only take centre stage to the extent that it is generic policy about changing state governance, such as outsourcing processes, or introducing performance targets, or deploying individual employment contracts. Such an account would not be very different from the multitude of studies of New Public Management (NPM) and governance within the public administration literature. It would recognise that policy reform always involves governance reform, in that new policies require new processes of governance to be introduced in order to implement, administer and check compliance with the policy.

The second story starts from the idea that all policy, in this case welfare reform, must be understood as the complex intertwining of the formal substance of policy (for example, eligibility rules, pay rates, services provided), the discourses of policy reform, reforms to public administration and governance, and the practices and technologies of policy reform as experienced in welfare agencies and welfare subjects. Welfare reform is produced in the nexus of these four intersecting and interdependent dimensions. This story seeks to speak of the policy produced by the confluence and confrontation of changes in both the substance of formal welfare policy and public sector organisational structure and practice. Accordingly, it throws light onto not only welfare policy reform as reflected in government documents and discussion papers, but also in the subjects and spaces of welfare practice. In this account, policy reform is always governance reform because policy is inseparable from governance. Indeed, policy is governance, and vice versa. It is in this manner that, I hope, the chapters in this edited collection are to be read.

If one is to construct such a story of welfare reform, how might one go about it? The fast-growing governance literature growing out of public administration provides some extremely useful observations about the changes in the institutional context, practices and technologies in which contemporary welfare policy is produced. However, such literature is often quite abstract and not sufficiently detailed about the day-to-day, on-the-ground realities of welfare production. Furthermore, its preference for a 'manager's' focus means that the realities for citizens and welfare subjects remain invisible and largely irrelevant. Finally, the governance literature takes no account of the substantive policies that are being implemented by changing governmental relations. Governance, it seems, is a technique that is independent of the policy that it operates on and with.

A more promising literature for constructing a 'welfare reform as governance reform' story is that drawn from street-level research (Lipsky, 1980). Drawing from ethnography and participant observation, street-level research:

> allows the researcher to get inside street-level practice, understand its logic on its own terms, and explore the policy experience at the ground-level.… It offers a lens through which to acquire a fuller picture of how policy is produced and acquires its 'practical' meaning in everyday life. (Brodkin, 2000, p 13)

In understanding the production of welfare reform, such research offers a very important supplement to analyses of formal policy and policy reform discourse. Due to the great utility of street-level research to the project of understanding 'welfare reform as governance reform', it is no surprise that many chapters in this book draw upon, either directly or indirectly, such research. However, in adopting such an approach, one must remain cognisant that one is not simply examining the administration or implementation of policy, but rather the very production and co-constitution of policy. Accordingly, if we are wanting to understand the effects of policy, we cannot do so without taking into account the effects of the policy's governance. The advantages of a street-level perspective are as a methodology. It redefines the way the study of welfare is conducted and the rich and detailed data set that results. Intrinsically, it gives attention to the practices and local peoples (staff and clients) involved in welfare. However, it defines a limited (if not no) analytic of the data it produces. To support and enhance the work of street-level research, this chapter argues that the Foucault-inspired governmentality analytic provides an ideal approach to analyse welfare reform as governance reform.

Governmentality

The governmentality framework must be contrasted with the governance framework. If the language of 'governance' offers a descriptive and often normative engagement with welfare administration, the language of 'governmentality' offers an *analytic* of welfare administration.[1] Indeed, governmentality offers a critical analytic of governance. Thus, in contrast to Daly's (2003) implicit characterisation of governmentality as a post-structuralist account of governance, it is argued that the governmentality approach starts from a very different intellectual project to governance studies and has distinct objectives and methods. This distinctiveness of the governmentality approach is illustrated by its general avoidance of the term 'governance' and the preference for 'government'.

Although the governmentality approach rose to popularity in the 1990s, alongside the governance literature, its beginnings are to be found in the late 1970s in a series of lectures given by Michel Foucault.[2] In contrast to the contemporary equation of 'government' with the state, Foucault reinvigorates an older conception of governing that applies to activities throughout society. Monarchs govern kingdoms, capitalists govern the working class, patriarchs govern households and individuals govern themselves. Quoting the 16th-century writings of Guillaume de La Perrière, Foucault observes how 'government is the right disposition of things, arranged so as to lead to a convenient end' (1991, p 93). According to Colin Gordon, Foucault rephrased this conception as the 'conduct of conduct' (1991, p 2).

Thus, in contrast to the governance literature, which mobilises the notion of governance as either an extension or opposite to state government, Foucault rehabilitates government to emphasise that governmental relations operate and emanate throughout society. There is thus a further contrast with the governance literature, the latter of which tends to focus attention on political governance by the state and quasi-state bodies.[3] For Foucault, the analysis of government is not simply about recognising the state's governmental activities 'by other means', but highlighting the range of state and non-state actors involved in governing for a disparate range of objectives. It should be recognised, however, that despite Foucault's advancement that governing is an activity of a range of actors, that his governmental literature is notable for its focus on the state. Only in his latter studies of self-governing practices is the depth of his approach evident (for example, Foucault, 1985, 1986, 1988a).

But the difference between the governance and governmentality literatures is not simply one of coinage of the semantics of government. Foucault's interest in government is to examine the logics, rationalities and technologies that constitute and justify particular forms of governing. Gordon (1991, p 3) summarises Foucault's analytical concern and conception of 'governmental rationality' or 'governmentality' as:

> a way or system of thinking about the nature of the practice of government (who can govern; what governing is; what or who is governed), capable of making some form of that activity thinkable and practicable both to its practitioners and to those upon whom it is practised.

As with much of his work, Foucault's academic project is not simply descriptive or normative, like that of the governance project; it is a critical and subversive project. It aims to understand the history of our present, while at the same time making visible the intellectual and conceptual bases underpinning the realities that we take for granted and naturalise. In doing so, Foucault's work highlights how our reality could be otherwise. Furthermore, Foucault's study of governing is inextricably tied to his analysis of power. Ideas of 'bio-power', 'pastoral' power, 'disciplinary' power, 'sovereign' power are discussed.[4] Thus, Foucault's governmentality analytic helps to highlight power relations where they might otherwise be invisible.[5]

Just as there has been a proliferation of studies using a governance framework, there has also been a proliferation of studies adopting and extending Foucault's governmentality analytic. Arguably, the most influential elaboration of governmentality has been by Rose and Miller (Miller and Rose, 1990; Rose and Miller, 1992). They articulate governmentality as the 'complex interweaving' of 'political rationalities' and 'technologies of government'.[6] According to Rose and Miller (1992, p 175), political rationalities are:

> the changing discursive fields within which the exercise of power is conceptualised, the moral justifications for particular ways of exercising power by diverse authorities, notions of appropriate forms, objects and limits of politics, and conceptions of the proper distribution of such tasks among secular, spiritual, military and familial sectors.

'Technologies of government', on the other hand, refers to 'the complex of mundane programmes, calculations, techniques, apparatuses, documents and procedures through which authorities seek to employ and give effect to governmental ambitions' (1992, p 175). To be sure, 'technologies of government' are not simply particular tools and techniques that correspond to 'political rationalities'. Rather, 'the characteristic of a technology of government is that it is an *assemblage* organised around a certain problem of conduct, and seeks to conduct that conduct according to particular norms and objectives' (Rose, 1995; emphasis added).

In summary, 'political rationalities' are the discursive, constructive and justificatory elements of government, whereas 'technologies of government' are the means with which such discourses are translated into action, or enacted. Miller and Rose (1990, p 8) describe the relationship between the two thus:

> If political rationalities render reality into the domain of thought 'technologies of government' seek to translate thought into the domain of reality, and to establish 'in the world of persons and things' spaces and devices for acting upon those entities of which they dream and scheme.

Rose and Miller's articulation of Foucault's original work has helped to highlight both the discursive and the technological elements of government, and to draw them both into analyses of governing.

As with the governance perspective, which pays attention to the practices and technologies of governance, governmentality draws attention beyond the self-descriptions of the way politicians say they govern. As Dean has recently argued (2002a, p 120):

> an analytics of government [that is, governmentality] does not claim that the intelligibility of political and social practices can be read off the writings of governors, policy writers and advisors. When applied to the contemporary government of the state ... it concerns not simply liberalism but also liberal ways of governing.

In doing so, governmentality maintains a critical perspective, which can be lacking in the governance framework. For example, governmentality analyses have demonstrated that the presence of illiberal or authoritarian forms of governing within liberal societies is not paradoxical or inconsistent, but very much part of a liberal rationality (Valverde, 1996; Hindess, 2001; Dean, 2002b).

A further critical element that governmentality brings to the study of governance is the examination of the conceptual basis upon which different types of government are justified and constituted, and even the way different governmental rationalities can be thought. In doing so, governmentality examines the intellectual technologies by which certain forms of governing become thinkable and thus practicable. Such domains are impossible to imagine within a governance framework. Indeed, the governmentality perspective highlights how the governance framework, especially in its normative form, is itself a governmental rationality that constitutes the governmental world, governing relations and the ends of government in a particular way. *Governance is governmental.*

Governmentality also points to the work of constituting government through the construction of governable subjects and spaces. It gives attention to the productive work of both rationalities and technologies in constructing certain types of identities, subjectivities, bodies and behaviours, and the way in which such identities are naturalised and taken for granted. For example, the language of 'risk' and the growth of actuarial technologies has redefined the way in which dangers of the world are viewed; they become calculable and, therefore, governable (for example, Ewald, 1991; Dean, 1999, ch 9). Both a new space and a new way of enacting on that space are established. As a result, other ways of viewing the world are displaced. In the governance literature, this work of construction and their 'micro-politics' are not within its analytical scope.

In summary, the governmentality analytic provides both a different and more critical perspective of contemporary governing than the governance concept. It does so by drawing attention to: the 'political rationalities' that define and justify a particular mode of governing and make it thinkable and amenable for governing; the 'governmental technologies' that are the very mechanisms by which governmental dreams and schemes are realised; the forms of power embodied in various modes of governing; and the identities, subjectivities, spaces, bodies and behaviours that are constituted and acted upon. We now turn to the application of this framework in an examination of welfare reform.[7]

Towards a governmentality of welfare reform

When studying welfare reform, the joint analytical focus of governmentality on both rationalities and technologies of governing attunes one to both the formal policy and the practice of welfare. In doing so, it rejoins the elements that have been the focus of the disciplines of social policy (and public policy) and social administration (and public administration) (compare Daly, 2003). More specifically, such an analytical framework helps to draw together under the same microscope the work of social policy on welfare reform with the work of public administration on welfare governance reform. In doing so, it provides a lens with which to critically assess the new power relations being forged.

What then might a governmentality of welfare reform ask and

examine? Following from Rose and Miller's dichotomy, this chapter examines the political rationalities and governmental technologies of welfare reform. To be sure, it is misleading to imply that there is only one governmentality of welfare reform. There are, of course, a myriad of objectives for welfare reform that differ from policy domain to policy domain and from location to location (be it nation, province or locality). Furthermore, there are competing governmentalities and practices of resistance to dominant discourses.

In looking at the *political rationalities of welfare reform*, a governmentality of welfare reform would seek to identify and problematise the narratives that tell of the need for welfare policy and administration reform.[8] How, for example, is it that reforming welfare comes to be seen as activity and a solution to a crisis (for example, O'Connor, 1973; Offe, 1984)? For example, such an analysis would highlight the shifting spatial imaginaries, from nation state to Europeanisation and globalisation (Hindess, 1998; Walters, 2004) to regionalisation, localisation and individualisation (Rose, 1996; Dale, 2004). The study would analyse the discourses and modes of rule that offer to solve the welfare state crisis (for example, 'privatisation', 'workfare', 'markets', 'mutual obligation', 'participation', 'inclusion'). Indeed, how is the very idea of 'welfare' conceptualised, and what aspects of welfare fall under the reforming discourses gaze? Such an analysis would highlight, for example, how in the US 'welfare' specifically relates to benefits for poor unmarried mothers, whereas elsewhere 'welfare' refers to a wider range of benefits. Furthermore, a governmentality of welfare reform would undertake a genealogy[9] of 'welfare', noting today's usage has become unlinked to the concept of 'well-being' or to 'fare well'. How does the 'active'–'passive' welfare dichotomy displace and mobilise differing forms of welfare? How do such discourses constitute the problem and the solution? In what ways are the problems constructed (for example, 'welfare dependency', 'welfare queens', overloaded political demands, labour market inflexibility, inefficient bureaucracies, poor macro-economic settings)? What identities and subjectivities do these discourses construct in terms of welfare organisations, welfare workers and welfare recipients? What welfare rationalities are displaced by these newer discourses? For example, how does the shift in language from client and citizenship to consumer, customer and taxpayer reconstitute the nature of welfare power relations?

A governmentality of welfare reform would also give attention to the language of 'risk' as a new organising concept for thinking about social welfare policy. In particular, it would show that with the new focus on statistical probabilities and possible futures, 'need' has been displaced by 'risk', and policy naturally becomes targeted (O'Malley, 1992; Ericson and Haggerty, 1997; Kemshall, 2002; Henman, 2004).

Another target for analysis is the 'rights and responsibilities' language, such as 'mutual obligation', in which the objective of policy is reconfigured and transformed, and so is the identity and activity of (particular types of) welfare subjects (Harris, 2001).

In examining the political rationalities for reforming welfare administration, a governmentality of welfare reform would importantly look to the way 'governance' as an imaginary defines the nature and practice of the state. It would, in other words, examine 'governance' as a governmental rationality (compare: Larner and Walters, 2004a). It investigates the way in which 'governance' constitutes specific notions of the state, contemporary governmental problems and entities for state action. It would highlight the work of the terms 'partnership', 'networks' and 'community' in problematising the space of government, while constituting, mobilising and naturalising new governmental forms (Rose, 1996; Schofield, 2002). It would ask how 'governance' and public sector reform discourses construct the nature and difference of state, private and third sector entities, and their relative contributions to welfare delivery. It would examine the way in which the language of 'participation' and 'consumer rights' constitutes new modes for governing welfare subjects (Bessant, 2003). Furthermore, a governmentality of welfare reform would point to the circuits of power through which governments seek to link the governance of organisations, managers, staff, clients, money and things.

The *governmental technologies of welfare reform* have started to be documented and analysed in academic research. Apart from the aforementioned discourses, which seek to constitute, configure and shape identities, relations and spaces, technological practices and apparatuses co-constitute government. They include auditing practices whereby the instalment of 'audit is a particular manner of *(re)presenting* administrative problems and their solutions'. Audit sits well with the decentralisation and managerial rhetoric, as it 'shifts monitoring practices from direct inspection towards the control of control', and in doing so, actively redefines and reconstructs the auditable domain (Power, 1994, pp 299, 303; compare: Power, 1997). In a similar manner, the widespread introduction of performance indicators, performance targets and benchmarking cannot be viewed simply as a way in which to enhance productivity (Newman, 2001, ch 5; Larner and Le Heron, 2004). Rather, such practices articulate, through what is measured and what is not, that which is important in welfare practice, and in doing so actively reconstitute the welfare domain (for example, Wright, Chapter Eight of this book). Technologies of audit and performance measures define circuits of power that transform and link the governance of welfare agencies, managers, workers and clients, seeking to inscribe new ways of thinking and bodily practice. Such regimes (along with contracts[10]), thereby form the very material foundation for 'government at a distance'[11] through the deployment of quasi-market and partnership models of welfare delivery.

A governmentality of welfare reform would accordingly not simply take dominant discourses for markets and partnerships at face value as more efficient, responsive and effective forms of welfare delivery. Its analysis would dig deeper and seek to bring to light the ways in which technologies (and also rationalities) reconfigure the role and nature of the state, the idea and practices of accountability (Chan, 1999), the role and relationships with citizens and claimants, practices of appeal and review (Dean, 1991), the relations of power among and between the state and non-state providers, and so on. To undertake such an inquiry requires a critical analysis of technologies of audit and performance, the various contracts between states and citizens, the information and communication technologies (ICTs) – both the advanced electronic ones and the more mundane trails of paper (compare: Latour, 1987) – that form the information and control infrastructure of governing beyond the state, the technologies of governing which welfare providers apply to welfare subjects, and much more. A governmentality analysis of partnership and market forms of welfare provision would unearth the differing power positions of participants (states, welfare providers, workers and welfare subjects), the conflicting objectives of participants in contractual arrangements, the levels of formal and informal discretion and associated non-compliant behaviours of all involved, the vertical and horizontal conduits of control and accountability, the inherent breakdowns, miscommunications and misunderstandings inherent in cross-agency work, and so forth (Newman, 2001, ch 6; Glendinning et al, 2002).

An examination of the technologies of welfare reform cannot overlook the role of electronic ICTs in reconstituting and governing welfare agencies, staff and subjects. This is not simply about the Internet (and digital telephony) making government accessible 24 hours a day, 365 days a year in your own home. As computers increasingly automate processes of eligibility determination and monitoring of clients, the role and importance of welfare staff is reconfigured and even eliminated and administrative discretion in formal and informal policy is correspondingly curtailed[12] (Henman, 1999; Bovens and Zouridis, 2002). Furthermore, computer technologies mesh with governmental rationalities to intensify the surveillance of welfare agencies and staff – through the automatic recording and analysis of performance indicators (Adler and Henman, 2001) – and of welfare subjects (Henman, 2004). Concomitant with risk discourses, to which they give rise, such electronic apparatuses also provide the means to think about, implement and intensify targeted forms of governing welfare (Henman, 2004, 2005). It is because of the key constitutive role of electronic ICTs in welfare practices, that a governmentality of welfare reform must examine the governmental practices embodied in and promulgated by such technology to observe both the micro-politics of power and the ways in which such electronic power is enmeshed with (and even in tension with) dominant political rationalities of welfare reform (Henman and Adler, 2003; Henman and Dean, 2004; Dearman, 2005).

An analysis of the governmental technologies of welfare reform cannot bypass the techniques through which welfare subjects, their identities, subjectivities and capacities, are formed, governed and self-governed. Such an analysis would highlight the work of government policy, the practices of welfare agencies and their staff, and the work of welfare subjects on constituting and transforming themselves. Reinforcing political rationalities, policy reforms of greater and more restrictive means testing, new and stricter time-limited benefits, new choices for clients in welfare services, and redefined workforce incentives (through tax credits, reduced replacement rates and reduced effective marginal tax rates), have all sought to reconstitute the welfare subject as a rational, self-maximising, entrepreneurial agent so beloved of neo-liberalism (Rose, 1992; Burchell, 1996). New welfare policy – as a governmental technology – works to construct calculative agents who respond to the various incentives and disincentives, rewards and penalties, defined by the policy domain. Welfare subjects increasingly take on their own risks individually, as risks increasingly are defined as a personalised phenomenon (Beck and Beck-Gernsheim, 2001). Within this context, the behaviour and decisions of welfare subjects are increasingly informed by new welfare experts (Rose, 1993), such as private pension advisors, financial counsellors, employment trainers and life trainers. To the analysis of these entrepreneurial technologies, must be added the surveillance technologies, which increasingly make visible the activities of welfare subjects. These include the mundane – increased reporting technologies, home visitations, worksite visits and fraud hotlines – to the more high-'tech' – data matching, DNA and drug testing, psychological profiling and online reporting. Allied with increasingly vehement public exhortations against welfare fraud, public advertisements saying 'you are being watched' and increased penalties for non-compliance, welfare reform seeks to internalise welfare subjects' self-government to ensure that they comply with all the requirements and requests of welfare agencies. Clearly, welfare reform is a self-disciplinary technology. This is no better illustrated than in the domain of workfare, to which we now turn.

Workfare: participants, practices, processes, power

Having outlined the shape of how governmentality analyses would approach welfare reform, we turn to a brief example of a governmentality analysis. Following this book's analytical structure of welfare participants, practices and processes, the following governmentality analysis will give attention to each of these elements.

Much of the previous section's broad account of how a governmentality of welfare reform might be conducted is clearly of relevance to a more specific analysis of the governmentality of workfare. For example, many of the political rationalities constructing a crisis in the welfare state and the location of problems and solutions in the behaviour of welfare recipients are especially pertinent in examining workfare. Analyses of the political rationalities of workfare have ably demonstrated the way in which the two previously separate domains of welfare and work (as well as their policy domains of social protection and employment services) have become merged, intertwined and are no longer thinkable as distinct (Harris, 1999; Walters, 2000, ch 6). Such discourses redefine the nature of work to refer to only paid work, while simultaneously reconfiguring conceptions of citizenship and devaluing unpaid work. The discourse of workfare, with its attendant phrases of 'mutual obligation' and 'no rights without responsibilities', also introduces a new conditionality into social protection that cuts across and destabilises its logic through its new coupling with the policy logic of employment services. As a result, social protection becomes unlinked from citizenship, its connection fractured (Harris, 2000; Moss, 2001).

Participants

Such political rationalities are not simply exhortations of politicians spoken at welfare staff, recipients and the broader public, but discourses that constitute a way of thinking and acting on the world which reconfigures the identities, subjectivities and forms of subjugation of the unemployed, in particular. Although occasionally encountering resistance and competing welfare rationalities, rationalities of workfare have captured the imagination and ways of being for many welfare recipients, and have thereby constituted new 'active' welfare subjects. Furthermore, due to this pervading discourse, welfare subjects increasingly experience welfare receipt in terms of 'obligation', rather than in terms of alternative welfare rationalities.

Workfare discourses also transform and constitute new participants. To begin with, the reconfiguration and conflation of social protection and employment services, creates new welfare agencies, their staff, their role, activities and objectives (see Part One of this collection). Indeed, it is not incidental that the introduction of workfare has often been accompanied with new organisational names. Although they may be the same individuals, they are no longer the same welfare workers as previously. No longer is their job distinctly defined to assess benefit entitlement and distribute those benefits, or to advise and support through employment services. Workfare involves a new welfare worker whose job is to monitor entitlement through the very delivery of employment services, a job that both Howard (Chapter Seven of this book) and Wright (Chapter Eight) report is difficult to balance with the inherent tensions conceived within the previous welfare rationality (of needs, rights and citizenship).

Practices

Such workfare subjects and welfare workers are constituted not simply through discourse, but also by 'regimes of practices', namely the administrative practices and subject–agency engagement that have been recreated as part of workfare. For example, Dean (1995, 1998) notes that in Australia, the 'work test' has been replaced with an 'activity test' to highlight the new active welfare subject of workfare. These are reinforced by the use of job 'compacts' (or contracts) that unemployed people make with the government, a 'dole diary' in which job seekers record their engagement with prospective employers, and 'job clubs' where unemployed persons learn and discuss techniques for improving their employability and success with job applications. More recently in Australia, the 'work for the dole' programme has been instituted. It is defined by community work activities, in which welfare beneficiaries are required to undertake 'voluntary' work to pay for their benefit. Ostensibly, this practice operates to instil a work ethic (and possibly work skills) in unemployed young people.

The conditionality of welfare that is central to workfare, cannot be conceived or realised without new and heightened practices of penalties for non-compliance. It is no coincidence that workfare has been universally accompanied by enhanced penalty regimes. Consequent to a renewed focus on penalties, is the introduction of new practices of surveillance, such as the 'dole diaries' mentioned above, intensive frequent reporting mechanisms for both clients and their welfare advisors, regular review interviews with welfare agencies, data matching, and the like.

Welfare workers are also enmeshed in new practices as a result of workfare. While the governmental practices of auditing, performance indicators, performance-based pay, individual contracts, and so on, are overt practices introduced as part of new welfare governance, there are also less observable practices that operate as a consequence of the introduction of workfare. Authors have noted the introduction and intensification of 'creaming' of good clients for job vacancies, the focus on easy-to-place clients rather than on those in need, and not advertising jobs until they are placed.[13] These are practices welfare staff have developed as a way in which to manage the various demands placed on them in the new workfare policy and governance environment.

Processes

The processes of workfare refer both to those broad socioeconomic processes that give rise to and reinforce workfare as a policy solution and to the processes by which workfare is carried out. The former are well known. Discursively constructed they include increasing numbers of people receiving government income support, greater average length of receipt, high replacement rates and low workforce incentives, greater fiscal tightening by the state, changes in demography and the nature of the labour market, and a change in political culture. Less discussed are the processes of individualisation, which both create the ground for and reinforce workfare policy. According to Beck and Beck-Gernsheim (2001), such processes highlight and reinforce the individual for understanding and responding to social problems. As a result, unemployment and welfare receipt is experienced as a result of psychological disposition or frame of mind (that is, 'job-snob', 'work ethic', laziness, dependency culture), which in turn highlights the need for the conditionality and compulsion that characterises workfare.

The processes by which workfare is carried out include the full range of management and governance processes and techniques required to implement workfare policy. This may involve the creation, development and maintenance of partnership relationships between government organisations and private and not-for-profit organisations. It includes the training processes of welfare workers and the development of information systems and workflows that support and make real production of policy.

The space of workfare processes is an important area for analysis. While the individual unemployed person has been a key focus of workfare, other changing spaces of governance are evident. In contrast with the previous focus on the state, workfare has tended to focus its governmental activities on the local and regional, while at the same time being engaged in global and European discourses and debates (Jessop, 1999). The discourses that give rise to and justify these governmental spaces are perhaps well known, however, the technologies that make them knowable and governable are perhaps less well investigated. These would include the generation, circulation and analysis of statistics to form Geographical Information Systems, the deployment of local partnership agreements and contracts, and the use of managerial flexibility.

Power

Ultimately, a governmental analysis of workfare would seek to uncover the operations of power. Governmentality analyses have repeatedly emphasised the neo-liberal character of workfare, and welfare reform, more broadly. Such neo-liberal power is said to operate by governing at a distance, by using choice and actively enrolling the subjectivities of those who are governed. However, such a characterisation of neo-liberalism must recognise the punitive and coercive elements that lie at the heart of workfare. To appreciate this seemingly paradoxical nature of liberalism, we must recognise that liberalism has always been infused with authoritarianism and illiberalism (Hindess, 2001; Dean, 2002b).

We must also recognise that welfare is also infused with a concern to care and to support. To this we must recognise the operation of what Foucault denoted 'pastoral power' (1981, 1982). Pastoral power emphasises the care for the welfare of each individual, which involves a detailed knowledge of every person. However, pastoral power is not always benevolent. It can often involve a paternalistic pressure to be reformed for 'one's own good', an invasion of the sphere of personal autonomy, and so on.

Conclusions

This chapter has advanced the Foucault-inspired governmentality perspective as a critical analytical approach to examining welfare reform as governance reform. The burgeoning governance literature has highlighted the need to place a greater emphasis on the practical, organisational and administrative aspects of welfare reform, and not simply the formal policies defined by politicians. This chapter thus argued that an examination of welfare reform that seeks to appreciate its full substance and effect must integrate into the analysis what has been the traditional focus of public and social policy on the one hand, with public and social administration on the other. We need to recapture a broader notion of policy, which includes policy as practice. The chapter then recognised street-level research – with its focus on the local production of policy – as providing an invaluable research method for bringing together these separate elements. However, as a research method, street-level research does not provide an analytical framework to analyse and interpret the findings of that research. Governmentality was advocated as a fruitful analytic. Its strengths include a critical consideration of both political rationalities and technologies of government, which is attuned to the formation and practices of power. As a post-structuralist analytic, governmentality seeks to excavate the discourses and rationalities that form and inscribe new domains – subjects, subjectivities, agencies – and make them governable.

Although the chapters in this book do not adopt a governmentality analytic, their work provides fresh and original insights into the nature and effects of the administration and governance of welfare reform, and how it is enmeshed with the formal policy defined by governments. This is the very material from which a governmentality analysis can emerge. How the observations from this book can be incorporated into a governmentality approach is taken up in the book's conclusion.

Notes

[1] Rhodes (1997, pp 5-7) does, however, argue that 'governance' acts as an 'organising perspective' that shapes the focus of study and poses particular research questions.

[2] The key writings are Foucault (1981, 1988b, 1991, 1997-2001 vols 1, 3). Other important contributions to the literature are Burchell et al (1991), Gordon (1991), Barry et al (1996), Dean and Hindess (1998), Dean (1999), Rose (1999), Larner and Walters (2004b).

[3] There is, however, a significant literature on corporate governance (for example, Monks and Minow, 2001).

[4] For an introduction see Dean (1999).

[5] A good example of this is Cruikshank's (1993, 1994) analysis of empowerment.

[6] In contrast, Gordon (1980, pp 246-55) examines Foucault's use of 'strategies', 'technologies' and 'programmes' in relation to rationalities of power/knowledge.

[7] Clarke (2004, ch 6) outlines some limitations of the governmentality approach, including how it overlooks conflict and is not explanatory, that is, it does not seek to explain change in governmental activities (see also O'Malley et al, 1997).

[8] Larner and Walters (2004a) do a similar job in problematising the narrative of 'globalisation'.

[9] Genealogy is an analytical method devised by Foucault to interrogate the history and meaning of concepts in our present (Smart, 1985, ch 2).

[10] See, for example, Yeatman (1998).

[11] See Latour (1987) for the argument that technology is 'action at a distance'.

[12] See Howard (Chapter Seven of this book) and Dearman (2005) for a different perspective on discretion.

[13] See, for example, the three chapters in Part Two of this book.

References

Adler, M. and Henman, P. (2001) 'e-Justice: a comparative study of computerization and procedural justice in social security', *International Review of Law, Computers and Technology*, vol 15, no 2, pp 195-212.

Barry, A., Osborne, T. and Rose, N. (eds) (1996) *Foucault and political reason*, London: UCL Press.

Beck, U. and Beck-Gernsheim, E. (2001) *Individualization*, London: Sage Publications.

Bessant, J. (2003) 'Youth participation: a new mode of government', *Policy Studies*, vol 24, no 2/3, pp 87-100.

Bovens, M. and Zouridis, S. (2002) 'From street-level to system-level bureaucracies: how information and communication technology is transforming administrative discretion and constitutional control', *Public Administration Review*, vol 62, no 2, pp 174-84.

Bridgman, P. and Davis, G. (2004) *The Australian policy handbook* (3rd edn), Sydney: Allen and Unwin.

Brodkin, E. (2000) *Investigating policy's 'practical' meaning: Street-level research on welfare policy* (online), Joint Center for Poverty Research, Working Paper No. 162, Chicago, IL: Northwestern University/University of Chicago, available at: www.jcpr.org/email_return.cfm?id=2107

Burchell, G. (1996) 'Liberal government and techniques of the self', in A. Barry, T. Osborne and N. Rose (eds) *Foucault and Political Reason*, London: UCL Press, pp 19-36.

Burchell, G., Gordon, C. and Miller, P. (eds) (1991) *The Foucault effect*, Chicago, IL: University of Chicago Press.

Chan, J. (1999) 'Governing police practice: limits of the new accountability', *British Journal of Sociology*, vol 50, no 2, pp 249-68.

Clarke, J. (2004) *Changing welfare, changing states*, London: Sage Publications.

Cruikshank, B. (1993) 'Revolutions within: self-government and self-esteem', *Economy and Society*, vol 22, no 3, pp 327-44.

Cruikshank, B. (1994) 'The will to empower: technologies of citizenship and the war on poverty', *Socialist Review*, vol 23, no 4, pp 29-55.

Dale, R. (2004) 'Forms of governance, governmentality and the EU's Open Method of Coordination', in W. Larner and W. Walters (eds) *Global governmentality*, London: Routledge, pp 174-94.

Daly, M. (2003) 'Governance and social policy', *Journal of Social Policy*, vol 32, no 1, pp 113-28.

Dean, H. (1991) *Social security and social control*, London: Routledge.

Dean, M. (1995) 'Governing the unemployed self in the active society', *Economy and Society*, vol 24, no 4, pp 559-83.

Dean, M. (1998) 'Administering asceticism: re-working the ethical life of the unemployed citizen', in M. Dean and B. Hindess (eds) *Governing, Australia*, Melbourne: Cambridge University Press, pp 87-107.

Dean, M. (1999) *Governmentality*, London: Sage Publications.

Dean, M. (2002a) 'Powers of life and death beyond governmentality', *Cultural Values*, vol 6, no 1-2, pp 119-38.

Dean, M. (2002b) 'Liberal government and authoritarianism', *Economy and Society*, vol 31, no 1, pp 37-61.

Dean, M. and Hindess, B. (eds) (1998) *Governing Australia*, Melbourne: Cambridge University Press.

Dearman, P. (2005) 'Computerised information systems and professional autonomy: the record of social work', PhD thesis, Monash University.

Ericson, R.V. and Haggerty, K.D. (1997) *Policing the risk society*, Toronto: University of Toronto Press.

Ewald, F. (1991) 'Insurance and risk', in G. Burchell, C. Gordon and P. Miller (eds) *The Foucault effect*, Chicago, IL: University of Chicago Press, pp 197-210.

Foucault, M. (1981) 'Omnes et singulatim: towards a criticism of "political reason"', *The Tanner Lectures on Human Values*, vol 2, pp 223-54.

Foucault, M. (1982) 'The subject and power', in H. Dreyfus and P. Rabinow (eds) *Michel Foucault*, Brighton: Harvester, pp 208-26.

Foucault, M. (1985) *The history of sexuality, volume 2: The use of pleasure*, New York: Vintage.

Foucault, M. (1986) *The history of sexuality, volume 3: The care of the self*, New York: Vintage.

Foucault, M. (1988a) 'Technologies of the self', in L.H. Martin, H. Gutman and P.H. Hutton (eds) *Technologies of the self*, London: Tavistock, pp 16-49.

Foucault, M. (1988b) 'Politics and reason', in L.H. Martin, H. Gutman and P.H. Hutton (eds) *Technologies of the self*, London: Tavistock, pp 145-62.

Foucault, M. (1991) 'Governmentality', in G. Burchell, C. Gordon and P. Miller (eds) *The Foucault effect*, Chicago, IL: University of Chicago Press, pp 87-104.

Foucault, M. (1997-2001) *The essential works 1954-1984*, 3 vols, New York, NY: Free Press.

Glendinning, C., Powell, M. and Rummery, K. (eds) (2002) *Partnerships, New Labour and the governance of welfare*, Bristol: The Policy Press.

Gordon, C. (1980) 'Afterword', in M. Foucault, *Power/knowledge*, New York, NY: Harvester Press, pp 229-59.

Gordon, C. (1991) 'Governmental rationality: an introduction', in G. Burchell, C. Gordon and P. Miller (eds) *The Foucault effect*, Chicago, IL: University of Chicago Press, pp 1-51.

Harris, P. (1999) 'Public welfare and liberal governance', in A. Petersen, I. Barns, J. Dudley and P. Harris (eds) *Poststructuralism, citizenship and social policy*, London: Routledge, pp 25-57.

Harris, P. (2000) 'Participation and the new welfare', *Australian Journal of Social Issues*, vol 35, no 4, pp 279-300.

Harris, P. (2001) 'From relief to mutual obligation: welfare rationalities and unemployment in 20th-century Australia', *Journal of Sociology*, vol 37, no 1, pp 5-26.

Henman, P. (1999) 'The bane and benefits of computers in Australia's Department of Social Security', *International Journal of Sociology and Social Policy*, vol 19, no 1-2, pp 101-29.

Henman, P. (2004) 'Targeted!: population segmentation, electronic surveillance and governing the unemployed in Australia', *International Sociology*, vol 19, no 2, pp 173-91.

Henman, P. (2005) 'E-government, targeting and data profiling: policy and ethical issues of differential treatment', *Journal of E-government*, vol 2, no 1, pp 79-98.

Henman, P. and Adler, M. (2003) 'Information technology and the governance of social security', *Critical Social Policy*, vol 23, no 2, pp 139-64.

Henman, P. and Dean, M. (2004) *The governmental powers of welfare e-administration* (online), Australian Electronic Governance Conference 2004, Melbourne: Melbourne University, available at: www.public-policy.unimelb.edu.au/egovernance/papers/15_henman.pdf

Hindess, B. (1998) 'Neo-liberalism and the national economy', in M. Dean and B. Hindess (eds) *Governing Australia*, Melbourne: Cambridge University Press, pp 210-26.

Hindess, B. (2001) 'The liberal government of unfreedom', *Alternatives*, vol 26, no 2, pp 93-111.

Jessop, B. (1999) 'The changing governance of welfare: recent trends in its primary functions, scale, and modes of coordination', *Social Policy and Administration*, vol 33, no 4, pp 348-59.

Kemshall, H. (2002) *Risk, social policy and welfare*, Buckingham: Open University Press.

Larner, W. and Le Heron, R. (2004) 'Global benchmarking: participating "at a distance" in the globalizing economy', in W. Larner and W. Walters (eds) *Global governmentality*, London: Routledge, pp 212-32.

Larner, W. and Walters, W. (2004a) 'Globalization as governmentality', *Alternatives: global, local, political*, vol 29, no 5, pp 495-514.

Larner, W. and Walters, W. (eds) (2004b) *Global governmentality*, London: Routledge.

Latour, B. (1987) *Science in action*, Cambridge, MA: Harvard University Press.

Levin, P. (1997) *Making social policy*, Buckingham: Open University Press.

Lipsky, M. (1980) *Street-level bureaucracy*, Cambridge, MA: MIT Press.

Marsh, D. and Smith, M.J. (2000) 'Understanding policy networks: towards a dialectical approach', *Policy Studies*, vol 48, pp 4-21.

Miller, P. and Rose, N. (1990) 'Governing economic life', *Economy and Society*, vol 19, no 1, pp 1-31.

Monks, R. and Minow, N. (2001) *Corporate governance* (2nd edn), Malden: Blackwell.

Moss, J. (2001) 'The ethics and politics of mutual obligation', *Australian Journal of Social Issues*, vol 36, no 1, pp 1-14.

Newman, J. (2001) *Modernising governance*, London: Sage Publications.

O'Connor, J. (1973) *The fiscal crisis of the state*, New York: St Martin's Press.

Offe, C. (1984) *Contradictions of the welfare state*, London: Hutchinson Education.

O'Malley, P. (1992) 'Risk, power and crime prevention', *Economy and Society*, vol 21, no 3, pp 252-75.

O'Malley, P., Weir, L. and Shearing, C. (1997) 'Governmentality, criticism, politics', *Economy and Society*, vol 26, no 4, pp 501-17.

Power, M. (1994) 'The audit society', in A. Hopwood and P. Miller (eds) *Accounting as a social and institutional process*, Cambridge: Cambridge University Press, pp 299-316.

Power, M. (1997) *The audit society*, Oxford: Oxford University Press.

Rhodes, R.A.W. (1997) *Understanding governance*, Buckingham: Open University Press.

Rose, N. (1992) 'Governing the enterprising self', in P. Heelas and P. Morris (eds) *The values of the enterprise culture*, London: Routledge, pp 141-64.

Rose, N. (1993) 'Government, authority and expertise in advanced liberalism', *Economy and Society*, vol 22, no 3, pp 283-99.

Rose, N. (1995) personal communication.

Rose, N. (1996) 'Death of the social? Re-figuring the territory of government', *Economy and Society*, vol 25, no 3, pp 327-56.

Rose, N. (1999) *Powers of freedom*, Cambridge: Cambridge University Press.

Rose, N. and Miller, P. (1992) 'Political power beyond the state: problematics of government', *British Journal of Sociology*, vol 43, no 2, pp 173-205.

Sabatier, P. and Jenkins-Smith, H. (eds) (1993) *Policy change and learning*, Boulder, CO: Westview Press.

Schofield, B. (2002) 'Partners in power: governing the self-sustaining community', *Sociology*, vol 36, no 3, pp 663-83.

Smart, B. (1985) *Michel Foucault*, London: Routledge.

Valverde, M. (1996) ' "Despotism" and ethical liberal governance', *Economy and Society*, vol 25, no 3, pp 357-72.

Walters, W. (2000) *Unemployment and government*, Cambridge: Cambridge University Press.

Walters, W. (2004) 'The political rationality of European integration', in W. Larner and W. Walters (eds) *Global governmentality*, London: Routledge, pp 155-73.

Yeatman, A. (1998) 'Interpreting contractualism', in M. Dean and B. Hindess (eds) *Governing Australia*, Melbourne: Cambridge University Press, pp 227-42.

Part One:
Participants: reforming the agents of welfare delivery

THREE

State–third sector partnership frameworks: from administration to participation

Deena White

Since the end of the last century, throughout much of the world, institutional relations between welfare states and the third sector, otherwise known as the voluntary and community sector, have been undergoing a multifaceted transformation. One apparent sign of change has been the signing of formal, national 'partnership' agreements or policies, to regularise relations between governments and third sectors. Non-governmental, non-profit, voluntary or grassroots organisations have always played significant roles in most welfare states. However, in the past, they tended to occupy fragmented or unrelated social spaces, only partially and unevenly regulated by the state; their relations with governments and public organisations tended to be ad hoc; and their role in the welfare state was largely invisible. As deliverers of public services, they were generally not distinguished from public sector organisations. As providers of charity, they represented the absence, failure or weakness of the welfare state, or a vestige of pre-welfare state institutions. Analysts of the welfare state studiously ignored them.

In 1997, something new happened: Tony Blair, newly elected Prime Minister of the UK, came to power promoting a new view of 'Third Way' welfare state governance. One of his first acts was to mandate the development of a series of 'Compacts' to be signed between the governments of England, Scotland, Wales and Northern Ireland and their respective voluntary and community sectors. The Compacts, signed in 1998, officially recognised the 'voluntary and community sector', formally defined and described it, designated it a 'partner' of government, and drew up a set of principles to govern the relations between the two parties. Oddly, this formula quickly spread to other countries with very different governments, different traditions of governance, and very different histories of civil society organisation. The British template has inspired agreements either signed or under consideration in at least 14 other jurisdictions, including Estonia, Germany, New Zealand and Spain (Phillips, 2002). Canada and France both signed similar accords in 2001 (Government of Canada and Voluntary Sector, 2001; Premier Ministre et CPCA, 2001). The Canadian province of Québec, as well as Wales, has adopted government policies that cover much the same ground, but are actually more binding on government than the original Compact-style agreements.

This international rash of activity, and the surprising similarities and differences between the various 'partnership frameworks' that have been devised, urge us to carefully consider their significance for the sector and for societies in general. The trials and traps of 'partnership working' among community-based and government actors has received considerable attention (Balloch and Taylor, 2002). Here, we pose a larger question: what is the significance of this potentially global trend towards formalising relations between the state and third sector for the future governance of welfare states? More specifically, what are the possible implications for the design and implementation of social welfare? One answer, at least to the first question, is that the formalisation of state–third sector relations represents a strategy for rebuilding the capacity of the welfare state in the wake of the neo-liberal attack of the 1980s and 1990s. Claire Ullman (1998) developed this argument in the case of France, to explain why the socialist government of the early 1980s, expected to favour the reinforcement of state monopolies, uncharacteristically turned towards local community associations to implement its social agenda, notably, the *revenu minimum d'insertion* (RMI). But state capacity theory can only be part of the story. Collaboration with the third sector may indeed broaden governments' ability to implement new social policies without 'growing' the public sector. But partnerships of this order have long existed in countless areas of public intervention, from culture and amateur sports to health and welfare, and have not required formal, cross-cutting, national framework agreements in the past. Furthermore, these formal agreements have, more often than not, been called for and drafted by civil society actors, not by governments.

This may explain why, surprisingly, the framework agreements speak relatively little of the potential service role of voluntary and community organisations. Instead, they identify what distinguishes the third sector from the market and the state, and draw attention to it as a collective actor in the defence of democracy and social justice. Through this discourse, the frameworks work to construct a more or less coherent identity for the third sector that most did not enjoy before the idea of the framework agreements took off – indeed, an identity that may belie and efface their ideological diversity. This chapter will argue that, despite the frustration of making government–community partnerships work in the field, the appearance of these national-level, formal agreements both *reflects* and *reinforces* the emergence of a new relationship between welfare states and civil society.

Social citizenship regimes in transition

The concept that will allow us to elaborate on this point is that of the 'social citizenship regime' (Jenson and Phillips, 1996; Jenson, 1997; Jenson and Papillon, 2000; Phillips, 2002). Originally developed as a way of describing national variability in the sorts of relations that welfare states establish with their citizens, the concept calls attention to four dimensions of those relations:

- What social rights are guaranteed by the state? This is the distribution question: what does the welfare state guarantee to its citizens, and under what conditions?
- How are these social rights provided or delivered, or, in other words, what is the responsibility mix between the state, the family, the market and the third sector?
- Who can legitimately claim these rights, or who is officially recognised as a bearer of rights?
- Who has a say in the way that they are designed and delivered, or, in other words, who can legitimately participate?

Traditional theories of welfare tend to focus only on the first two questions, dealing with policies and programmes and their implementation. Discussion of 'partnerships' between governments and third sectors or the market are equally limited to these terms of analysis, therefore focusing increasingly on the implementation of national partnership frameworks at the local level, where they count, and neglecting to pursue further the original significance of these agreements. A 'social citizenship regime' approach also emphasises the place and role of citizens in the citizenship relation. It focuses on the recognition of various social groups as bearers of rights (for example, lone mothers, immigrants, children, workers) and on their participation in shaping the social policy agenda and programme design, through claims-making activities, consultation, or other forms of citizen engagement. Thinking in terms of the social citizenship regime will allow us to identify non-superficial similarities between the agreements signed in vastly different social and political contexts, suggesting that the agreements are part of a broad shift in the structure and operation of welfare states. It will also allow us to distinguish between traditional relations between welfare states and third sectors as providers of services, and the new relations that, it is argued here, are implied by the discourse of the partnership framework agreements.

These partnership agreements are not necessarily the first formal step in this transformation process. The establishment of the contract culture in state–third sector relations during the 1990s, borrowed from the realm of market relations and propagated in large part by the Organisation for Economic Co-operation and Development (OECD) and by European guidelines regarding the regulation of the service sector, was almost universally a prior step (Wistow et al, 1996; 6 and Kendell, 1997; Evers and Strünck, 1998; Bode, 2004). The imposition of a contracting regime was based on the principles of New Public Management (NPM) (Dunleavy and Hood, 1994; Aucoin, 1995; Polidano et al, 1998; Rouban, 1999). It replaced long-term partnerships allowing for considerable autonomy on the part of service organisations, with systems of short-term, vertical accountability to government agencies. But like other market-inspired policies for the governance of social welfare (for example, privatisation[1]), the introduction of the contract culture was necessarily an interim step in the transformation process; necessarily, because the so-called 'partners' in these new relations were not simply service providers, but simultaneously, civically engaged social actors and often the representatives or 'agents' of otherwise voiceless social and consumption groups. This is why that first step in the institutionalisation of new government–third sector relations drove vastly disparate voluntary and community organisations to coordinate nationally, often for the first time, in order to re-establish more realistic ground rules for these relations. The emergence and multiplication of national partnership framework agreements is the result.

The following section of this chapter will present four short stories of the development and design of the agreements in different contexts: England, France, Canada (at the federal level) and the Canadian province of Québec. These cases vary on several important dimensions, including the origins, history, constitution and roles of their third sectors, as well as of their states, accounting for very different relations between the two. Institutional theories would predict that, on these grounds, the agreements negotiated in each context would be sufficiently tied to embedded interests and dominant ideas that they would be unlikely to introduce anything significantly *new* in state–third sector relations.

Despite these major differences, there are nonetheless some similarities among contexts, which help explain the emergence and transfer of national partnership framework agreements. For example, Québec community organisations are perhaps the most financially dependent on the state, while, in England, commercial activities and fundraising are important for most of the larger voluntary organisations. But in both cases – indeed, in all four cases – government is the most significant funder of the third sector. In all four cases, relations with the state began to deteriorate in the eyes of third sector actors about a decade before the adoption of partnership frameworks in the wake of NPM reforms, even though in at least one context, that of Québec, the contract culture never penetrated. In three of the four cases (again, with the exception of Québec), this resulted in third sector leadership calling for a formal accord with government to acknowledge the autonomy of voluntary and community organisations, recognise their distinctive role in society and preserve their capacity to act. In these three cases, the initial draft of the partnership framework was drawn up by the sector under the auspices of a leadership coalition and with broad and deep consultation among the hugely diverse voluntary and community organisations that constitute their respective civil societies. It is evident that the Québec case stands out. It is especially interesting because of both its differences and similarities with respect to the other cases.

One of the most striking similarities among the cases, including Québec, comes to light when we compare the framework agreements in terms of the social citizen regime that each one reflects. Each takes a stand not only regarding the distributive and productive service functions of the third sector, but also, and indeed more importantly, regarding its recognition of social groups and their right to participate in the development and design of policies affecting them. In our view, this represents an important shift in the operation of welfare state democracies.

Formalising relations between states and third sectors

The four partnership agreements between governments and third sectors analysed in this chapter all share a similar format with the exception of Québec, which opted for a unilateral government policy rather than a joint agreement. Each – including the Québec policy and despite its far greater detail and length – contains a statement of values and principles shared by the government and third sector, followed by a set of reciprocal commitments. Aside from the similarities in form, there are also numerous similarities in the content of the frameworks. All the agreements begin by paying homage to a set of basic, shared ideals, such as equality of opportunity, social development, inclusion, active citizenship or 'liberty, equality and fraternity'. All recognise the independence of the sector, its right to dissent, its diversity, its unique contributions to society as distinct from the state and the market, and the importance of volunteering. All include a commitment on the part of third sector organisations to accountability and good governance, and, usually, a commitment to participate, when appropriate and in line with their means, in consultations about government policies and programmes. Most include a commitment on the part of government to consult with the sector at the point of policy development and design as well as implementation, to review or reform funding practices, to recognise the costs of, and support to, volunteers and sector capacity building, to encourage public awareness of the contributions of the sector, and to take into consideration the impact that other policies and programmes may have on the sector. These agreements are not to be understood as government positions on the role of the third sector in their societies. They are rather the fruit of hard negotiation in every case. Québec's government policy, while not an 'agreement' because it was not co-signed by the two parties, was nonetheless also devised in a context of significant, highly visible and, ultimately, effective consultation.

The similarities between the agreements and the Québec policy are a clear case of policy transfer from the UK to both France and Canada, with the usual caveat associated with this interpretation. Policy transfer is not akin to 'cloning', where a policy developed in one context is simply copied in another. The right opportunities and conditions must be present for a foreign policy to be noticed and considered as a possible solution to some problem, and then the policy will be transformed in the transfer process, to conform to the new institutional and political context. To a large extent, this policy transfer seems to have been facilitated by a shared concern within Europe and North America about social cohesion and welfare state renewal, as well as by domestically defined opportunities, such as a change in government or an election, the centenary of the French legalisation of 'association' (2001) or the International Year of the Volunteer (2001). Nonetheless, there are important distinctions between the agreements[2] with respect to the vision that each projects of the nature of citizenship, and the role of the third sector in promoting it.

The first partnership agreements were the British, adopted within one month of each other in the autumn of 1998 (the Scottish Compact first, then the English and the Welsh (Scottish Office, 1998; Home Office, 1998; Secretary of State for Wales, 1998)). They all followed a general guideline that had been published a year earlier by the British Labour Party before coming to power in 1997. Their form is therefore similar: they are brief (five to eight pages) and non-binding, but are explicitly founded on the moral authority extended by the government's endorsement and by the apparent legitimacy of the Party signing for the third sector, after wide consultation. Each contains a statement of values and principles shared by the state and the third sector, followed by a recitation of reciprocal state and third sector commitments. This format is almost exactly reproduced in the French *Charte d'engagements réciproques entre l'état et les associations* (Premier Ministre et CPCA, 2001), and in the Canadian *An accord between the government of Canada and the voluntary sector* (Government of Canada and the Voluntary Sector, 2001), despite very different third sectors, and different histories between them and their respective states. Several sections of the Québec policy are clearly also inspired by this format.

Service delivery, although slightly more prominent in the English Compact than in others, is hardly mentioned, and funding commitments usually make promises well beyond service contracts (for example, core funding and the funding of umbrella organisations). More salient than contributions to social care, in all the frameworks, is the role attributed to the third sector in promoting citizen engagement, social cohesion and social development.

The English Compact between the government and the third sector

Britain was the first country to enter into a formal agreement with its voluntary sector, and served as a model for the others. The political conditions that led to this innovative strategy can perhaps be summarised in a single word: Thatcherism. Thatcher's National Health Service and Community Care Act of 1990 was the first serious government effort to radically change the traditional close relationship between the British welfare state and the large, venerable voluntary organisations that provided largely publicly funded social services. This Act notably imposed quasi-market contracting and managerial systems on the National Health Service (NHS), decentralised administrative responsibility for social services to local authorities, and effectively led the way to an explicitly mixed economy of care as the future of the neo-liberal welfare state. In the same year, the Home Office published a policy targeting the third sector: *Efficiency scrutiny of government funding of the voluntary sector: Profiting from partnership* (Home Office, 1990); it was strictly in the spirit of the new managerialism introduced by the 1990 National Health Service and Community Care Act. It sought to re-engineer government funding practices with respect to third sector organisations by cutting core and project funding in favour of contractual payment for services. Public Sector Contract regulations published in 1993 (United Kingdom, 1993) further elaborated on and justified the contract culture in the context of a mixed economy of care, where voluntary organisations compete with private for-profit enterprises for contracts with local authorities (Wistow et al, 1996). While a hallmark of the discourse on decentralisation and community care was the emphasis placed on 'local voices', the traditional, institutionalised practices and influence of the voluntary sector were under serious pressure and threat throughout the Conservative era.

It was the sector's reaction to this cold, Conservative climate that led the way to the Compact. The National Council for Voluntary Organisations (NCVO) commissioned Nicholas Deakin, a respected academic, to head a commission and report on its conclusions, which, ultimately, urged not a return to the comfortable old ways, but an alternative way forward. It defended the autonomy of the sector that was threatened by the new contract culture, as well as the sector's right to speak for itself through its own umbrella organisations, and it called for a 'concordat' to be drafted between the government and the sector as equal partners, each with their own interests and constituencies, with a view to a better definition of their complementary roles (Commission, 1996). New Labour swept into power the following year, already inspired by the Deakin Report. It had already responded to the Report with its own manifesto, *Building the future together* (1997), while still in opposition and now it took up NCVO's challenge to enter into a partnership agreement with the voluntary sector. This became one of Blair's first projects upon taking over the reins of government later that year.

The resulting *Compact on relations between government and the voluntary and community sector in England* (Home Office, 1998) as well as the Scottish (Scottish Office, 1998) and Welsh (Secretary of State for Wales, 1998) Compacts signed the same year, all follow the guidelines proposed in the 1997 Labour manifesto. The English Compact begins by stating that it is non-exhaustive, that it is but a general framework that needs to be filled in, and that it is not legally binding, but rather a 'memorandum ... [whose] authority is derived from its endorsement by Government and by the voluntary and community sector itself through its consultation process' (Home Office, 1998, art 2). This consultation process had been ensured under the auspices of the NCVO. The process had begun with a conference of leading umbrella groups and a 65-member reference group, and once a draft agreement had been developed, it was distributed to over 1,000 organisations for consultation purposes. The Compact was co-signed by the chair of the NCVO working group and the Home Secretary, and presented to Parliament in November 1998.

The *Compact on relations between government and the voluntary and community sector in England* presents the voluntary and community sector as promoting 'citizenship' through its contribution to 'the development of the society and to the social, cultural, economic and political life of the nation' (Home Office, 1998, art 6). Its 'underlying philosophy' is that voluntary and community action is 'fundamental to the development of a democratic, socially inclusive society' (art 5). This is because voluntary and community organisations 'enable individuals to contribute to the public life and the development of their communities' (ibid) and because 'they engage the skills, interests, beliefs and values of individuals and groups'. The Compact pledges 'to take account positively of the specific needs, interests and contributions of those parts of the sector which represent women, minority groups and the social excluded' (ibid). Black and minority ethnic organisations are specifically recognised as feeling 'outside the traditional structures of the sector', and are assured that 'support for, and involvement of, these organisations are mainstream issues for both the Government and the ... sector' (art 13). They are promised 'the opportunity to be directly involved in partnerships, consultation and decision making' (ibid). The Compact also reaches out to those local, community-based organisations that are poorly represented by the large, traditional, national voluntary organisations that took the leading role in the development of the Compact. Finally, it promises to encourage the signing of similar agreements between local levels of government and community-based groups. This is an image of citizenship, then, that calls attention to diversity and local citizen engagement. It clearly acknowledges 'the importance of promoting equality of opportunity for all people, regardless of race, age, disability, gender, sexual orientation or religion' (art 8.8). The various Codes of Good Practice that have been published since the adoption of the Compact have aimed to facilitate and promote more dense relations between black and ethnic minority groups and government, between grassroots community groups and government, and between local governments and the full range of civil society groups in their communities.

The French Charter of mutual commitment between the state and associations

The French *Charte d'engagement réciproque entre l'état et les associations* (Premier Ministre et CPCA, 2001) represents a clear symbolic break with both the French statist tradition as well as with its traditional 'social economy' consisting of 'mutuals', important actors in the development and delivery of social insurance. Although decentralisation and contracting with local community organisations had begun in the 1960s, this official recognition of their role in the French welfare state was new. Although long associated with the Church and held in great suspicion by the state, the Charter now envisages 'the associative life' as a means of access to full citizenship for an increasing number of citizens, particularly youth and minority groups with relatively little voice. The Charter even goes beyond claiming to champion voluntary and community action within France alone. It invites French associations to promote the activities of civil society groups throughout Europe to support their development particularly in relations between the north and the south. The model French citizen, then, is also a responsible citizen of the world.

In the Charter, associations are recognised as agents of social and economic transformation. It notes that associations mobilise their resources towards a new, more 'human' conception of wealth, 'to the creation of social, cultural or economic wealth' (Premier Ministre et CPCA, 2001, art 2.4 – author's translation), helping to ensure that 'the market economy does not degenerate into a market society, but rather, leaves plenty of room for the reinforcement of solidarity' (Preamble to the Charter). Like the English Compact, then, the French Charter recognises a social cohesion role for the sector. But it also explicitly recognises its role in promoting social change through its critical social advocacy work. This vision contrasts somewhat with that expressed in the English Compact, where the voluntary organisations' role in helping in 'ensuring the continued capacity of voluntary and community organisations to respond to Government initiatives' (Home Office, 1998, art 9.2) is stressed more than its role in social innovation.

The French Charter is no more binding a contract than the English Compact, although it is not quite as forthright in so stating. Signed by Prime Minister Lionel Jospin himself, rather than a designated representative as in the case of England, it stipulates that the 'signatories commit themselves to put in place whatever is needed to achieve [the] objectives' of the Charter (Premier Ministre et CPCA, 2001, Preamble to the Charter). To this end, the *Conférence Permanente des Coordinations Associatives* (CPCA) is officially recognised as the expression of the 'associative movement' and designated its interlocutor with the state, much as the NCVO has taken on that representative role in England. But in a more neo-corporatist tradition, the CPCA is charged with 'putting in place whatever intermediary associations and modes of representation that may be needed to allow state authorities to be able to count on certain representative structures, for purposes of civic and social dialogue, consultation on public policy and the possible negotiation of contractual arrangements' (Premier Ministre et CPCA, art 4.7). In this sense, the Charter appears to take as its model for a state–third sector partnership, the types of institutional relations that it has established with its other 'social partners', including unions and business.

The Accord between the government of Canada and the third sector

Canada's Accord (Government of Canada and the Voluntary Sector, 2001) was born of conditions less conducive to partnership than those that existed in England in 1997, when New Labour had just come to power and, after more than a decade of Thatcherism, was seen by the voluntary sector as representing a promising fresh start.

In Canada, that is, at the level of the federal government, the Liberal Party in power first expressed an interest in the voluntary sector in 1997, at about the same time that Tony Blair's opposition Labour Party did in the UK. But in Canada, this was followed by more than four years of social spending cuts by the very same Liberal government, as well as attacks on the credibility and accountability of the third sector, and the imposition of contract relations and accountability regulations that were reminiscent of Thatcher's Conservatives, which were crippling the capacity of voluntary organisations to carry out their missions. Thus, when the Prime Minister sang the praises of the voluntary sector during his 1997 re-election campaign, a coalition of national voluntary organisations[3] had already begun to work towards a coherent strategy to defend the sector. It took over two years for this strategy to come into line with the government's about-face, which took the form of a joint Voluntary Sector Initiative (VSI). The development of an Accord similar to England's was one of many items on the agenda of the VSI.

The Accord that was finally signed in December 2001 dedicates itself to 'improving the quality of life of all Canadians'. In a context where polls showed an overwhelming prevalence of the idea that 'government doesn't care much what ordinary people think' (Nevitte, 2000, pp 13-14), voluntary action was held as proof that citizens had the means to influence the state of affairs. Thus, a shared value announced in the Accord is that of active citizenship, or 'active involvement or engagement of individuals and communities in shaping society, whether through political or voluntary activity or both' (Government of Canada and the Voluntary Sector, 2001, p 7). It draws attention to those individual and collective rights enshrined in the Canadian Charter of Rights and Freedoms (Government of Canada, 1982) and the Canadian Human Rights Act (Government of Canada, 1985).

The Accord upholds 'shared values' of diversity, 'respecting the rich variety of cultures, languages, identities, interests, views, abilities and communities in Canada' (p 7), and of inclusion, 'welcoming the expression and representation of diversity' (ibid). This is similar to both the English Compact and the French Charter, which give a nod to the more prominent fault lines in their own societies (black and minority ethnic communities in England; youth, women and the excluded – 'those with no voice' – in France). However, the lesser lever of a cohesive sector identity is evident in the Canadian case, where it is recognised that Canada's classic regional, provincial and national fault lines are not well represented by the coalition that signed the Accord on behalf of the voluntary and community sector. This is brought home in the letter of transmittal of the Accord, where the process of consultation leading up to the signing, is defended by pointing out that 'special efforts' were made 'to reach rural Canadians and visible minorities, Provincial and territorial officials and representatives from Aboriginal groups. The private sector [and] labour unions ... were consulted' (Government of Canada and the Voluntary Sector, 2001, p iv). Likewise, the idea is expressed in the introduction to the Accord, rather than in its actual text, that 'by encouraging people to participate and work together for common causes, the sector strengthens citizen engagement, gives voice to the voiceless, allows for multiple perspectives to be heard on a variety of issues, and provides opportunities for people to practice the skills of democratic life' (p 2).

Rather than specify the importance of consultation on issues of public policy and programmes, as the Compact and the Charter do, the Canadian Accord refers vaguely to respectful dialogue, flexible cooperation and the sharing of ideas and perspectives. In many ways, then, the Accord does not appear as firm in its intent to announce an important new vision and era of government–third sector relations, as the English Compact and French Charter seem to do. Phillips (2002) has called this a case of 'incomplete policy transfer', insofar as the conditions (for example, both third sector and state leadership) were not ripe for the Canadian Accord to take a significant step in the redesign of Canada's citizenship regime.

Québec's government policy on independent community action

Strong Catholic cultural and institutional roots, ethnic class divisions and nationalist aspirations and policies have all contributed to the autonomous development of Québec's state and civil society in relation to English Canada. Traditional French ideas of the 'social economy' have been influential, but, otherwise, the third sector has been actively engaged with the Québec provincial government for centuries, first in the form of a 'compact' between government and the Catholic Church, and, since the 1960s, in the form of a collaborative–conflict relationship between the state and combative grassroots organisations. This made for a very different scenario than that seen in France, where, traditionally, the state monopolised the public sphere. It is also different from the other two cases where relatively large and traditional voluntary organisations have been far more visible and significant actors in the development of partnership frameworks, than have been local, activist, grassroots groups. Indeed, we have seen in the English and Canadian (federal-level) cases, some recognition that local grassroots groups had been marginal in the construction of the Compact and the Accord. In Québec, these sorts of groups were the principles of the third sector.

From the early 1990s, the government of Québec had begun a process of 'integrating' community organisations into its public system of health and social service delivery. Although the imposition of contractual relations was relatively rare, new government policies were increasingly designed to depend upon community sector involvement in service planning and delivery. The community sector had begun mobilising from the grassroots up in order to defend its autonomy in the face of this perceived appropriation of its self-defined missions. During the 1990s, it had begun to organise locally, regionally and provincially in single-mission and cross-mission roundtables. On the one hand, this organisation facilitated its effective participation in regional service planning and delivery. On the other hand, it also constructed a somewhat more coherent, autonomous identity for Québec's third sector than exists in the other cases we have examined, as well as the thick, vertically and horizontally integrated networks to defend it.

While the voluntary or associative sectors in England, France and Canada had all initiated work on government–third sector partnership framework agreements, the community sector in Québec had no interest in such an accord. It was not under the same sort of neo-liberal attack as had been the case in England and Canada, for example. Although it felt threatened both financially and in terms of its autonomy, contracting was rare compared to core funding, its positions were often taken seriously in the social policy domain, and, when they were not, it had the capacity to mobilise popular and social movements in the province to pressure the government. Thus, the government, seeking to introduce some order into its rapidly growing and diversifying relations with the sector, took it upon itself to develop a policy with respect to community action. In it, it recognised that the 'history and evolution of Québec has been strongly marked by the extent of community-level action' (Gouvernement du Québec, 2001, p 15, author's translation). Indeed, the policy itself admits that its offer of partnership with the sector was essentially opposed by that sector. Nonetheless, the government had strived for legitimacy by engaging in a vast, independent consultation on a draft of the policy, and by adopting numerous important changes in the wake of that consultation. In parts, the policy mimics the form of the Compact, but it is a far longer and more complete document, including a lengthy representation of the history and nature of community action in Québec, and a detailed plan for the financing of various types of community organisations.

Québecers are depicted in the policy as politically and socially engaged citizens whose activities are, above all, grounded in their communities. The 'originality' of the Québec third sector, it claims, is precisely the salience of the 'community milieu'. It explicitly excludes from the policy, philanthropic organisations (so central to the Anglo-Saxon tradition) and the cooperatives and mutuals (important in the French tradition), to concentrate on the specificity of independent, locally grounded grassroots activity. It explicitly identifies a 'community movement' grounded in civil society, that involves a significant proportion of the sector, while also recognising the existence of less politically engaged groups whose first mission is to provide a service rather than transform the society. The movement, however, is given the place of honour in the policy. It is defined as 'initiated by citizens and communities, with their democratic participation and their political or social engagement' and their 'empowerment' (p 21). Its aims are 'social solidarity and the transformation of life conditions and social relations' (ibid). It 'fights against poverty and discrimination and for sexual equality' (ibid). Moreover, this policy spells out binding government commitments, or at least as binding as any other government policy that is not supported by specific legislation. There are no parallel commitments being made by the community sector, which ultimately gave its assent to the policy and agreed to collaborate, despite serious misgivings and divisions about such collaboration within the sector.

From administration to participation?

A citizenship regime refers to the mutually understood relationship that is established between states and citizens, typically on the basis of institutionally supported civic, political and social rights and responsibilities. In this context, the significance of the partnership framework agreements discussed above lies in the fact that they are an important formal step in the institutionalisation of a new social citizenship regime that appears to be emerging throughout welfare states, in which the third sector is recognised not only as a producer and distributor of welfare, but, clearly, also as a representative and participating actor in the social policy process.

Evers (1993) long ago argued that the third sector is 'not only shaped by public policies but also [is] a proactive factor influencing public discourse and social realities'. Moreover, he reminds us that the historical record shows that the third sector significantly influenced welfare state developments:

> If the evolution of welfare provision involved a sequential order at all then it was of third-sector initiatives pushed forward by local or national social movements that usually came first. They pioneered concepts of the collective good and notions of social rights. Afterwards, in a second phase ... these nuclei of social welfare were taken up by public policy and integrated into more general social contracts or state welfare. The history of social insurance often illustrates such developments. (p 9)

This same process in no way slowed down during the years of welfare state development in which third sector participation was eclipsed by the growing role of the state. It was entirely evident in the systematic introduction of public services since the 1960s and, we would argue, after a hiatus during the years of neo-liberal retrenchment, the growing diversification of public services since the late 1990s. On the one hand, then, civil society organisations remain active in the areas of child poverty, immigration, disability, mental health, minority ethnic services, childcare, housing and women's shelters, all relatively recent examples of third sector development of innovative or alternative practices, and successful (or less successful) pressure to have states commit themselves to support them as a matter of policy. But on the other hand, their capacity to be effective in this role – to model alternative forms of interventions in the social domain, to advocate for new or different policies and to mobilise citizens to act with respect to their social and economic marginalisation – has been severely tested by the introduction of NPM techniques. Short-term government financing, government-fixed objectives, time-consuming, complex and costly accountability procedures, unpredictability, and competition among third sector organisations as well as, in some cases, between them and market enterprises, have all begun to cripple the sector in terms of both its capacity and its autonomy (Lewis, 1997; Dart and Zimmerman, 2000; Leduc Browne, 2000; Scott, 2003). The question of the significance and implications of state–third sector partnership framework agreements needs to be addressed in this sobering context.

If the welfare state is largely not only about granting and delivery of social rights, but equally about how these rights can be claimed and who can legitimately claim them, this would hardly be known from recent evaluations of the partnership framework agreements several years after their adoption. For example, one of the more significant results of the processes leading up to and following the signing of the English Compact in 1998, was the recognition of grassroots community organisations and black and minority ethnic groups, previously invisible in the traditional third sector. In two Codes of Good Practice[4] eventually published on each of these issues, these groups were publicly recognised and their specific characteristics and roles defined. Particularly in the case of black and minority ethnic groups, one of these designated roles was to 'present their concerns to government'. Nonetheless, the paramount concerns in these Codes of Good Practice are related to ensuring that the organisations can more efficiently contribute to the implementation of government policies. On this ground, a report of the Compact Working Group of NCVO, entitled *The paradox of compacts* (Craig et al, 2005), suggests that the Compact might already be becoming superfluous. Since the signing of the Compact, there has been an extremely high level of government activity in Britain, promoting myriad locally based policies and programmes, all organised around partnerships between local authorities and voluntary and community organisations and all acting to build up the level of trust between groups and government agencies that the very idea of the Compact was intended to promote. Thus:

> Instead of being the framework within which the range of new policy initiatives could be embedded, Compacts were taking a back seat while these more immediate imperatives were addressed.... While the Compact could have an important role to play in changing relationships between government and the sector ... it may paradoxically no longer be needed. Indeed ... its longer-term future might lie in becoming a template for local partnership working more generally. (Craig et al, 2005, p 5)

However, a survey conducted by a voluntary sector research organisation had a different, although equally paradoxical, take on the situation. It suggested that the voluntary sector 'feels locked into an unhappy relationship with the state, and often feels it is taken for granted ... but far from trying to extract itself, much of the sector is keen to get more deeply involved with government' (ThirdSector, 2005). The impression of being 'second among equals' in its dealings with the state appears to apply to the domain of service contracts, however, and not to campaigning or advocacy activities, where English voluntary and community organisations are not dependent on the state, but rely heavily on membership fees and donations. Still, with the massive flow of funding to credible organisations of the third sector since 1998, it is clear that some organisations that used to play an essentially advocacy role have turned to the more lucrative business of service provision.

In England, then, where the first partnership framework agreement was designed, service provision and service administration trump representation and advocacy as the principle issues highlighted by the Compact. In contrast, in both Canada and France, post-Accord and post-Charter activities have tended to focus as much or more on matters of participation as they do on technical matters, such as funding – although the latter remains problematic.

In the Canadian case, one of the principal issues has been the extent to which current funding laws limit the participation of government-funded organisations in advocacy work (Harvie, 2002; Scott, 2003). The legitimacy of advocacy has been questioned by the federal government, which, in the past, has equated it with private as opposed to public interests. Few organisations in Canada have the capacity to raise independent funds that large organisations in England do. The Accord, while recognising the right to take independent views on issues of government interest, has not led to these important obstacles to advocacy being lifted. It is significant, then, that among the various achievements of the VSI's capacity-building round table is *Participating in federal public policy: A guide for the voluntary sector* (Voluntary Sector Initiative, 2003), a 60-page 'training' document designed to increase organisations' access to government for effectiveness in advocacy. While traditional forms of advocacy and community development are no longer government-supported (Richmond and Shields, 2004), many organisations have diversified their sources of funding in order to continue such activities (Meinhard and Foster, 2002). One development since the signing of the Accord is an upsurge in government consultation with the voluntary and community sector. This has transformed the sector's strategies for influencing policy development. Many now opt for developing and promoting their expertise and specialised knowledge in specific social fields as well as their capacity for performing effectively in various federal consultation contexts.

Consultation and advocacy are clearly not the same thing. Consultation typically takes place under conditions imposed by government or other authorities, at their whim and with little regard for accountability to those consulted. Advocacy is independent. Moreover, its practitioners usually have entire repertoires of collective action that they can resort to, to hold public agencies accountable. The distinction overlaps that between 'insider' and 'outsider' strategies for promoting change (White, 2000). By engaging increasingly in expert consultation with the voluntary sector, the Canadian government lives up to the Accord, enhances its policy capacity, stretches the boundaries of traditional policy communities, and, at the same time, tames collective action.

In contrast, in the French case, the promise of greater participation of the sector does not appear to imply recognition of the sector as an independent actor, but, rather, its recognition as a social partner. The idea that the third sector shares the territory of 'public interest' with the state was introduced in the Charter. It is a vision that is still supported by both government and the sector itself, although there is no evidence that headway has been made. Since the signing of the Charter in 2001, the sector has been particularly identified as an economic one and its development represents an important plank in the implementation of national social cohesion and inclusion policies (Ministère du travail, de l'emploi et de la cohésion, 2004). Both government (Lamour, 2004) and the sector leadership (CPCA, 2004) refer to it as a 'fully fledged intermediary body', suggesting that it serves to mediate interests between citizens and the state. The minister responsible for the sector has recently stated his intention to shift the state–third sector relation from a strictly administrative framework (which has been paramount since the signing of the Charter and which still remains problematic, especially with respect to financing) to one in which the sector participates fully in national debates around issues of public interest. This includes an intention to reinforce its place and role within the Economic and Social Council, an important advisory council to the government, and to strengthen the interministerial council on social innovation and the social economy (Lamour, 2004).

In France, then, where traditionally the state alone could represent the public interest, the Charter more clearly represented a step towards a new state–third sector relation, with the sector increasingly taking on the identity of a recognised, although junior, social partner. In contrast, in England, where a large and vital third sector has historically collaborated with the state as *both* a producer of welfare *and* an agent of welfare development, the Compact's impact appears to be more modest. It has allowed for a more effective mobilisation of voluntary and community groups to participate in government-initiated policies and programmes.

Finally, Canada's Accord may be contributing to changes in advocacy strategies, as funding regulations remain intact and the federal government reaches out to it, through consultation. As for Québec, the situation is sufficiently different for that case to serve as an alternative model to partnership framework agreements.

Administration and participation: the Québec case

In Québec, the government policy on independent community action may, paradoxically, have the most impact of all on administrative relations between the government and the third sector, and the least on participatory relations. With respect to welfare administration, it seeks primarily to inject some level of order into the government's myriad dealings with the sector, across ministries, and to streamline community groups' access to more stable, long-term government funding. This is indeed an institutionalisation of relations. But in terms of the sector's ability to confront and engage the government, the policy leaves that entirely up to the sector itself. On the political level, the community sector has always been a significant vehicle for change in Québec and there is nothing in the policy to change that one way or another. The sector itself has committed itself to nothing, although it has indicated its willingness, for now, to cooperate with the implementation process. As in England, many groups questioned the need for a government policy or agreement. But in Québec, it was clear that it was the government that needed a policy, not the sector.

This difference between Québec and the other cases we have examined can only be explained by considering two dimensions. First, with respect to the state: like England, Québec has a socially active state, at least since the 1960s. The period of welfare state retrenchment in Québec did not take the form of cancelled or decimated policies and programmes, but, rather, of significant cuts at the margins of existing services and transfers. This was typically accompanied by reorganisations and reforms and while they created havoc in the social sector, they did not fundamentally change the government's view of the social role of community organisations in society. Their distinction from market enterprises was never seriously questioned before the late 1990s, and then, it was to recognise and support a new category of organisations, the social enterprise. Thus, contracting was very limited, compared to its massive introduction in the years prior to the signing of agreements, in the other cases we have looked at. Furthermore, for at least a decade before the adoption of the policy, community organisations were recognised for their expertise in given areas and were drawn into programme planning and design committees at the local and regional levels, as fully fledged members rather than ad hoc consultants. England has been adopting similar strategies since the signing of the Compact.

Second, and perhaps more significant, is the way in which civil society organises itself in Québec. The sector, while almost wholly dependent on the state for its financial resources, nonetheless has the power to mobilise local constituencies and coalitions with the women's movement, the youth movement, the environmental movement and even the union movement. In response to disorienting cuts and reforms in the 1990s, community organisations of all stripes organised into networks at local and regional levels to represent their common interests. When the government announced its intention to develop a policy with respect to them, they organised at the provincial level and provided the government with a structured and legitimate, if recalcitrant, interlocutor. These self-organised structures claim to represent only their members, not the sector as a whole. In short, the strategies adopted by Québec's third sector itself have been very different from those adopted in England, France and English Canada. But, then, the sector has operated within a different institutional environment.

Conclusions

This chapter has argued that the signing of partnership framework agreements between governments and third sectors in several countries needs to be understood in two ways. First, as a shift in the administration of welfare, where the pressure to increase welfare services calls for increasing involvement of third sector organisations in public programmes, and new financial and other arrangements compatible with both government and sector needs. Second, it needs to be understood as a step demanded, in most cases, by the sector itself, as it defensively reorganised in the face of increasing demands and the unilateral transformation of existing arrangements. In this sense, the agreements, like Québec's policy, reflect the need to adapt to a changing situation for both government and the sector. But do they contribute to the emergence of a new social citizenship regime, implying (1) new policies or programmes, (2) new modes of delivery, (3) new bearers or claimants of social rights, and (4) new actors in the social policy community?

Clearly, the answer is somewhat different for each case we examined here. Nonetheless, a premise of the emergence of all these agreements, including Québec's policy, was that the government's ability to introduce new policies and programmes had been decimated during the 1980s and 1990s, and that by the end of the 1990s, social renewal required new modes of service delivery involving third sector 'partners'. Legitimate, new rules of the game needed to be drawn up. But the extent to which the agreements imply new bearers of social rights and new policy actors is more uneven. Newly or differently recognised bearers of social rights seem to be identified to the extent that grassroots organisations are drawn into the picture. Thus, black and minority ethnic organisations in England have, in the Compact, a new tool to claim and deliver improved access to social rights for their constituents. This is a less likely outcome where the agreements ultimate manage to mobilise mainly traditional voluntary organisations, leaving the local 'upstarts' at the margins. Finally, while the agreements all appear to invite the third sector to add its voice to those already heard within the policy community, the paths provided for this differ from one case to another. One of the factors involved is the manner and extent of self-organisation within the sector. For example, both reaching out too broadly and not broadly enough may inhibit cohesive, effective voice. However, perhaps a more important factor in whether the sector will have an effective voice lies with state strategy: the more socially active the state, the more likely it is to multiply opportunities for effective input, not least because it feeds on that input. Finally, these opportunities may more or less be structured by the state or by the third sector itself.

In the end, the partnership framework agreements appear to have more life as administrative tools than as vehicles of new forms of welfare governance. Indeed, they may be less and less salient as time goes on and they have completed their job of naming and regulating a new situation. Yet the content of the agreements may prove to be far less important than the process that produced them. This process involved, in all cases examined, the consolidation and organisation of the third sector, the construction of a collective actor recognised, legitimated and empowered by government. The partnership framework agreements set down remarkably similar rules for the new game, but how the game is played by government and third sector actors alike will differ according to both their capacities and their strategies.

Notes

[1] Privatisation of social service delivery was attempted and had some success in some areas, in some countries; for example, in certain workfare programmes in the US and in supported housing for older people in many countries. However, as theory predicted, social welfare generally proved to be unattractive to the private sector and the third sector grew instead as governments attempted to reduce the size of their public sectors.

[2] The term 'agreement' will be used to refer to all four cases, despite the fact that in the Québec case, it is not an 'agreement' but a unilateral government policy.

[3] National voluntary organisations in Canada are involved principally in advocacy work, since health, education and social policies and services are all designed and delivered by the provinces. A few national voluntary organisations have provincial affiliates and all make efforts (for example, through membership) to represent all regions of the country. In some provinces, and in variable ways, aspects of health, social and educational responsibilities are devolved to municipalities. Thus, the majority of voluntary and community organisations work vis-à-vis the provincial or, to a lesser degree, municipal government, not the federal government.

[4] The exact dates of publication of these Codes are not recorded. The Code on Black and Minority Ethnic Voluntary and Community Organisations was published within two years of the original Compact (Active Community Unit, 2001), while the Code on Community Groups was not adopted until 2003 (Active Community Unit, 2003).

References

6, P. and Kendall, J. (eds) (1997) *The contract culture in public services: Studies from Britain, Europe and the USA*, Aldershot: Ashgate.

Active Community Unit (2001) *Black and minority ethnic voluntary and community organisations: A Code of Good Practice*, London: The Home Office.

Active Community Unit (2003) *Community groups. A code of good practice*, London: The Home Office.

Aucoin, P. (1995) *The New Public Management: Canada in comparative perspective*, Quebec: Institute for Research on Public Policy.

Balloch, S. and Taylor, M. (eds) (2001) *Partnership working: Policy and practice*, Bristol: The Policy Press.

Commission on the Future of the Voluntary Sector (1996) *Meeting the challenge of change: Voluntary action into the 21st century (The 'Deakin Report')*, London: NCVO (National Coalition of Voluntary Organisations).

CPCA (Conférence Permanente des Coordinations Associatives) (2004) *Position politique CPCA novembre 2004, Conférence permanente des coordinations associatives* (online), available at: http://cpca.asso.fr/docs/PositionpolitiqueCPCAnovembre2004.pdf

Craig, G., Taylor, M., Carlton, N., Gawbutt, R., Kimberlee, R., Lepine, E. and Syed, A. (2005) *The paradox of Compacts: Monitoring the impact of Compacts*, London: Home Office Research, Development and Statistics Directorate.

Dart, R. and Zimmerman, B. (2000) 'After government cuts: insights from two Ontario "enterprising nonprofits", in K.G. Banting (ed) *The nonprofit sector in Canada: Roles and relationships*, Kingston: McGill-Queens Press.

Dunleavy, P. and Hood, C. (1994) 'From old public administration to New Public Management', *Public Money and Management*, vol 14, no 3, July–Sept, pp 9-16.

Evers, A. (1993) 'The welfare mix approach. Understanding the pluralism of welfare systems', in A. Evers and I. Svetlick (eds) *Balancing pluralism*, Aldershot: Avebury.

Evers, A. and Strünck, C. (1998) 'The liberty which is given by retreat: The changing contract culture in the provision of social services in Germany', Paper presented at the 3rd International Society for Third Sector Research (ISTR) Conference, Geneva, July.

Gouvernement du Québec (2001) *L'action communautaire: Une contribution essentielle à l'exercice de la citoyenneté et au développement social du Québec, Projet de politique gouvernmentale* (document de travail), Québec: Ministère de l'emploi et de la solidarité sociale.

Government of Canada (1982) *Constitution Act*, http://laws.justice.gc.ca/en/charter/.

Government of Canada (1985) *Canadian Human Rights Act*, R.S. 1985, c.H-6/, http://laws.justice.gc.ca/en/H-6/.

Government of Canada and the Voluntary Sector (2001) *An accord between the government of Canada and the voluntary and community sector*, Ottawa: Government of Canada and the Voluntary Sector.

Harvie, B.A. (2002) *Regulation of advocacy in the voluntary sector: Current challenges and some responses*, Ottawa: Voluntary Sector Secretariat.

Home Office (1998) *Compact on relations between government and the voluntary and community sector in England*, London: The Stationery Office.

Home Office (1990) *Efficiency scrutiny of Government funding of the voluntary sector: Profiting from partnership*, London: HMSO.

Jenson, J. (1997) 'Fated to live in interesting times: Canada's changing citizenship regimes', *Canadian Journal of Political Science*, vol 30, no 4, pp 627-44.

Jenson, J. and Papillon, M. (2000) *The changing boundaries of citizenship: A review and research agenda*, Ottawa: Canadian Policy Research Networks.

Jenson, J. and Phillips, S.D. (1996) 'Regime shift: new citizenship practices in Canada', *International Journal of Canadian Studies*, vol 14, autumn, pp 111-38.

Lamour, J.-F. (2004) *Grands axes de la politique associative* (online), available at: www.jeunesse-sports.gouv.fr/vieasso/grandsaxes_JFL.pdf

Leduc Browne, P. (2000) 'The neo-liberal uses of the social economy: non-profit organisations and workfare in Ontario', in E. Shragge and J.M. Fontan (eds) *Social economy: International debates and perspectives*, Montréal: Black Rose Books, pp 65-80.

Lewis, J. (1997) 'Contracting: what does it do to voluntary and non-profit organisations?', in J. Kendall and T. Kendall (eds) *The contract culture in public services*, Aldershot: Arena.

Meinhard, A. and Foster, M. (2002) 'Responses of Canada's voluntary organisations to shifts in social policy: a provincial perspective', Paper presented at the 5th International Society for Third Sector Research (ISTR) Conference, Cape Town, 7-10 July.

Ministère du Travail, de l'Emploi et de la Cohésion (2004) *Plan de cohésion sociale*, Paris: République Française.

Nevitte, N. (2000) 'Value change and reorientations in citizen–state relations', *Canadian Public Policy*, vol 26, special supplement 2, pp S73-S94.

Phillips, S. (2002) 'Striking an accord: the limits of transnational policy transfer in Canada's voluntary sector', Federal Government Framework Agreement, Paper presented to the Annual Meeting of the Canadian Political Science Association, Toronto, 29 May.

Polidano, C., Minogue, M. and Hulme, D. (eds) (1998) *Beyond the New Public Management: Changing ideas and practices in governance*, Cheltenham: Edward Elgar.

Premier Ministre et CPCA (Conférence Permanente des Coordinations Associatives) (2001) *Charte d'engagements réciproques entre l'état et les associations regroupées au sein de la CPCA*, in Dossier de presse, Centenaire de la loi 1901, Paris: Bureau du Premier Ministre.

Richmond, T. and Shields, J. (2004) *Third sector restructuring and the new contracting regime: The case of immigrant serving agencies in Ontario*, Centre for Voluntary Sector Studies Working Paper Series, No. 24. Toronto: Ryerson University.

Rouban, L. (ed) (1999) *Citizens and the new governance: Beyond New Public Management*, Amsterdam: IOS Press.

Scott, K. (2003) *Funding matters: The impact of Canada's new funding regime on nonprofit and voluntary organisations*, Ottawa: Canadian Council on Social Development.

Scottish Office (1998) *The Scottish Compact: Principals underpinning the relationship between Government and the voluntary sector in Scotland*, London: The Stationery Office. (Revised edition published in 2003).

Secretary of State for Wales (1998) *Compact between the Government and the voluntary sector in Wales*, London: HMSO.

ThirdSector (2005) 'Working with the government: second among equals', *General Charity News*, January 26. www.thirdsector.co.uk/charity_news/full_news.cfm:ID×13379.

Ullman, C.F. (1998) 'Partners in reform: nonprofit organisations and the welfare state in France', in W.W. Powell and E.S. Clemens (eds) *Private action and the public good*, New Haven, CT: Yale University Press.

United Kingdom (1993) *The Public Service Contracts Regulations*, Statutory Instrument 1993 No 3228, London: HMSO.

Voluntary Sector Initiative (VSI). Capacity Joint Table (2003) *Participating in federal public policy: A guide for the voluntary sector*, Ottawa: VSI.

White, D. (2000) 'Consumer and community participation', in G.L. Albrecht, R. Fitzpatrick and S.C. Scrimshaw (eds) *Handbook of social studies in health and medicine*, London: Sage Publications, pp 465-80.

Wistow, G., Knapp, M.R.J., Hardy, B., Forder, J., Kendall, J. and Manning, R. (1996) *Social care markets: Progress and prospects*, Buckingham: Open University Press.

FOUR

Shifts in welfare governance: the state, private and non-profit sectors in four European countries

Menno Fenger

As we have seen in other chapters of this book, the administration and implementation of welfare involve a wide variety of state organisations, private commercial organisations and non-profit organisations. However, the roles and positions of these state, private and non-profit organisations in administering and implementing social policies vary significantly between countries. This variation is commonly attributed to the differences in welfare regimes (Esping-Andersen, 1990). However, in the era of welfare reform, everything is in flux. This includes the role and position of state, private and non-profit actors in social policies. The concept of governance, which is widely gaining popularity in social policies (see Newman, 2001; Daly, 2003; Ewalt and Jennings, 2004), refers to these changing relations between government and society (Daly, 2003, p 116). Governance is about 'sustaining co-ordination and coherence among a wide variety of actors with different purposes and objectives such as political actors and institutions, corporate interests, civil society, and transnational organizations' (Pierre, 2000, p 4). So there are many reasons to assume that welfare reform has affected the involvement of state, private and non-profit actors in administering and implementing social policy.

In this chapter, the key question is what shifts have taken place in the role and position of state, private and non-profit organisations in the administration and implementation of social policies since the early 1990s. To answer this question, I will focus on the role of the state, the private and the non-profit sectors in four European countries. More specifically, the attention is aimed at the delivery of unemployment benefits on the one hand and all activities that are focused on getting unemployed people back to the labour market (also known as 'active labour market policies') on the other hand.

As these two streams become increasingly interconnected in modern Europe, I use the concept of employment policy to refer to both activities (Lødemel and Trickey, 2001). In the next section, I will present four general perspectives on the shifts between the roles of the state, the private and the non-profit sectors in welfare governance. The third section contains a brief review of the literature on the three societal domains – state, private and non-profit sector. The shifts between these domains are the key focus of this article. In section four, an overview will be given of the developments that the four examined European countries have gone through since the early 1990s. In order to get a clear overview of the developments in the different welfare regimes, each type is represented by one country. The UK represents the Anglo-Saxon type, Sweden the Scandinavian welfare states and Germany the continental type. The Netherlands is added to these three countries because it is usually considered an interesting mix of the continental and the Scandinavian types (SCP, 2001). This mix of countries ensures sufficient variation in the involvement of state, private and non-profit actors in social policies in 1990, the starting-point of this analysis. In the final section, some general conclusions concerning the shifts in welfare governance and their implications for administering and implementing social policies are drawn.

Welfare governance: general trends and expectations

There are at least four different perspectives on the shifts in the role of the state, the private and the non-profit sectors in welfare governance. First, there are authors who perceive the introduction of market incentives as a dominant shift in all, or almost all, modern welfare states. For instance, Osborne and Gaebler (1992, pp 325-8) see the New Public Management (NPM) movement – in which the introduction of private mechanisms is fundamental – as both global and inevitable (compare: Pollitt, 2003). In the field of social security and welfare policy, this assumes a convergent trend towards market-based mechanisms of governance in various countries, independent of the institutional structure of these fields in the past.

Second, from a governance perspective, we would assume a move away from hierarchy – that is, governing by the state – towards alternative modes of governance. As has been stated in the first chapters of this book, one of the premises is the 'erosion of domestic political authority and the flow of authority (if not power) away from traditional institutions of government' (Daly, 2003, p 116).

Starting from this normative premise, it is advisable that states retrench, become less powerful, assume a low profile and operate in a network with private interests and groups as a partner scarcely more important than any other (Merrien, 1998). All actors who are involved in welfare administration and implementation should 'join together with the state institutions, pool their resources, expertise, skills and plans and form a new coalition for action based on sharing of responsibilities' (Merrien, 1998, p 58). In the case of welfare reform, the notions of self-governing and co-governing are especially important. In a self-governing welfare system, employees, employers and (potential) welfare recipients jointly give rise to a sustainable system for social protection and employment policy, whereas in a system of co-governing the coordination between various societal domains including the state results in a sustainable welfare system (compare: Kooiman, 2000, pp 147-50). There is, of course, some overlap between the concepts of corporatism and co-governance, because both point towards the importance of state–society interactions. However, in this perspective the concept of corporatism refers much more to formal, well-structured interactions in a closed circuit of employers' associations, trades unions and the state, whereas the concept of co-governance refers to more open, spontaneous and informal interactions between a wide variety of actors.

The third perspective can be associated with the notion of path dependency. A path-dependent process is one characterised by a self-reinforcing sequence of effects (Deeg, 2001). Pierson (2000) argues that positive feedback mechanisms promote a specific path. The first feedback mechanism relates to large initial or set-up costs. This implies that actors have an incentive to continue the given path in order to recover these costs. Learning is a second feedback mechanism. Over time, actors operating within a particular path become more adept and knowledgeable and use this to enhance the efficiency and effectiveness of the institutions. Another mechanism is coordination effects. In this mechanism, actors anticipate each other's behaviour within a specific path and thus reinforce the reproduction of the path.

The concept of path dependency explains institutional stability over time. However, it does not exclude the possibility of institutional dynamics. Major external events can cause critical junctures: 'off-path' change. However, when we use the notion of path dependency to formulate hypotheses on the shifts in the role of state, private and non-profit actors in employment policy, we would expect that even processes of welfare reform reinforce the existing institutional structure. The policies may change, but actual shifts in the involvement of state, private and non-profit actors cannot be straightforwardly related to the path-dependency theory.

Finally, some authors suggest that the introduction of the European Employment Strategy might lead to congruence in the development of the European welfare states (see Bertozzi and Bonoli, 2002; Dehousse, 2002; see also Chapters Ten and Eleven of this book). The fields of social and employment policy have long been neglected in the European Union (EU). Traditionally, the EU's focus has been on optimising the functioning of the internal labour market. However, since the Amsterdam Treaty of 1997, employment policy has been officially raised to the status of a common European concern. At the Luxembourg Jobs Summit following the adoption of the Amsterdam Treaty the member states of the EU agreed on the European Employment Strategy (EES). The EES consists of four integrated strands of action, the so-called 'pillars' of the Employment Guidelines: employability, entrepreneurship, adaptability and equal opportunities. These actions are intended to constitute a comprehensive response to the employment challenge in the EU. Unlike most other policy domains in the EU, governance in the EES does not take place through compulsory directives, but through the so-called Open Method of Coordination. Through a system of monitoring and benchmarking, this method 'promotes a ... "learning-friendly" environment for policy innovation and experimentation, while recognising that the national European welfare states are profoundly different' (Hemerijck, 2002, p 209). Although congruence between the European welfare states is explicitly not a goal of this Open Method of Coordination, it could be argued that a system which promotes the dissemination of best practices and mutual learning, promotes congruence as an inevitable outcome. Considering the relatively short history of European social and employment policy, its impact on the shifts in welfare governance is probably limited. Nevertheless, from this perspective, these shifts may gradually lead each of the nations towards a common – but not yet well-articulated – model of European welfare governance.

State, private and non-profit sectors: an overview

Streeck and Schmitter (1985) state that society consists of four different spheres: state, private, community and associations. The sphere of the associations is also referred to as the 'non-profit sector' or the 'third sector' (compare: Pestoff, 1992). In this chapter, the shifts in the role of three societal domains in administering and implementing social policies take a central place. The community, which refers to families and households, does not play a significant role in the administration and implementation of social policies and is therefore neglected in this chapter. According to Arts (1991, p 5), the concept of a state refers to a decision-making and coordinating mechanism that rests on a network of centrally coordinated activities of a large number of actors who make decisions collectively. Markets can be defined as decision-making and coordinating mechanisms that rest upon networks of actual and potential exchange relations between individual actors making independent choices, which feature compatibility (Arts, 1991, p 5).

Since the early 1990s there has been increasing scientific attention to the role of non-profit organisations' public governance. There is a wide range of definitions of the non-profit sector. In this article, the term non-profit sector is used to designate all organisations that are neither profit-oriented businesses nor governmental agencies or bureaucracies (Seibel and Anheier, 1990, p 7). According to Salamon and Anheier (1996, p 9), two factors seem to be especially important in shaping the scope and scale of the non-profit sector in a country:

(1) *Heterogeneity*. The more diverse the population, the more difficult it is for people to agree on what collective goods should be provided. The result would be unsatisfied demand for collective goods in different segments of the population. The function of the non-profit sector is to meet this unsatisfied demand for collective goods (Salamon and Anheier, 1996, pp 9-10).
(2) *Historical traditions*. Various historical and religious traditions can encourage or discourage the formation of non-profit sector organisations.

In this section, the most important features of the state, the private and the non-profit sectors have been presented. In the next section, we will analyse to what extent there have been shifts in the role of each of these societal domains. Therefore, we analyse recent developments in employment policies in the Netherlands, Germany, the UK and Sweden. This enables us to assess the value of each of the four perspectives (NPM, governance, path dependency and Europeanisation) on shifting welfare governance.

Shifting welfare governance in four countries

In this section, a brief overview will be given of the developments in the institutional structure of employment policies in four countries: the Netherlands, Germany, the UK and Sweden.

The Netherlands

In the Netherlands, until 1990, employers' organisations and labour unions together were responsible for the administration of unemployment insurance. The state only had a role as a supervisor in the Social Insurance Council. In the early 1990s the limited role of the state became the subject of heavy criticism, as a result of the ever-increasing claims for unemployment benefits, disability allowances and social assistance benefits and an ongoing discussion on the quality of the administration process.

As a result, radical changes in the institutional design of unemployment and disability benefits were implemented. Under these changes the involvement of employees and employers with the administration was limited. An Independent Board of Supervision of Social Insurance replaced the Social Insurance Council. A tender procedure for the administration of unemployment benefits was initiated. Trade associations had to contract administration agencies for administrating employee insurances for limited periods. Five private administration agencies were established, which competed to obtain contracts.

However, before the first contract period was finished, the policy of competition was replaced. There are two reasons for this. First, political parties feared that privatisation of benefits could lead to unfair situations. Second, private administration agencies had merged with conglomerates of banks, insurance companies, personal finance advisors, and so on. Politicians feared an intolerable mixture of public contributions to employee insurances with private capital (Fenger, 2001).

In 2000, a new law was submitted to Parliament: the law on the implementation structure of work and income. In this law, the five private administration agencies were merged into a national Administration Agency for Employee Insurance. The Independent Board of Supervision of Social Insurance lost its independence and became part of the national ministry.

There is a great difference in the institutional dynamics between labour market policy and the administration of unemployment benefits. Since the Second World War, employment policy has been a task of central government (in fact, this had been a 'heritage' of the German occupation) whereas the administration of unemployment benefits has been the domain of the social partners. In the new Public Employment Service Law of 1990, it was decided to have central government share its responsibility with organisations of employers and employees.

However, within a few years the performance of the Public Employment Service was criticised. Sol (2000, pp 281-4) even states that the experiment with the 'tripartite' governance can be called a failure. In 1995 the law was revised so that the role of central government was reinforced again.

The proposals for the SIWI law in 2000 involved another reorganisation of the Public Employment Service. The old Public Employment Service was abolished. Instead, new Centres for Work and Income (CWIs) were established. In the CWIs, the labour office and the intake for unemployment and welfare benefits was integrated. The activities of the old Public Employment Service aimed at reintegration of the unemployed into the labour market were privatised. The new organisation, Kliq, became one of the new players in the reintegration market established in 2000. This market for the reintegration of benefit recipients into work developed very quickly. By 2004, it consisted of over 700 suppliers with a large variation in size, degree of specialisation, level of operation (national, regional or local) and performance. The market share of the former state employment agency has fallen below 30%.

Table 4.1 summarises the developments described above and translates these into the theoretical concepts developed earlier in this chapter. After we have analysed the developments in the other three countries, we will reflect on these developments from a theoretical and practical perspective on welfare reform.

Germany

Compared with the Netherlands, two characteristics of the German developments in employment policy stand out. First, in Germany there is an institutional integration of the responsibility for unemployment benefits and labour market policy in the Public Employment Agency, the *Bundesanstalt für Arbeit* (BA). Second, the absence of institutional dynamics until 2002 is striking.

The foundations of German social insurance were laid in the 1880s with the introduction of health, accident and pension

Table 4.1: Welfare governance developments in the Netherlands

Year	Developments in active labour market policy	Developments in unemployment policy
1990	Initial situation: pure state activity	Initial situation: corporatist
1993	From state governance to co-governance	From corporatism to market incentives (NPM)
1996	Enlarging the role of the state in the co-governance arrangement	
2000	From co-governance (with an important state role) to competition between private enterprises (NPM)	From market incentives to state governance
2003	Present situation: competition between private enterprises (NPM)	Present situation: state governance

insurance. The rise of the welfare state was associated not with the replacement, but with the incorporation of the private associations that had sprung up since the mid-19th century (Bönker and Wollmann, 2000, p 328). Unlike in other countries, the Second World War did not lead to a clear break with pre-war social policy. Bönker and Wollmann (2000, p 328) even state that for social services, the 'German welfare state has been a frozen one, until recently characterised by a high degree of institutional stability and, to use a fashionable term, path dependence'. According to Bönker and Wollmann (2000, p 329) the creation and relative stability of the compromise between different social actors were encouraged by religious heterogeneity, as well as by institutional features such as federalism and the predominance of coalition governments. The fragmented structure stems from the various historical origins together with the emphasis on the federal constitutional imperative, which allocated the federal states (and thus, in addition, the communal level) the responsibility for organisational structures and processes of implementation (Grünow, 2000).

The stability of welfare governance in Germany is even more striking when we realise that a major external event such as German unification in 1990 – which also had enormous economic impacts – did not lead to fundamental shifts in the institutional structure. This is not to say that there is a complete absence of dynamics in the German welfare state. For instance, Trampusch (2003) shows that there has been a tendency of shifting expenditure burdens between the federal Public Employment Service, the pension insurance funds and the federal budget.

Table 4.2: Welfare governance developments in Germany

Year	Developments in active labour market policy	Developments in unemployment policy
1990	Initial situation: integrated with unemployment policy Corporatist	Initial situation: integrated with active labour market policy Corporatist
2002	Separated from unemployment policy Slightly less corporatist, towards co-governance	Separated from active labour market policy Corporatist
2003	Present situation: minor steps towards co-governance	Present situation: corporatist

Until recently, German employment policy has been the responsibility of the federal Ministry of Labour and Social Affairs (*Bundesministerium für Arbeit und Sozialordnung*). In October 2002, the tasks of the Ministry were divided between the new Ministries of Economy and Labour and of Health and Social Security. Collective social insurance companies that are governed by representatives of employers and employees perform the administration of the social insurances. Implementation of disability insurance, employment insurance and labour market policy is carried out by the BA. Representatives of employers, employees and federal, regional and local authorities govern this organisation. The majority of the financial resources come from contributions of employers and employees; only a limited amount comes from the Ministry. This system of employment policy has been highly stable over time.

In February 2002, the German Court of Audit published a highly critical report on the performance of the BA. It appeared that the BA deliberately overestimated its own performance indicators. The criticism on the performance of the BA led to the installation of the Hartz Commission. This Commission, led by Peter Hartz, head of the personnel executive committee of Volkswagen, presented its proposals for reform of the German labour market in August 2002.

It is still unclear what the future will bring for the institutional design of the labour market and employment policy in Germany. But the government's support for the proposals of the Hartz Commission suggests that the dominance of corporatism in employment policy is bound to come to its end. Some authors believe that market-based governance mechanisms will replace corporatism. This thesis is supported by the introduction of market incentives in other social policy sectors such as health and housing (see Bönker and Wollmann, 2000). However, considering the immobility of the German institutional setting for welfare policy since the early 1990s, we should be cautious in believing revolutionary changes will occur in the German welfare state.

The UK

As in other countries, at the start of the first arrangements for poor and disabled people, government activity in the UK was minimal. In 1906 a government was elected with a large Liberal majority and support from the emerging Labour Party. The 1911 National Insurance Act and legislation of the 1920s created social insurance benefits for old, sick and unemployed people. Limited benefits were paid by the state and did not involve any form of partnership with voluntary organisations or trades unions. New participants in the social policy system did not emerge and little was done to strengthen those already involved (Hill, 2000, p 310). Throughout its history, the management of British social insurance has not involved any sort of corporate arrangement with 'social partners' (Clarke and Hoggett, 2000, p 225). According to Wells (2001, p 242), a central feature of the UK system is its universal welfare state with an extended scope but a limited generosity. Much of the social protection system is paid for through general taxation and employee social insurance contributions, which explains the limited role of social partners in administering and implementing social policy.

After the Second World War, the role of the state was expanded in the UK. Webb and Wistow (cited in Hill, 2000, p 316) write of 'the surprisingly cohesive and widely accepted "pure doctrine" of state welfare which underpinned the development of the post-war welfare state'. From the 1980s, the British Thatcher period, the role of the private sector in delivering social services was expanded. At the end of the 1980s, the Department of Social Security was subject to a radical process of restructuring in line with the Conservative government's 'Next Steps' reforms – that is, the 'agencification' of central government. The administration of most social insurance and social assistance benefits was devolved to the state-owned Benefits Agency. Since the creation of the Benefits Agency in 1991 the delivery of social security services has been subject to a series of sweeping reforms exemplifying nearly all of the main features of NPM (Clarke and Hoggett, 2000, p 225). In the period from 1991 to 1995, much value was placed on the quality of the service delivery by the Benefits Agency. In the period from 1995 until now, more emphasis has been placed on the introduction of market incentives (Clarke and Hoggett, 2000, p 231).

When the welfare state was set up in the late 1940s, compulsory labour exchanges were considered as a crucial counterbalance to any scheme of unemployment insurance. Requirements of active job search and availability for work were the key reasons for creating and maintaining a public Employment Service in the UK. Still in 1995, despite the government's predisposition towards greater private sector involvement, abolition of the public Employment Service was ruled out. Privatisation was not considered feasible, because charging for placing would undermine the help for the unemployed (Wells, 2001, p 247).

However, in 1997 the role of the Employment Service changed radically, becoming responsible for the delivery of the New Deal programmes. The New Deal is one of the initiatives that the British government has taken in its Welfare-to-Work strategy. For the implementation of the New Deal strategy an open tendering procedure is followed. The regional offices of the Employment Service organise these tenders. Table 4.3 provides an overview of the recent developments of active labour market policy and unemployment policy in the UK.

Sweden

Despite its unique reputation, the Swedish welfare state is 'clearly derivative, borrowing heavily from Beveridge in Britain and from the German social insurance approach developed in the late 1800s under Bismarck' (Olsen, 1999, p 241). Unemployment insurance has two distinct levels. First, there is a system of unemployment benefits restricted to members of unemployment insurance funds administered by the trades unions. Second, alongside the union funds, a public unemployment assistance programme provides flat-rate benefits for those not eligible for the union funds (Olsen, 1999; Anderson, 2001). According to Anderson (2001), in 1991 about 80% of the labour force belonged to a union fund.

In the field of unemployment insurance, little changed in the 1990s. In the early 1990s mass unemployment made its debut in Sweden. Developments that were a response to this are lower levels of spending in certain areas, declining public sector employment, and a decrease in the availability and quality of various social services. However, this has not yet led to dramatic changes in the institutional

Table 4.3: Welfare governance developments in the UK

Year	Developments in active labour market policy	Developments in unemployment policy
1990	Initial situation: state governance	Initial situation: state governance
1991		Introduction of market incentives Creation of Benefits Agency
1995		Stronger emphasis on market incentives
1997	Introduction of New Deal programmes, implemented by agents through tender procedure	
2003	Present situation: competition between private enterprises (NPM)	Present situation: governance based on market incentives (NPM)

structure of the Swedish welfare state (Olsen, 1999). Unemployment benefits were cut, but attempts to limit the role of the unions in the administration of the unemployment programmes failed.

Employment policy also has been a task for the Swedish state, with a strong emphasis on the local level. The Swedish National Labour Market Administration is responsible for the implementation of employment programmes. It formulates directives that have to be carried out at the regional and local levels. The local office of the Public Employment Service is the most important actor for the implementation of Swedish labour market policy. Its task is to match job vacancies and job seekers and to offer services that can facilitate the job matching. Sweden has over 400 local Employment Offices (Struyven et al, 2002, p 205). Table 4.4 provides an overview of the recent developments of active labour market policy and unemployment policy in Sweden.

Few institutional changes can be observed in this field, although Struyven et al (2002) rightfully argue that some privatisation has been introduced with regard to employment training. In 1986, the state authority for public employment training was transformed into an autonomous agency (AmuGruppen) and the market for state-financed employment training was opened up for public and private training institutions. In 1993, a second step of privatisation was taken. The AmuGruppen was transformed into a state enterprise. Level playing-field conditions for competition were introduced. However, this is the only element in the field of labour market policy in which the introduction of market incentives can be observed.

Table 4.4: Welfare governance developments in Sweden

Year	Developments in active labour market policy	Developments in unemployment policy
1990	Initial situation: state governance	Initial situation: co-governance of state and trades unions
1993	Introduction of market incentives in employment training	
2003	Present situation: state governance, with minor steps towards market incentives	Present situation: co-governance of state and trades unions

Analysis: general trends in welfare governance?

In this chapter, the issue of welfare governance takes a central place. The key question is what shifts have taken place in the involvement of state, private and non-profit organisations since 1990. In the wider context of this book, this issue connects to the shifting participants in welfare administration and implementation. Undoubtedly the most striking observation in this chapter is the divergence in developments in the four European countries in the last decade. None of the four perspectives that have been formulated in the second section of this chapter seems to adequately explain the development in each of the countries that have been described. We do not observe an overall trend towards privatisation or NPM models of welfare state governance, nor are all the countries moving towards a 'governance' model of welfare state governance or a European social model. And even path-dependency theory fails in explaining the development in each of the countries, although it does seem to apply to the German and Swedish cases.

Now we have analysed the shifts in four countries, we can try to assess the value of each of the four explanations offered in section two. Osborne and Gaebler (1992) consider the NPM movement as both a global and inevitable trend. When we focus on the field of employment policy, this statement seems not to hold true. In the UK a clear move from the state as principal mechanism of governance towards the introduction of market-based incentives can be observed. In the Netherlands, a partial shift towards the market as a mechanism for governance has been introduced. However, in Sweden and Germany there have not been significant moves towards a heavy role for private companies and market incentives in welfare governance. Even more striking is the fact that, in the Netherlands, the introduction of competition in the provision of unemployment benefits has been abandoned in favour of an integrated state-based structure.

Since 1990, all countries have been confronted with the limitations of central steering and state control in the field of social policies. However, this has not led to a general adoption of governance models of administering and implementing social policies. In Germany and the Netherlands, reforms that can be characterised as co-governance have been introduced. This is not surprising, considering the fact that these countries have extensive experience with corporatist models of social policy making. Although we have argued that there are important differences between corporatism and co-governance, the experiences with sharing responsibilities and pooling resources under corporatism could facilitate the adoption of co-governance arrangements.

The cases of Sweden and Germany at first sight seem to be excellent illustrations of path dependency. Both welfare states have been confronted with major challenges – of which the German reunification is the most striking – but the institutional structure has followed a path-dependent line of development. A strong argument for using path dependency to explain the developments in Germany and Sweden lies in the distinctiveness of the path in these countries. In Germany, the non-profit sector traditionally has played and still plays an important role in employment policy. Until recently, Germany has been one of the purest examples of the corporatist welfare state that can be found in Europe. All kinds of feedback mechanisms, including the financial interconnectedness of employment policy, pension insurance funds and the federal budget (see Trampusch, 2003) have reinforced the corporatist character of German employment policy. This explains the institutional stability in a turbulent environment. The notion of path dependency can also be used to explain the Swedish case. As the purest example of the social-democratic welfare state, with a large involvement of the state in the administration and provision of employment policy, even major economic, technological and demographic changes have not led to significant reforms in the governance of the welfare state. However, the shifts that have been observed in the UK and the Netherlands prevent the adoption of path dependency as the universal driving force in processes of welfare reform.

In the second section I argued that the history of European social policy probably would be too short to critically assess its impact on the direction of reforms in welfare governance in Europe. As expected, we are indeed unable to distillate the fundamentals of a common European social framework out of this four-country comparison. Whether this is the result of a still-limited role of Europe in the social policy domain, or confirms the claim of some protagonists that the Open Method of Coordination does not impose a specific model, is a question that cannot be answered on this data. We can, however, conclude that there is no discernable trend towards a common European framework for welfare governance.

Power struggles: the missing link?

It could be argued that the theoretical perspectives on welfare governance discussed in the second section of this chapter, do not take into account the political processes in different countries. Despite possible general trends, the actions that are taken, the reforms that are adopted, and the shifts that are implemented to a large extent depend on the struggle of different groups with different interests, ideologies and resources. These power struggles make the processes of welfare reform unpredictable, sometimes seemingly irrational, and always exciting.

The starting point of a power-based explanation is situated in the idea of a balance between groups with different ideological and practical ideas on the courses of action that should be taken. This idea can be found both in Paul Sabatier's advocacy coalition framework (Sabatier, 1993) and in Baumgartner and Jones's punctuated equilibrium theory (Baumgartner and Jones, 2002). In the advocacy coalition framework, policy-oriented learning is considered as the primary source for policy change. Factors that are external to the policy domain, like socioeconomic developments or changes in the governing coalitions, also might cause policy changes. Fenger and Klok (2001) argue that in addition to the cognitive explanations for policy change, power-based explanations also have to be incorporated into Sabatier's framework. They also propose to take into account the shifts in interdependencies between actors as an important trigger for policy change. In Baumgartner and Jones's theory, attention shifts can open up policy monopolies, which might result in policy change. In policy monopolies, a limited group of actors has dominated a policy domain for some time. When this policy domain for some reason becomes the subject of attention from the media or the public, the monopoly is broken. New actors enter the domain, often resulting in a new approach.

In addition to the explanations that have been previously discussed, we could try to assess to what extent these power-based approaches account for the (absence of) shifts between private, state, and non-profit-based welfare governance. Considering the Dutch case, struggling coalitions might have determined the outcome of the process of welfare reform. In contrast with the UK, where a clear preference for the introduction of market incentives can be identified and with Sweden where there seems to be consensus on the status quo, in the Netherlands various positions in this debate can be distinguished. There are organisations with a deeply rooted distrust against the introduction of market-based governance mechanisms, and organisations that believe that the market will lead to a more efficient administration and provision of employment services and unemployment benefits. Varying opinions on this topic can be found even within two of the most important political parties: the Christian-Democratic Party and the Labour Party. The fact that the power balance between the advocacy coalitions for and against the introduction of market incentives varies in different arenas and over time, might explain the different directions the process of welfare reform has taken in the Netherlands since 1990.

To explain the changes that followed the publication of the Court of Audit's report on the federal Employment Service in Germany, it is also necessary to take into account the struggle for power. The Hartz Commission presented its strategy only three months before German national elections, and it was clear that unemployment would be a key topic in the elections. The Hartz Commission's plans perhaps did not fit with the ideology of Chancellor Schröder's Social-Democratic Party. However, the German population widely supported those plans (Hilmer, 2002). A prompt implementation of the Hartz Commission's plans would show the Social-Democrats' determination to fight unemployment.

It seems that, next to the potential general trends of NPM, governance and (in Europe) Europeanisation, and the institutional context of history, we should not neglect the political process at the domestic level as an important factor, which gives shape to welfare reform. This is not a new, let alone revolutionary, insight. It is an insight, however, that is easily being overlooked in our search for general patterns of reform in welfare governance.

Shifts in welfare governance: final reflections

In this chapter, we have seen that there is no overall trend concerning the role of state, private and non-profit actors in welfare governance. Different theoretical foundations suggest different directions in welfare governance: a general trend towards a market-based model of administering and implementing social policies; a trend towards a governance-based model in which the interactions between state and society take a central place; a 'European model'; or institutional continuity. However, we have not found evidence that supports any of these claims in particular. From a welfare reform point of view, where does this conclusion leave us? The fact that there is no dominant trend towards a single model illustrates the ideological and political variety of opinions on how to organise welfare governance in contemporary Europe. Although the common developments that have been outlined in Chapter One of this book challenge all modern welfare states, the responses to these challenges have been diverse. This diversity is not only restricted to the diversity in changes in policy programmes (see also Scharpf and Schmidt, 2000), but is also visible in the modes of governance that play a role in the administration of the welfare state. The interplay of domestic characteristics and the institutional characteristics, the political process and power relations seems to play an important, although not decisive, role in changing welfare administrations' participants.

References

Anderson, K.M. (2001) 'The politics of retrenchment in a social democratic welfare state: reform of Swedish pensions and unemployment insurance', *Comparative Political Studies*, vol 34, no 9, pp 1063-91.

Arts, W.A. (1991) *Community, market and state: Reflections on their potential for achieving economic justice*, Bratislava: Bratislava School of Economics.

Baumgartner, F.R. and Jones, B.D. (2002) 'Positive and negative feedback in politics', in F.R. Baumgartner and B.D. Jones (eds) *Policy dynamics*, Chicago, IL: Chicago University Press, pp 3-27.

Bertozzi, F. and Bonoli G. (2002) 'Europeanisation and the convergence of national social and employment policies: what can the open method of co-ordination achieve', paper presented to the joint sessions of the European Consortium for Political Research, Turin, 22-27 March.

Bönker, F. and Wollmann, H. (2000) 'The rise and fall of a social service regime: marketisation of German social services in historical perspective', in H. Wollmann and E. Schröter (eds) *Public sector reform in Britain and Germany: Key traditions and trends of modernization*, Aldershot: Ashgate, pp 327-50.

Clarke, J. and Hoggett, P. (2000) 'Regressive modernisation: the changing patterns of social service delivery in the United Kingdom', in H. Wollmann and E. Schröter (eds) *Public sector reform in Britain and Germany: Key traditions and trends of modernization*, Aldershot: Ashgate: pp 224-43.

Daly, M. (2003) 'Governance and social policy', *Journal of Social Policy*, vol 32, no 1, pp 113-28.

Deeg, R. (2001) *Institutional change and the uses and limits of path dependency: the case of German Finance*, MPIfG Discussion Paper 01/6. Köln: Max-Planck-Institut für Gesellschaftforschung.

Dehousse, R. (2002) 'The Open Method of Coordination: a new policy paradigm?', paper presented at the 1st Pan-European Conference on European Union Politics, Bordeaux.

Esping-Andersen, G. (1990) *The three worlds of welfare capitalism*, Princeton, NJ: Princeton University Press.

Ewalt, J.A.G. and Jennings Jr., E.T. (2004) 'Administration, governance, and policy tools in welfare policy implementation', *Public Administration Review*, vol 64, no 4, pp 449-62.

Fenger, H.J.M. (2001) *Sturing van samenwerking: Institutionele veranderingen in het beleid voor werk en inkomen*, Amsterdam: Thela Thesis.

Fenger, H.J.M. and P.-J. Klok (2001) 'Interdependency, beliefs and coalition behavior: a contribution to the advocacy coalition framework', *Policy Sciences*, vol 34, no 2, pp 157-70.

Grünow, D. (2000) 'Social administration in Germany: basic structures and reform history', in H. Wollmann and E. Schröter (eds) *Public sector reform in Britain and Germany: Key traditions and trends of modernization*, Aldershot: Ashgate, pp 244-63.

Hemerijck, A. (2002) 'The self-transformation of the European social model(s)', in G. Esping-Andersen (ed) *Why we need a new welfare state*, Oxford: Oxford University Press, pp 173-213.

Hill, M. (2000) 'Trends in the marketisation of British social services', in H. Wollmann and E. Schröter (eds) *Public sector reform in Britain and Germany: Key traditions and trends of modernization*, Aldershot: Ashgate, pp 304-26.

Hilmer, R. (2002) *The political situation in Germany before the general elections on 22 September 2002*, Working Paper 6/2002, London: Friedrich-Ebert-Stiftung.

Kooiman, J. (2000) 'Societal governance: levels, modes and orders of social-political interaction', in J. Pierre (ed) *Debating governance: Authority, steering and democracy*, Oxford: Oxford University Press, pp 139-64.

Lødemel, I. and Trickey, H. (eds) (2001) *'An offer you can't refuse': Workfare in international perspective*, Bristol: The Policy Press.

Merrien, F.-X. (1998) 'Governance and modern welfare states', *International Social Science Journal*, vol 50, no 155, pp 57-68.

Newman, J. (2001) *Modernising governance: New Labour, policy and society*, London: Sage Publications.

Olsen, G.M. (1999) 'Half empty or half full? The Swedish welfare state in transition', *The Canadian Review of Sociology and Anthropology*, vol 36, no 2, pp 241-68.

Osborne, D. and Gaebler, T. (1992) *Reinventing government: How the entrepreneurial spirit is transforming the public sector*, Reading: Addison Wesley.

Pestoff, V.A. (1992) 'Third sector and co-operative services – an alternative to privatization', *Journal of Consumer Policy*, vol 15, no 1, pp 21-45.

Pierre, J. (2000) 'Introduction: understanding governance', in J. Pierre (ed) *Debating governance: Authority, steering and democracy*, Oxford: Oxford University Press.

Pierson, P. (2000) 'Increasing returns, path dependence, and the study of politics', *American Political Science Review*, vol 94, pp 251-67.

Pollitt, C. (2003) *The essential public manager*, Maidenhead, Open University Press.

Sabatier, P.A. (1993) 'Policy change over a decade or more', in H.C. Jenkins-Smith and P.A. Sabatier (eds) *Policy change and learning: An advocacy coalition approach*, Boulder, CO: Westview Press, pp 13-39.

Salamon, L.M. and Anheier, H.K. (1996) *The emerging non-profit sector. An overview*, Manchester: Manchester University Press.

Scharpf, F.W. and Schmidt, V.A. (2000) 'Introduction', in F.W. Scharpf and V.A. Schmidt (eds) *Welfare and work in the open economy. Vol. 2. Diverse responses to common challenges*, Oxford: Oxford University Press, pp 1-18.

SCP (Social and Cultural Planning Office of the Netherlands) (2001) *On worlds of welfare: Institutions and their effects in eleven welfare states*, The Hague: Social and Cultural Planning Office of the Netherlands.

Seibel, W. and Anheier, H.K. (1990) 'Sociological and political science approaches to the third sector', in H.K. Anheier and W. Seibel (eds) *The third sector: Comparative studies of non-profit organizations*, Berlin: Walter de Gruyter, pp 8-20.

Sol, E. (2000) *Arbeidsvoorzieningsbeleid in Nederland: De rol van de overheid en de sociale partners*, Den Haag: Sdu-uitgevers.

Streeck, W. and Schmitter, P. (1985) 'Community, market, state – and associations?', in W. Streeck and P. Schmitter (eds) *Private interest government: Beyond market and state*, London: Sage Publications, pp 1-29.

Struyven, L., Steurs, G., Peeters, A. and Minne, V. (2002) *Van aanbieden naar aanbesteden: Marktwerking bij arbeidsbemiddeling en reïntegratie in Australië, Nederland, Verenigd Koninkrijk en Zweden*, Leuven: Acco.

Trampusch, C. (2003) *Ein Bündnis für die nachhaltige Finanzierung der Socialversicherungssysteme: Interessenvermittlung in der bundesdeutschen Arbeidsmarkt- und Rentenpolitik*, Discussion Paper 03/1, Köln: MPIfG.

Wells, W. (2001) 'From restart to the New Deal in the United Kingdom', in OECD, *Labour market policies and the Public Employment Service*, Paris: OECD.

FIVE

From charity to 'not-for-profit': changes in the role and structure of voluntary social service agencies

Jo Barnes

> Justice is not about measurable outcomes, justice is about opportunity, justice is about access, justice is about getting your right to a whole lot of basic life things. (Faith-based agency director)

From 1984 to 1999, New Zealand underwent 15 years of significant welfare reform and welfare state restructuring. In the US, President Clinton took office in 1993 declaring his commitment 'to end welfare as we know it' and in 1996 signed into law the Personal Responsibility and Work Opportunity Reconciliation Act (see Chapter Six of this book). This Act dramatically changed the welfare system. In the wake of these reforms, this chapter discusses changes regarding welfare governance as they relate to the role of the third sector or voluntary social service agencies. The chapter presents the results of a study into the organisational changes of non-government social provision agencies as they move from being charities to 'not-for-profit businesses' as state support for welfare declines in New Zealand and the US.

This chapter discusses findings from a study undertaken in 2001-02 on not-for-profit social service organisations in the regional city of Hamilton, a city of 166,000 people, in the context of changes in New Zealand welfare governance from 1984 to 1999 and in Tampa, Florida, a city of just over 300,000 people, following the US welfare reforms of the Clinton administration.

It is argued that the move from being charities to 'not-for-profit businesses' affected both the way that agencies were structurally organised in terms of their management and the types of clients that they were able to help. It is argued that because of the fiscal and procedural accountability that was demanded of them, the agencies made deliberate decisions to become 'managerialist' in their way of working and at the same time, albeit unconsciously, initiated a new concept of the deserving and undeserving.

The chapter is structured as follows. It starts with a description of the changes that occurred as New Zealand moved from a welfare state based on Keynesian philosophy to a market-led user-pays economy and the effects of the Clinton administration's welfare reform. Next, an overview is given of the research undertaken in Hamilton, New Zealand, and Tampa, Florida, US, of not-for-profit social service agencies. Then it focuses on the changes that have occurred in the structure and philosophies of these agencies and their move to managerialism and professionalisation. The chapter then discusses the re-emergence of the concept of the 'deserving poor' and argues that the requirement to demonstrate 'successful' programmes has resulted in a need to target those clients who are willing and able to change their behaviour in a particular way.

The change in governance from 'Keynesian welfare' to the 'free market'

The transformation of the public sector in many western industrialised countries has been mirrored in New Zealand. Indeed, writing in 1998, John Gray argues that 'The neo-liberal experiment in New Zealand is the most ambitious attempt at constructing the free market as a social institution to be implemented anywhere this century' (Gray, 1998, p 39). Larner and Craig (2002, pp 8-10) describe the three phases of 'New Zealand's restructuring project'. The first stage saw a return to power of a Labour government, which, when faced with a deepening financial decline, abandoned New Zealand's Keynesian managed economy in favour of a pure neo-liberal model of lean government and a free-market economy. From 1984, the Labour Party implemented policies of deregulation that involved abolishing controls on prices, wages and interest rates, removing export subsidies and reducing tariffs. Many state-owned enterprises and assets were privatised and the principle of full employment was replaced by a monetarist goal of price stability (Gray, 1998). Despite a doctrine of 'rolling back the state' economically, the Labour government attempted to preserve its socially liberal policies on education, healthcare and Maori affairs. However, following the 1987 election such 'social policies were made more compatible with its [the government's] economic reforms and these were also shifting further in the direction of market liberalism' (Cheyne et al, 2005, p 39).

The second phase in the early 1990s under a conservative National government continued and extended the market reform process and additionally reformed the welfare state in a major way. 'The reforms were aimed at reducing dependency on the state, instituting a more modest safety net, and eliminating the vestiges of universal access to welfare' (Cheyne et al, 2005, p 39). The government's core business was seen as making policy and funding essential services; service delivery was to be transferred to the private market and the community. Public hospitals became commercial enterprises required to compete with private medical providers, delivery of education became the responsibility of local school boards and entitlement to welfare benefits was severely reduced. The State Housing body, which provided public housing, underwent a number of structural and name changes. Also, in 1993 housing rentals were calculated according to market values, rather than the cap of 25% of income, which had previously allowed low-income families access to decent housing. The balance between targeted and universal benefits, which had in the late post-war period ensured that everyone benefited from the welfare state in some way, now tipped towards further targeting. For example, entitlement to the non-taxable universal family benefit was combined with family assistance and means tested. Community Services Cards were introduced for low-income families and only those families were entitled to a number of health subsidies that had previously been universally available (St John, 1994). 'In less than a decade, New Zealand had gone from a bastion of welfare interventionism to a neo-liberal's paradise' (Kelsey, 1995, p 297).

The third phase, according to Larner and Craig (2002, p 9) is one in which 'local partnerships have come to the centre stage politically'. With the return of a Labour government in 1999 this phase of governance is characterised by a distancing from the market and individualised approaches of the 1980s and 1990s neo-liberalism and a 'joining up' of levels of government with the community and 'formalising of these relationships around shared values and place based goals ... a broad project in which every organisation ought to be involved, and which will benefit all' (Larner and Craig, 2002, p 9). In its 2005 Statement of Intent, the New Zealand Ministry of Social Development emphasised this viewpoint:

> The priorities and strategies outlined recognise that successful social development involves: ... government working in partnership with local authorities, with the community and voluntary sector, and with the private sector to develop 'joined up' local services. (MSD, 2005, p 9)

Since Labour came to power in 1999, a number of reforms have taken place in terms of welfare protection. Nevertheless, the emphasis on partnership does not diminish the increased role that non-governmental organisations had undertaken during the previous years.

The US and PRWORA

Welfare in the US does not mirror that of New Zealand. 'In the United States welfare has always meant one thing: means-tested assistance paid primarily to lone mothers and their children' (Deacon, 2002, p 5). In 1996, President Clinton signed into legislation the Personal Responsibility and Work Opportunity Reconciliation Act (PRWORA). This Act signalled major changes to the US welfare system. 'At the heart of these changes was the abolition of the right to welfare' (Deacon, 2002, p 91). The basis of the PRWORA was to move the existing welfare system 'into one that requires work in exchange for time-limited assistance' (US Department of Health and Human Services, 1996, p 1). In the preamble of the PRWORA the goals of the legislation were:

> to provide assistance to needy families so that children may be cared for in their own homes or in the homes of relatives; to end the dependence of needy parents on government benefits by promoting job preparation, work, and marriage; to prevent and reduce the incidence of out-of-wedlock pregnancies and establish annual numerical goals for preventing and reducing the incidence of these pregnancies; and to encourage the formation and maintenance of two-parent families. (PRWORA, 1996)

Until the implementation of PRWORA cash assistance had been paid to single mothers under the Aid to Families with Dependent Children (AFDC) Programme. Although each state was required by law to pay AFDC to those whose income fell below certain limits, the level of payment was left to those individual states. The PRWORA abolished AFDC and replaced it with the Temporary Assistance for Needy Families (TANF) Programme and thus lifted the states' obligation to pay cash assistance. As Deacon notes, 'The relevant part of the Act began with a declaration that it should not "be interpreted to entitle any individual or family to assistance under any state program funded under this part"' (Deacon, 2002, p 91; see also Weaver, 2000, p 456). There is no doubt that the changes made to the US welfare system in the 1990s had a significant impact. While the reforms were successful in diverting people from public assistance and the combination of a strong economy and intensive welfare-to-work policies reduced caseloads, the general consensus was that the policies were substantially less effective in helping families move out of poverty (Acker et al, 2002). The demand on the non-governmental agencies continued to increase as they struggled to cover the unmet needs of families throughout the US.

The research

Field research was undertaken in 2001-02. The objective of that research was to identify the organisational changes within non-governmental social provision agencies that had taken place during the neo-liberal era of the successive Labour and National Governments of the 1990s in New Zealand and during the Clinton era in the US. These organisational changes not only involved a philosophical upheaval as non-governmental agencies moved from being 'charities' to 'not-for-profit businesses', but the changes also resulted in a new view of the services that the agencies could provide.

Representatives of seven community social service agencies in Hamilton, New Zealand, and two in Tampa, Florida, US, took part in interviews. All of the agencies were 'faith-based' organisations. Although their programmes are similar to other community programmes, these may be shaped by significant differences in what the social service means to the staff and volunteers (see Hartford Institute for Religion Research, 2000). The agencies involved in this research offered a number of different services. Eight of the nine provided accommodation serving various groups – families, women and children, ex-prisoners, people with mental health problems, night shelters, and so on. All of them provided some type of counselling services, six provided food delivery services (foodbank or feeding sites) and five of them ran opportunity shops selling used clothing, furniture and the like.

Interviews of one to two hours' duration were conducted with men and women who held management positions in their organisations. The titles of these positions ranged from director to manager. Interviews followed a semi-structured, in-depth format focusing on four issues:

- Had the organisational structure changed and, if so, how?
- Had any changes been made in the philosophical direction of the agency?
- Had the services provided by the agency changed?
- Had the structure of the workforce changed?

Although a list of general topics to guide the interview was constructed, the intention was to provide the participants with an opportunity to frame their own priorities and speak freely about their agency and changes in its structural organisation. To initiate the dialogue respondents were asked for an overview of what they did in their positions and what services their agency provided to the community.

Often during this first conversation, a great deal of information was gathered pertaining to the general topics on the researchers' list and it was often not necessary to ask direct questions. With the consent of the participants, each interview was tape-recorded and transcribed for analysis. The analysis involved reading and rereading the transcripts with the above issues in mind.

The studied agencies

In the New Zealand neo-liberal era contracts between government and subcontracting agencies were negotiated with a strong emphasis on accountability. Accountability was measured in the language of outputs and outcomes, and the new arrangements influenced relationships among agencies and between agencies and the state:

> Social service organisations, including notable church based not-for-profit entities, found themselves re-cast as 'little arms of the state' and, to a certain extent, forced into competition with each other. (Larner and Craig, 2002, p 18)

In addition, the contractual requirements often demanded that not-for-profit agencies put in place operational and reporting frameworks that agencies found onerous and costly in both time and financial resources. The managerialism of this era is clearly evident in the profile of the representatives of not-for-profit agencies in Hamilton who participated in this study. The directors and managers interviewed were responsible for as few as 16 to as many as 100 staff members. The titles of those who work in the agencies indicate the managerial focus that has overtaken many such organisations. For example, one interviewee described herself as one of seven in the management team responsible to the general manager. Another was a director responsible for three administration managers and a public relations manager. The director of the smallest organisation reported that she had six office staff, a financial administrator and a funding officer. The director of a medium-sized agency described her role in this way:

> 'My role is really a dual role. It has got a number of facets but I guess it is primarily seen as a managing role and a directing role and in the managing role is an expectation that I manage the day-to-day affairs of the agency and give support to the staff. I have oversight of the financial well-being of the agency and I am responsible for policy development. So that is at a management level, that is what I am expected to do and that takes a lot of time on a daily basis because there are always issues coming up. And on another level I am expected, in the director's role, to be aware of social policy, to be aware of the socioeconomic political kind of environment that we are in, and be able to make sudden strategic responses to that.' (Agency No. 1)

> 'I always talk about it as like standing on top of a hill and looking out and trying to see beyond the horizon and see where we might be going and given all the factors – social, political, economic – where's the trend taking us and how will we respond to it and, more importantly, how will we be sustainable in the long term.' (Agency No. 1)

The majority of community welfare agencies in Hamilton are faith-based. An enquiry as to why there is a lack of secular large-scale agencies in Hamilton elicited this response:

> 'I think now that if you are not seen to have a strong infrastructure that has been around a while, you won't get funded. It's a question of sustainability.' (Agency No. 1)

Although each of the agencies interviewed had a religious background, the agencies were independent of their churches and received funding from various sources. One was not financially supported by its church at all; the others received church funding ranging from 10% to 30% of their annual incomes. All of the agencies were dependent on government funding (in contracts to provide services) ranging from 10% to 45%, grants from Community Trusts, and income from their operations (for example, childcare fees, accommodation rentals and opportunity shops).

Financial information was not available to gauge the size of the organisations but staffing provides an indication. Staff ranged from five full-time and part-time workers with a number of volunteers to 100 full- and part-time staff with no volunteers. In Tampa, US, both organisations had recently undergone managerial changes. Both interviewees had recently been appointed to newly created positions in order to carry out new programmes to cater for the increased numbers of homeless families. Both agencies received funding primarily from the community. Private donations and United Way funds were the main source of funding as well as specific fundraising events held on a regular basis. Both agencies received a small amount of government funding but, at the time of the interviews, the new Bush administration was planning to introduce his faith-based initiatives, which would result in moving more of the social service functions into the private and not-for-profit sectors and would result in increased government monies being allocated to these organisations. As in New Zealand the titles of the interviewees indicate the managerial tone of the organisations. Both the director of the human services department in one agency and the director of programmes in the other were responsible to a governing board of directors:

> 'First of all our big boss is our board of directors and our president of the board, of course, is the big, big boss.

They meet, I believe, every other month and we have an Executive Committee that meets monthly and they are the decision-making body, made up of community leaders.' (Agency No. 6)

Both Tampa organisations employed over 100 paid workers and recruited teams of volunteers:

> 'We have two types of volunteers ... one of them we call them Full-Time Equivalency Volunteers ... they take the place of the staff person and of course it depends on the skill level of the individual. Some of them are counsellors at our office, office receptionists at different desks, maybe teaching classes to clients, you know, wherever their skills are, and the idea is that they will actually take the place of having to hire staff for us.... And then we have our group volunteers. Those are the civic groups, the church organisations, the youth groups, the schools, where they've come as a group usually, sometimes youth, sometimes adults, and they'll do a big project for us.' (Agency No. 6)

Changes in structure and philosophy

All of the agencies reported that, over a period of time, changes had been made in the management of their daily activities:

> 'We changed the structure about, I think, about five years ago. There was a strategic decision made and that was that we couldn't operate in a charity way any more, you know, because the charitable dollar has been so stretched now by different demands.' (Agency No. 2)

> 'We have a general manager and under that a role of like a senior management team really – set up with myself in the practice consultancy division, we have two operational managers who operate regionally and two practice leaders, which is kind of equivalent to my old role, who operate in conjunction with the operations managers regionally, and then that's supported now by a business manager, by a funding and marketing person.' (Agency No. 2)

> 'There was a deliberate decision made to retrain, so jobs got disestablished but in other jobs like the frameworks of how teams were, it was different, but the agency put a huge amount of money into training, internal training, and we spent two years retraining people.' (Agency No. 2)

Philosophically, Agency No. 2 made what the director referred to as a 'huge change':

> 'We've moved into a kind of a way of working that we call strength-based practice, which kind of sits outside the traditional ways of working that are more around psychological areas. So that's been a significant paradigm shift really, for us as an organisation.'

Strength-based practice focuses on the competencies, skills and interests of clients in order to find solutions rather than attempting to correct deficiencies. This approach is not only taken by the agency in relation to service delivery, but is also evident in how the agency staff structured organisational change. The staff at this agency are expected to work cooperatively in a team setting. The team incorporates therapists, social workers and community workers, as well as administrative and managerial staff: 'Our belief is that everybody has strengths and abilities ... and we believe that about organisations as well' (Agency No. 2).

The director of Agency No. 2 reported that their change in focus had brought some conflictual issues with other agencies, particularly government services:

> 'Well, their [the government's] ways of working would be more what we call deficit based. They would be looking for what people were doing wrong and finding ways to fix it. We look at what do people do right and how do you grow it. So it's just a different kind of focus, so that kind of often calls us into conflict with the way that we work, and in lots of instances, because we do the same thing looking from different ways.'

> 'So we're having to work with people who believe in different things but work with them in a way that is non-adversarial. So there are real challenges in that.'

Traditionally, faith-based agencies have been funded by their own communities. But as the director of Agency No. 2 reported, the number of church-goers is decreasing:

> 'The people who are still there are aging and that kind of funding resource in a way was dying off. So we had to make some strategic decisions. If we are going to be around, you know, we have to look at an alternative source rather than being able to rely on that kind of funding.'

The new way of working also had ramifications for funding in that the requirements of the funders and the desire for the agency to work in this new way produced tensions for the agency:

> 'There are challenges for us at a funding level because all the funding structures are set up around contracts that operate in a way that we don't choose to operate. We really need the money so do we go back to operating in the traditional way to fulfil the contract and the reporting requirements or do we work hard to change the way that these funding people think, so that they will fund us for what we do, not what they want?' (Agency No. 2)

The director of Agency No. 1 is passionate about justice and had made it a key focus of the agency:

> 'The shift in philosophy has been to focus and to really underscore that this agency is primarily in pursuit of social justice and we do that through the delivery of social services. So this might be our action, social services is the action, the pursuit through and the philosophical underpinning for the agency is social justice oriented.'

> 'Justice is not about measurable outcomes, justice is about opportunity, justice is about access, justice is about getting your right to a whole lot of basic life things.'

A year after the interview, Agency No. 1 had changed its name to a short catchy title, and mailed out brochures and produced fridge magnets to promote its new image.

This agency had also dramatically changed its way of working.

The director discussed extra pressures that were affecting the work staff wanted to do:

> 'With the devolution of government responsibility back into the community for a lot of the social services, I think that we have picked up more and more of what was formally seen as statutory responsibilities. A lot of our work now comes out of direct referral from government agencies so the whole devolution process by government is a real factor.
>
> We work now in a sort of managerialist model that imposes extra demands upon us in terms of developing commercial systems and working with them keeps us extraordinarily busy because we are under-resourced. It's not just about delivering services, it's about creating systems and structures and maintaining them. Doing all that, who gets any time or energy for activism?' (Agency No. 1)

Agency No. 3 made this comment:

> 'Compliance has become a major, major issue, you know, and is a major cost. In the time I've been here, this place and many social agencies would be like it, you know, social agencies got on with the job and all they were interested in was the clients, and the workers were only really dealing with that. Over the past, with contracting, you've got this whole business of being responsible and having things that can be audited and so therefore you have to [have] manuals, you have to have processes. All these kinds of things have to be codified.'

In the US, as a result of the Clinton administration initiatives one of the Tampa agencies had made major changes in the way it worked. Two years prior to the interview, the agency, which had traditionally supplied short-term accommodation and residual financial aid, introduced a completely new programme:

> 'What we found is that our old programme wasn't working any more for people. There wasn't any public housing to put them into any more. There wasn't any

> safety nets of any income that they could get to subside on, and we really had to redesign our programme to give them an opportunity for self-sufficiency without government supports, because that's really the reality of the world these days. So two years ago we redesigned our programme into a self-sufficiency model.' (Agency No. 6)

This programme comprised longer-term family accommodation accompanied by training in order that individuals learn employment, parenting and coping skills together with receiving addiction and violent behaviour counselling:

> 'The goal is to provide everything that is needed to actually bring a person to self-sufficiency at their own best level, without any government supports.' (Agency No. 6)

Professionalisation

Traditionally, these not-for-profit social service agencies have been supported by voluntary labour, which has steadily decreased while the call for credentialised workers has increased:

> 'I recall way back, 15 years ago, when I first agreed to take on this role, that it was sufficient for employees to do the work provided they'd had the experience of their own children. Over the years the onus has been placed on the employees not only to up-skill, to train, but now today they have to be registered. This is the latest enforcement.
>
> There might be the odd volunteer but, no, I think that it is generally accepted that people have a qualification.' (Agency No. 2)

> 'I think for a whole lot of reasons the volunteer pool that is out there now is still a much older age group. We are talking about people who are 60 plus and 70 plus actually who still work out of the philosophy of the common good.' (Agency No. 1)

> 'People now coming in are expected to have professional qualifications. They are expected to have associations with the bodies that they are working under and they are expected to have a sense of professionalism that they didn't formally need to have.' (Agency No. 1)

In one agency director's opinion this shift was due to funding requirements, which in turn have resulted in statutory requirements:

> 'I think it has been because of a funding requirement. I think that, you know, people now say if they are going to fund us they want to be sure that the people who are working in the field are qualified to do it.' (Agency No. 4)

This was echoed by another agency representative who said:

> 'It's a requirement now for all of our staff to have membership of a professional body. If they don't have it when we hire them, then their training and development plans are geared towards getting it.' (Agency No. 2)

And a third agency:

> 'Well that's your problem, you see, the moment you have standards, then in a sense you're into the business of having to update qualifications. Now basically from this year on, you've got to have somebody with a diploma and you know that the next step is that somebody will have to have a degree.'
>
> The use of volunteers has become more of a difficulty with agencies because you can only really accommodate certain people within your programmes. Some agencies have programmes where volunteers can do a lot, and if you're giving meals or feeding people, you can use volunteers in those kinds of areas. But the moment you come into a place like us [childcare], we can't use too many. You've got to go through police checks and all that kind of thing, to make sure that they are safe. Anybody that comes to this place goes through police

> checks; we won't have any volunteers or anyone who has not had a police check.' (Agency No. 4)

The Tampa agencies in the US told a similar story:

> 'I have very few positions that do not require a college diploma in terms of direct provision of services, you know. We have, of course, administrative support positions; we have lower functional positions that while are not unskilled positions do not require that higher level of education ... they require a different group of skills and knowledge.' (Agency No. 7)

The deserving poor

An additional dimension to the funding issue is the perceived need to specify explicit outputs when agencies are negotiating contracts. These outputs, in turn, become measures of success. In order for funded programmes to generate the specified outcome, they are often targeted at clients who, it is felt, will be 'successes'. The result of this model of funding is a new type of deserving poor. Just as in Victorian times when charitable organisations were encouraged to divide the poor into categories of deserving and undeserving, not-for-profit organisations are dividing their clientele. From the beginnings of state support for paupers and the destitute, the distinction between non-disabled people and the defenceless poor has been a moral distinction between the unworthy and worthy – the undeserving and deserving poor.

The notion of deserving and undeserving continues to influence contemporary views on supporting the poor (Cook, 1979; Coughlin, 1980; de Swaan, 1988; Will, 1993; van Oorschot, 1998). Van Oorschot (1998) has argued that there is 'deservingness criteria' comprising control, need, identity, attitude and reciprocity. Van Oorschot referred to control as the control that poor people have over their own neediness. The deserving poor are those whose situation is beyond their control; the undeserving are those 'who could make a living on their own, if they only tried or tried hard enough' (van Oorschot, 1998, p 3). Will's (1993) study on who the public perceives as the deserving poor in America found that the highest level of support was for large families, unemployed people and physically disabled people, and particularly for those who actively strived to help themselves.

The deserving are also distinguished from the undeserving poor on the basis of level of need – the greater the need, the more deserving people are. Cook (1979) found that, generally, willingness of others to help was based on the level of neediness. Thus there was more willingness to support those who were in greater need of help.

The moral identity of the poor is based on their 'location' relative to 'in-group favourability' (Messe et al, 1986). Deservingness is based on the degree to which the poor belong to 'Us' (van Oorschot, 1998, p 3). The 'Us' may be identifiable groups such as family, town and church, and 'in modern, national societies this criterion might result in an unwillingness to support needy people from ethnic minorities or foreign residents in general' (van Oorschot, 1998, p 3).

The attitude criterion refers to the attitude of those in need. De Swaan's (1988) 'docility' and Cook's (1979) 'gratefulness criterion' describes the level to which poor people acknowledge the help they are given: 'the gratefulness criterion holds that the inclination to support is higher towards those people in need who respond gratefully for help' (van Oorschot, 1998, p 3).

The criterion of reciprocity is an extension of attitude. The idea of reciprocity in social relations – giving and taking – is the basis of this criterion. While the poor may have little to reciprocate with at the time except for their compliance or gratefulness, they may have previously earned support. The almost universal acceptance that older people who have already contributed to society are deserving of help is a clear example of this notion of reciprocity.

The deserving and undeserving poor in New Zealand

Referring to the concept of the deserving and undeserving poor in New Zealand in the 1990s, Cheyne et al (2005, p 21) argue that:

> Nineteenth-century debates of laissez-faire and charitable aid have a similarity to the rhetoric that underpins the retrenched welfare state of the 1990s. There is a common stress on self-help and non-interference in the market-place.

The New Zealand government's funding criteria for welfare agencies and the need for successful outcomes reflect this continuing dichotomy of deserving and undeserving poor. In order to access funding, agencies are obliged to show 'success' in what they do. But the agencies face the issue of what is meant by 'success':

> 'I mean, how do you measure success? That's the thing that has been difficult for us because generally contracts have been measured by how many people you put through, you know, that's the traditional way. You know, you get three sessions and then you're out and next person is in. But we know that's not successful, and so we work with our own measures of success knowing that they're not going to be fully funded, because they're still being funded on the basis of output not outcome.' (Agency No. 2)

> 'The resources are limited, I mean we can't keep on pouring money in, in ways that, you know, that haven't been well thought out, haven't been targeted, haven't been coordinated. We've noticed that for the government funding that we do have, reporting for that used to be a matter of filling in a form, you know, they give you the money at the end of the year and you fill in a form. Well now we have stringent audits, they come along and they want to not just look at how you spent the money, they want to look at your professional practice and how you know that you've been successful and what kind of internal support systems you have. I think the government is demanding a lot more for their money now.' (Agency No. 2)

> 'One of the things that seems to be coming through is that this whole evaluation area, you know, proving that you actually do people some good and measuring that is difficult really.' (Agency No. 5)

> 'What is success in addiction programmes? Drying the guy out? Is that success? Getting their health back, because often they've sluiced all the vitamins out of their system and that kind of thing and so therefore you restore their health and you might get them back to a state of sobriety, is that success? Or do they need to do one week's sobriety or do they need to do three months, or do they need to do six months, or 12 months? You know,

> what is success with addiction? And with counselling, what is success?' (Agency No. 5)

Despite the dilemma of defining what success means, agencies have changed their way of working in order to meet these criteria by targeting their clientele:

> 'A lot of it is about funding. If you can demonstrate that you have a specialist way of working and that you will target a particular group. And so that is what is tending to happen. We are getting a lot of specialist agencies now who are saying that they work from specialist models and target a particular group in the community and you could say that's part of the "deserving poor" model. That's a funding requirement that still comes out of that whole 15 years of producing results. We were told we would get so much money and we had to demonstrate that three months down the track this family was cured or that there were good outcomes for this family. Significant outcomes, not just minor outcomes. And so with the funding, as with professionalisation, it starts to get targeted.' (Agency No. 1)

> 'The reality is a lot of people access our [counselling] services because it's affordable. It's based on donation and ability to pay. Generally the people who come can't afford to pay and the income they're getting is really low, and there's a real debate even internally in the agency because you're constantly pressured into prioritising people who can come attached with funding. So that there's always the pull for us if we want the contract. Does that mean that we can only take people who are bad enough to fit the criteria?' (Agency No. 3)

The deserving poor in Tampa

When asked about the notion of the deserving poor, the interviewees in Tampa, US, both acknowledged that the public at large perceived people as deserving and undeserving but did not connect that notion to the programmes in their agencies. The director of the agency that had introduced the completely new programme said: 'I'd say usually the wealthy business-type successful professionals are the ones that are most likely to want to help the deserving and not the undeserving'.

While the director of the second agency said of the first:

> 'We have another major provider here in the area who last year, unannounced, closed their emergency shelter so that they were no longer going to be providing services to street people because to provide emergency shelter services was just enabling them to remain where they were. If they wanted to make the choice to enter a transitional programme and to do the things they needed to do to get their lives on track then they could come into their programme. So I guess that would be consistent with that of providing services for the deserving poor.' (Agency No. 7)

This first agency had an ethos of self-help in order for its programme to be judged successful:

> 'Basically they can come and stay with us when they're ready to make a change in their life. We can't let them propagate what they've been doing if it's been drinking, if it's been drugging, if it's them refusing to work or whatever, but once they get to a point in their life where they say "Okay, I'm ready to make a change", that's when they are most appropriate for our programme.' (Agency No. 6)

The director of the second agency acknowledged the connection between funding and success:

> 'Perhaps some services should be restricted to individuals that are ready to change and I think that we have an ethical responsibility to utilise resources where they are going to be the most productive. I mean, you know, the people that are providing our resources have that in mind when they give it. They want to help people to improve their situation.' (Agency No. 7)

Conclusions

This chapter has examined non-governmental agencies in two cities, one in New Zealand and one in the US, which have taken up the growing residual welfare that comes out of a neo-liberal idea of less government and more individual responsibility on the part of their populations. Over the past 15 years the argument that the economic difficulties faced by industrial countries have been caused by welfare systems using resources that could otherwise be invested in industry has gained momentum. Political parties of both the left and the right have advocated a neo-liberal reliance on market forces and subsequently limited welfare spending to programmes that are cost-effective, targeted and which can demonstrate quantifiable outcomes.

The change in governance in New Zealand to a deregulated, market-led state that relied on community welfare resulted in a non-governmental sector struggling to cope with a burgeoning responsibility exacerbated by a demand (by government funders) for fiscal responsibility and proof of measurable success. In order to cope with those demands, agencies were forced to mirror the private sector by restructuring their management systems and seeking to make a 'profit' by ensuring that their services and programmes were not wasted on the 'undeserving'. In the US, changes in one agency's way of working due to the Clinton administration initiatives resulted in similar outcomes. Although the character of the reforms were not as potent as those in New Zealand, the need to create programmes that accomplished more than merely housing and feeding people as a temporary measure, meant that those who were targeted for the programme were those who were committed to changing their personal behaviour and thus become deserving of welfare.

As we progress through the first decade of the 21st century, the non-governmental sector continues to encounter greater demands on its time, resources and energy. The ideology of individualism, personal responsibility and welfare-generated dependency creates an atmosphere very much like that dominant in the late 18th century. Economic rewards are governed by the operation of the free market and 'every man [sic] should be free to pursue his fortune and should take responsibility for its success or failure' (Conley, 1982, p 282).

References

Acker, J., Morgen, S. and Gonzales, L. (2002) *Welfare restructuring, work and poverty*, Eugene, OR: Center for the Study of Women in Society, University of Oregon.

Cheyne, C., O'Brien, M. and Belgrave, M. (2005) *Social policy in Aotearoa New Zealand: A critical introduction* (2nd edn), South Melbourne: Oxford University Press.

Conley, M. (1982) 'The "undeserving" poor: welfare and labour policy', in R. Kennedy (ed) *Australian welfare history: Critical essays*, South Melbourne: Macmillan, pp 281-303.

Cook, F. (1979) *Who should be helped: Public support for social services*, Beverly Hills, CA: Sage Publications.

Coughlin, R.M. (1980) *Ideology, public opinion and welfare policy: Attitudes towards taxes and spending in industrial societies*, Institute of International Studies, Research Series No. 42, Berkeley, CA: University of California.

De Swaan, A. (1988) *In care of the state*, Amsterdam: Bakker.

Deacon, A. (2002) *Perspectives on welfare*, Buckingham: Open University Press.

Gray, J. (1998) *False dawn: The delusions of global capitalism*, London: Granta Publications.

Hartford Institute for Religion Research (2000) *How do people perceive religious meaning in faith-based social services? Congregations, Communities and Leadership Development Project* (online), available at: http://hirr.hartsem.edu/research/research_churchoutreach_perceptions.html

Kelsey, J. (1995) *Economic fundamentalism*, London and East Haven, CT: Pluto Press.

Larner, W. and Craig, D. (2002) *After neoliberalism? Local partnerships and social governance in Aotearoa/New Zealand*, Research Paper No. 3, Auckland: University of Auckland.

Messe, L., Hynmes, R. and MacCoun, R. (1986) 'Group categorization and distributive justice decisions', in H.W. Bierhoff, R. Cohen and J. Greenberg (eds) *Justice in social relations*, New York and London: Plenum Press.

Ministry of Social Development (MSD) (2005) *Leading social development*, Ministry of Social Development Statement of Intent 2005/6, Wellington: Ministry of Social Development.

PRWORA (Personal Responsibility and Work Opportunity Reconciliation Act) (1996) Washington, www.acf.dhhs.gov/programs/ofa/prwora96.htm

St John, S. (1994) 'The state and welfare', in A. Sharp (ed) *Leap into the dark: The changing role of the state in New Zealand since 1984*, Auckland: Auckland University Press, pp 89-106.

US Department of Health and Human Services (1996) *Administration for children and families*, Fact Sheet, 22 August.

van Oorschot, W. (1998) 'Who should get what, and why? On deservingness criteria and selectivism vs universalism among the Dutch public', paper presented at the 2nd International Research Conference on Social Security of the International Social Security Association (ISSA), Jerusalem, 25-28 January.

Weaver, K. (2000) *Ending welfare as we know it*, Washington, DC: Brookings Institute.

Will, J. (1993) 'The dimensions of poverty: public perceptions of the deserving poor', *Social Science Research*, vol 22, pp 312-32.

Part Two:
Practices: the welfare governance of street-level practices

SIX

'Ending welfare as we know it': welfare reform in the US

Joel F. Handler

When President Bill Clinton signed welfare reform into law in 1996, he fulfilled his campaign promise to 'end welfare as we know it'. In the US, the term welfare most commonly refers to the public assistance programme for poor single mothers and their children. Although this chapter will focus on changes made to Temporary Assistance for Needy Families (TANF), the cash aid programme for poor single mothers and their children, significant changes have also been made or are being proposed for other welfare programmes, including the social security pension system, government health insurance programmes (Medicaid and Medicare) and unemployment insurance. This chapter will examine the effects of welfare reform on states, welfare delivery organisations and welfare recipients. Specifically, it will address whether giving states increased flexibility has improved their ability to respond to local conditions and needs. The chapter will also examine the new strategies adopted by welfare agencies to implement welfare-to-work programmes in addition to their responsibility to determine eligibility and control fraud, and whether these strategies created the desired results of increasing recipients' participation in the paid labour force. Last, this chapter will consider the effects of welfare reform on recipients. It will specifically examine recipients' ability to enter into the paid labour force and to stay off welfare after finding employment.

The US social security framework

In the US, the social security system gives monthly cash benefits to people over the age of 65 who paid into the system as well as to people with disabilities and to widows and their children. Unlike TANF, the benefits for social security are set by the federal government, not the states. Since its enactment, social security has significantly reduced poverty among older people. In fact, in 1999, the proportion of older people in poverty was 10.5%, a proportion lower than the population as a whole (Katz, 2001). Although social security used to be considered an 'untouchable' aid programme, President George W. Bush has made social security reform one of the priorities of his second term. Under his proposed changes, younger workers would be allowed to put some of their payroll taxes into Individual Savings Accounts instead of into the Social Security Trust Fund. It is unclear what the long-term results of Bush's plan will be. However, the transition costs to Bush's proposed system are estimated to add US$4 trillion by 2040 (Aaron, 2004).

At the time of writing in January 2005, Democratic lawmakers are vowing to block any attempts to privatise the social security system.

Unlike other industrialised nations, the US does not have a government health insurance programme covering all of its citizens. There are currently two primary government health insurance systems. Medicare is run by the federal government and provides older and disabled people with prepaid hospital insurance and supplemental medical insurance. Medicaid was designed for the poor, including TANF and Supplemental Security Income (SSI) recipients. The federal and state governments jointly fund the Medicaid programme, but states administratively control the programme. The costs for both the Medicare and Medicaid programmes have grown substantially since the 1990s. However, recent changes have been made to both programmes. In 2004, the federal government added prescription drug coverage to Medicare. This new coverage is expected to add between US$395 to US$534 billion in expenditures over the budget period of 2004 to 2013 (Kaiser Family Foundation, 2004). The Medicaid programme has undergone significant reforms due to changes in eligibility criteria and to funding reductions made by state governments. Before the passage of welfare reform in 1996, TANF recipients were automatically enrolled in the Medicaid programme. In order to ensure that women who reached the TANF time limits could still be eligible for Medicaid, in 1996, lawmakers de-linked the two programmes. Thus, women and children now had to fill out a separate application for Medicaid when applying for TANF. (The same de-linking also occurred with food stamps.) After the passage of welfare reform, about two thirds of adults who left welfare also lost Medicaid because they either did not know about or did not want to go through the separate application procedure (De Parle, 2004). Another significant change to the Medicaid programme has been rooted in reductions made by states facing budget crises in the early 1990s. As mentioned above, Medicaid is jointly financed by the US state and federal governments. A survey of state governments sponsored by the Kaiser Commission on Medicaid and the Uninsured (2004) found that in response to increasing fiscal pressures, 49 states as well as the District of Columbia have implemented or are planning Medicaid reduction during the 2004 fiscal year, marking the third year of Medicaid reductions. These reductions include limiting coverage, decreasing reimbursement rates to providers and restricting eligibility for the programme.

Unemployment insurance in the US is also a state-administered programme run under federal guidelines. In order to receive aid, an applicant must meet at least three general requirements: (1) the applicant must have been employed in a job covered by Unemployment Insurance and be currently looking for work; (2) the applicant must be unemployed for a specified time period that is longer than the waiting period and less than a maximum duration; and (3) the claimant must have received a minimum amount of earnings or worked for a specified number of hours in a time period (Handler and Hasenfeld, 1997). Although there have not been significant changes to unemployment insurance, the programme has not been updated to face the changing employment status of many workers. Therefore, fewer and fewer workers are qualifying for benefits. Some of the changes in the employment sector affecting benefits are rising levels of earnings inequality, growing instability of income over time, increased employment that is part time and contingent and increased structural unemployment (Hacker, 2004).

The 1996 legislation, the Personal Responsibility and Work Opportunity Reconciliation Act (PRWORA), replaced Aid to Families with Dependent Children (AFDC) with TANF. Significant changes were made. Temporary Assistance for Needy Families (TANF) ended public assistance as a federal entitlement by enacting a system of block grants to states based on state caseloads at various points in the 1990s. In order to receive federal funding, states must fulfil a variety of federal requirements, the most important of which was moving increasing proportions of mothers into the paid labour force. The legislation created two sets of time limits: a two-year limit on continuous aid and a cumulative lifetime limit of five years. Although the federal government gave states flexibility in deciding how to encourage welfare recipients to work, most states enacted a 'work first strategy', which encourages recipients to take any job, even a low-wage entry-level job, rather than offering recipients education and training programmes.

The TANF reforms reflect the long tradition in American ideology that blames the individual for poverty rather than structural conditions in society. Throughout US history, poor mothers have always been considered as 'undeserving poor', a suspicious category, and blamed for their own poverty. In the US the failure of a non-disabled person to support themselves and their family has historically been viewed as a moral failure. The first statutes enacted by states, called Mothers' Pensions Programs, reflected this belief. These programmes primarily aided white widows. All other mothers, including immigrants, divorced, deserted and unmarried mothers, were excluded, and thus dependent on the paid labour market (Gordon, 1988). Even the recipients had work requirements tied to their benefits (Abromovitz, 1988).

Starting with the end of the Second World War, there were large migrations of African Americans from the South to the Northern and Western cities looking, mostly unsuccessfully, for work and a better life. For a variety of reasons, the welfare rolls exploded with large increases in unwed, single-mother African Americans. Civil rights activists reclassified welfare as a 'right' for all those in need regardless of marital status or race/ethnicity. Women, who were previously excluded, were accepted onto the welfare rolls (Piven and Cloward, 1977). To the usual suspicions of single mothers was the explosive mixture of race. It was President Ronald Reagan in the 1980s who coined the term 'welfare queen', which fed the stereotype of welfare recipients as inner-city, unwed African-American mothers, having children to stay on welfare, generational dependence, substance abuse and sexually promiscuous, in short, breeding a criminal class (Handler, 2004).

In response to the increasing rolls, in 1967, the US federal government enacted the Work Incentive Program, which combined incentives and mandatory work requirements. The Work Incentive Program, as well as subsequent work programmes, was never enforced. The rolls continued to grow and 'welfare' was increasingly attacked. It became one of the central issues of politics. At first, liberals opposed work requirements. Then, in the 1980s, they changed. They gave two reasons. Since most married mothers were now in the paid labour force, it seemed reasonable to expect unwed welfare mothers to work also. And second, a series of studies showed that families were materially and socially better off when the adults were gainfully employed. Both conservatives and liberals agreed that current welfare policies were detrimental to poor families, that it had to be changed, and that the best solution was to make them enter the paid labour force.

In response to the pressure to do something about welfare, the federal government began granting waivers to the states allowing them to alter AFDC. These waivers became common in the 1980s under President Reagan, and increased under subsequent administrations. Nevertheless, the political pressure continued to mount. President Clinton promised to 'end welfare as we know it'. In 1996, the PRWORA was passed. Temporary Assistance for Needy Families (TANF) replaced AFDC. State discretion was increased through block grants. States were required to move increasing percentages of single mothers into the paid labour force. There were strict time limits (two consecutive years and five years cumulative on aid). There were also 'family value' provisions, including the ability to deny aid to teenage parents unless they live with an adult and attend school, increased funding to abstinence-only sexual health education programmes, the requirement to establish the paternity of children in order to receive aid, and states being able to decide whether to deny aid to persons convicted of drug-related felonies. As Brodkin et al (2002, p 1) state, 'The 1996 legislation established what states must do [require work], but largely left to them the decision of how to do it'.

The state response to welfare reform

Under block grants, states were free to design their own cash assistance programmes as long as they complied with two federal rules: they could not use federal funds to provide assistance for more than two years at any one time and for more than five years cumulatively and states had to meet federal work participation requirements (Greenberg, 2004). Specifically, states were required to move an increasing proportion of welfare recipients into the workforce starting with 25% of adults in single-parent families in 1997 and increasing to 50% by 2002. These work requirements are enforced by the threat of funding cuts to block grants. Lawmakers believed that states could use this increased flexibility to make their welfare-to-work programmes more effective by tailoring them to local needs and preferences. However, opponents of making AFDC a block grant programme contended that states would use their increased flexibility to make significant cuts to their programmes.

To examine how devolution influences state welfare policy

innovation, Lieberman and Shaw (2000) analysed data on AFDC waivers granted to states from 1977 until welfare reform was enacted in 1996. They tested what state and national characteristics influenced states' decisions to apply for waivers. When examining the timing of applying for waivers, they found that states seemed to apply for waivers in response to national welfare trends, instead of changes in local caseloads. They determined that states that were wealthier and more ideologically conservative applied for waivers more frequently than states with high poverty levels and liberal ideologies. Cumulatively, their data suggests that when states applied for waivers, they 'were responding not to particular local conditions of need but to the political pressure of wealthy, conservative voters, buttressed by state capacity and policy legacies favouring innovation' (Lieberman and Shaw, 2000, p 229). Furthermore, the policy innovations that states wanted to make – including modifying earned income rules, increasing work requirements, imposing time limits, and limiting cash assistance to children born while the mother was receiving welfare – were similar, regardless of local and regional factors that may have led them to make different policy decisions.

Since the 1996 welfare reform, states have adopted similar provisions despite their increased flexibility. In general, states have used their increased flexibility to enact stricter provisions than required by PRWORA. Most have implemented sanction policies that are stricter and more extensive than required under TANF. In 37 states, the entire family loses its benefits if the adult violates work or other requirements – called full-family sanctions. In 15 of these states, the full-family sanction is imposed immediately; in the remaining 22, the grant is initially reduced as a warning. Six states only eliminate the adult portion of the grant for non-compliance while continuing the child's portion, called a partial sanction. In the remaining eight states, the amount of the sanction is increased, but the whole family does not lose its entire grant. In these states, the remaining assistance may take the form of vendor payments, instead of cash aid (Pavetti and Bloom, 2001). With regard to time limits, states have also enacted stricter policies than required by the federal legislation. Although PRWORA sets a cumulative lifetime limit of five years, at least 20 states have time limits that are less than five years. In 10 of these states, the time limit is only two years (De Parle, 1997). These results show that states have not yet started using their increased flexibility to respond to local needs and preferences. Instead, states created their policies in response to the popular perception that previous policies had not provided strong enough incentives for participation in work activities or penalties for non-compliance (Wu et al, 2004).

The response of welfare delivery organisations to welfare reform

To understand how welfare offices have implemented their welfare-to-work programmes, one must first consider welfare office culture before the 1996 legislation. When the welfare rolls exploded in the 1960s, one of the charges was that the programme was wracked with 'waste, fraud and abuse'. Both the federal government and the states imposed strict quality control measures. The result was a change in mission of the offices from service to minimising eligibility errors by requiring extensive documentation, including frequent reporting of income and assets, birth records, social security numbers and other eligibility data. When PRWORA was signed into law, some of its proponents recognised the changes that would have to be made in the offices to develop individualised welfare-to-work plans, monitor progress and impose sanctions. The 'culture' of the office had to be changed from being solely concerned with eligibility and compliance to individual, service-oriented, intensive casework.

In a study of 11 local welfare offices, some changes appear to have been made or at least attempted. In Texas, case managers are called Texas Work Advisors; in Michigan, Assistance Payment Workers are now Family Independence Specialists. Sometimes, jobs actually changed as well. Still, at the front line, the central tasks of eligibility determination and compliance with rules remained – getting the work done in a timely fashion, and eliminating fraud (Gais et al, 2001). Rather than changing welfare office culture of eligibility and compliance, the work programme was instead added to it. Adding this component has made the already complicated process of applying for and maintaining benefits even more complicated. Welfare-to-work programmes require recipients to accept offers of suitable employment or participate in various kinds of pre-employment activities (for example, job search, job preparedness classes, and so on); if, without cause, they fail to do so, they are subject to sanctions. Within these seemingly simple requirements, lie volumes of rules, regulations, standards and interpretations. There are scores of regulations attempting to spell out every element in the programme from what determines inability to work to whether a recipient should be sanctioned for missing an appointment. There is an enormous amount of paperwork; everything has to be documented. Despite the quantity of rules, a great many of the most crucial decisions require judgement or discretion on the part of field-level workers.

There is a rich literature on the attitudes of American welfare workers towards recipients. The workers practise what Yeheskel Hasenfeld has described as 'moral typification' (1983). The core activity of welfare agencies is to process or change people. Poor unwed mothers must be transformed from dependent recipients to active participants in the labour force. The very nature of selecting, processing and changing people conveys a judgement as to the *moral* worth of the person. However rule-bound the decision, somewhere along the line, a value judgement has been made about the client. Cultural beliefs determine what values are legitimate and appropriate in working with clients. The welfare agency selects those clients who fit organisational needs and compartmentalises clients into 'normal' service categories. Other client problems will be considered irrelevant. Employment and training programmes select and train the most promising students and somehow defer or deflect those who may need the services the most. Welfare agencies punish those who do not or cannot comply. Many welfare agency workers see themselves as but a short step away from welfare themselves; yet, they work hard, 'play by the rules' and no one is giving them benefits and favours. Workers trained, socialised and supervised in this manner will apply rules strictly, impose sanctions, avoid errors and get through the day as quickly and painlessly as possible. Requests for change or required change consume scarce administrative time and run the risk of error. Clients with problems become problems (Hasenfeld, 1983).

The work contract

The culture of welfare offices and values of workers influence decisions over which the client should have at least some influence: the work contract. In theory, a contract should be drawn up between the welfare recipient and agency that spells out the mutual obligations of both and makes them accountable to the terms of the contract. However, as demonstrated in a study by Evelyn Brodkin (1997), the state stacks the cards in such a way that the clients have few opportunities to influence the terms of the contract. The caseworkers used their discretionary power to force the clients to comply with their interpretation of the contract. The caseworkers constructed their own conception of the welfare contract, which 'excluded a client's right to help in job-finding and denied a state obligation to assure that decent job opportunities existed or could be found' (Brodkin, 1997, p 13). During assessment of the clients' needs, the workers fitted the clients into available slots and ignored information about service needs to which they could not respond. Not infrequently, caseworkers sent clients on job searches even though the clients did not meet the required level of education or literacy proficiency. The findings by Brodkin are not surprising and are replicated in many other instances. For the average caseworker, the pressures are 'to cream' – to deal with those clients who more easily fulfil the programme's requirements and, above all, not cause any problems. This means concentrating on the most readily employable. In the past, the workers would deflect the most troublesome cases. Now, they are sanctioned.

Another important change resulting from welfare reform is a significant increase in the privatisation of welfare services. In order to meet the rapidly increasing employment quotas specified in the 1996 legislation in the short time allotted, states needed to substantially increase their capacity to provide welfare-to-work services. To do so, states started contracting with private organisations. The degree and form of contracting has varied by state. While Texas and Florida implemented large-scale privatisation of welfare services, other states created a mixture of public–private provision of services (Brodkin et al, 2002). Over 30 states have entered into contracts for various welfare services. Maximus Inc., probably the most successful welfare contractor to date, runs welfare-to-work programmes in nearly a dozen states and childcare and Medicare programmes for dozens of local governments (Hartung and Washburn, 1998). Proponents of contracting have asserted that private businesses will be able to improve the efficiency and effectiveness of welfare delivery (Brodkin et al, 2002). However, research has shown that private contractors suffer from many of the same inefficiencies and problems as public agencies. One study examining the practices of private and public agencies administering welfare-to-work programmes in Chicago found that the performance goals set by the state rewarded agencies for obtaining job placement targets at the lowest marginal cost, while indirectly rewarding or not at all rewarding agencies for service quality or appropriate placements. The results were that private agencies faced the same problems previously documented in public agencies – creaming, restricting the options available to clients and offering clients inappropriate placements (Brodkin et al, 2002). Documenting what happens in private agencies is becoming more difficult as they have become increasingly reluctant to collect or disclose information on their programmes (Handler, 2004).

Thus, in both public and private organisations, welfare workers are creating welfare-to-work contracts that meet the needs of welfare agencies instead of recipient needs. One way to understand why one sees the same problems in both public and private organisations is to understand the differential power held by caseworkers and recipients. The principal source of caseworker power derives from the resources and services controlled by the agency. If the recipients want these resources, then they must yield at least some control over their fate. Additionally, caseworkers have other sources of power, including expertise, persuasion and legitimacy – all of which are used in various combinations to exercise control over recipients. A great deal of organisational power is exercised through its standardised operative procedures such as the type of information that is processed, the range of available alternatives and the rules governing decisions. On the other hand, recipients have power only if they possess desirable characteristics. The exchange relationship between the agency and the recipient can be voluntary or involuntary depending on the degree of choice that each possesses. Workers are constrained by rules and regulations, and to various degrees, professional norms and values.

With vulnerable groups, relationships tend to be involuntary. Welfare recipients are told that they must go to specific agencies in order to maintain their benefits. As mentioned above, the agency is not dependent on providing quality services to recipients for its resources; rather, it must meet employment quotas. Workers in public or private welfare offices have large caseloads, face massive numbers of regulations and requirements and must place clients in paid employment or other positions. Their response will be to secure their own survival as well as the agency's survival, and not necessarily to provide appropriate services to recipients. All of these factors mean that poor clients will receive poor services (Hasenfeld, 1983). Although recipients have the right to appeal the decisions of their worker, few file grievances due to lack of resources, time and knowledge and due to fear of retaliation from the worker. Therefore, the relationship between caseworker and welfare recipient is structured so that the client must fulfil their side of the contract or face consequences while there are no negative consequences if workers do not meet client needs.

Effects of welfare reform on recipients

Since PRWORA was enacted in 1996, the welfare rolls have fallen from 12.2 million people to 5.3 million (Pear, 2002). White people left the welfare rolls faster than African Americans and Latinos; declines have been slower in urban areas (Katz, 2001). And of 1.6 million parents still on assistance, nearly one third are working, a threefold increase from 1992 (Healy, 2000). Based on these results, almost all politicians have declared welfare reform a success. However, there are doubts about how much of these results are due to changes in welfare policy. Jeffrey Grogger et al (2002) estimate that about 15% of the decline in welfare caseloads is due to welfare reform, but about half of this is because of sanctions and diversion, rather than help with job search and employment. The other factors that led to the reduction in welfare rolls include national economic growth (until the recent recession), minimum wage increases and the expansion of the Earned Income Tax Credit (EITC) (Greenberg, 2004).

This section will examine the effects of welfare reform on both families who are still receiving aid and on families who have left the welfare rolls. One of the most significant changes to the welfare programme faced by current recipients is the imposition of sanctions. As mentioned above, if an adult fails to comply with new work requirements, they are subject to a sanction, which can either terminate cash assistance altogether or reduce the cash aid given to the family. Although the numbers of families vary from state to state, studies have revealed that high numbers of families are sanctioned at any given time. A recent General Accounting Office study (1997), found that an average of 135,800 families each month (4.5% of the national TANF caseload) received a full or partial sanction. Partial sanctions were used more frequently than full sanctions, but still an average of 16,000 families lost their benefits completely. A US Department of Health and Human Services study (1999, Table 9:31, p 108) reported an average of 15,000 monthly case closures due to sanctions. One study estimated that 540,000 families lost benefits due to full-family sanctions from 1997 to 1999, and that 370,000 remained off assistance at the end of 1999 (Hasenfeld et al, 2001).

This loss of benefits accounted for about a quarter of the total reduction in cash assistance nationally in this period (Wu et al, 2004). Cohort studies have shown that sanction rates are quite high: one quarter to one half of families subject to work requirements are sanctioned over a 12- to 24-month period. When New York City adopted a more stringent welfare programme, over 400,000 people were dropped from the rolls; 69% of recipients in its workfare programmes were sanctioned and removed from the rolls for at least several months (Brito, 2000). Based on data collected after Wisconsin implemented its welfare-to-work programme, Wu et al (2004) found that four years after entering the programme, 64% of their sample was sanctioned, 25% of these had full sanctions. It is important to note that many families are sanctioned due to bureaucratic errors, not because they do not comply with welfare regulations. If the computer fails to record a required appointment, then the recipient is automatically sanctioned (Diller, 2000).

Sanctions

Who gets sanctioned? Several studies have shown that recipients who may be least able to succeed in the labour market are the most likely to be sanctioned. Sanctioned recipients have been shown to have several employment barriers, including cognitive and health-related barriers, and certain aspects of home life (for example, lack of transportation, three or more children, childcare problems, domestic violence) (Hasenfeld et al, 2001; Pavetti and Bloom, 2001). According to a General Accounting Office report (1997), sanctioned recipients had less education, more limited work experience and longer welfare receipt than non-sanctioned recipients. In Tennessee, 60% of sanctioned recipients lacked a high-school diploma or General Education Diploma compared to 40% who left welfare for work. In South Carolina, 36% of high-school dropouts were sanctioned, compared to 22% of high-school graduates. Studies in Arizona and Minnesota report that more than half of the families receiving full sanctions had an adult with less than a high-school education. In Maryland, 41% of sanctioned families had no employment history, compared to 31% who left welfare for other reasons (Hasenfeld et al, 2001). Many sanctioned families also experience personal and family challenges at a higher rate than other recipients, including chemical dependency, physical and mental health problems and domestic violence. These studies have been replicated in Utah, Connecticut, Minnesota and Wisconsin (Hasenfeld et al, 2001; Wu et al, 2004).

Despite the extensive use of sanctions, the evidence is contradictory as to whether sanctions are effective in encouraging compliance with welfare programmes or encouraging poor unwed mothers to work. Many agency staff firmly believe that sanctions 'work' – they communicate the seriousness of the requirements. Some studies show that neither the threat of sanctions nor the imposition of sanctions change behaviour. Other studies show that severe sanctions are no more or less effective than moderate sanctions (Kaplan, 1999). However, a recent study conducted among welfare recipients in Wisconsin shows that most sanction spells are short and that most recipients re-obtain their full level of welfare benefits after facing a full-family sanction. The authors believe this shows some evidence that sanctions have their desired effect of increasing compliance with programme requirements (Wu et al, 2004). However, the authors contend that it is still important to consider whether the imposition of sanctions led to significant hardship among families. Taken as a whole, studies suggest that sanctions influence the behaviours of many TANF recipients but not others, even with the loss of all assistance (Pavetti and Bloom, 2001).

The other significant change in welfare policy is the imposition of strict time limits on aid. The federal five-year time limit was reached on 1 October 2001. Even before the federal time limit was reached, approximately 60,000 families reached the time limits in seven states with shorter periods. Most of these families reside in three states: Connecticut, Massachusetts and Louisiana (Pavetti and Bloom, 2001). Research about the characteristics and outcomes of families who have reached their cumulative lifetime limit on aid is starting to be released. These families, like families that are sanctioned, face multiple barriers to obtaining and keeping employment. A recent study examining characteristics of families who are approaching the federal time limit revealed that a variety of characteristics distinguish these families from those who are on welfare for shorter periods of time, including persistent maternal and child health problems, persistent domestic violence, persistent drug use, lack of a partner, low levels of education and increases in the number of children (Seefeldt and Orzol, 2004). Even though most observers thought that states would somehow extend benefits, most, in fact, have not and benefits have been terminated. Many of the families who were terminated were working, but many were not (Haskins and Blank, 2001).

Effects of welfare reform

When determining whether welfare reform was successful, it is also important to consider the effectiveness of welfare-to-work programmes. Rather than education and training, the dominant strategy emphasises 'work first' – take any job, even a low-wage job, stick with that job, and the person will move up the economic ladder. Studies of state welfare-to-work programmes reveal that they are not having their intended results. In a survey of 20 welfare-to-work programmes, Manpower Demonstration Research Corporation found that participating in the programmes increased earnings by only about US$500 per year more than the controls. Welfare payments were reduced by nearly US$400 and food stamps by US$100, thus resulting in welfare savings for the government, if the expenses of other supportive services are not included in the analysis (Michalopoulos and Schwartz, 2000). While earnings of the most disadvantaged groups (long-term recipients, those who lack a high-school diploma, those with three or more children and those with no recent work experience) increased, they still remained far below the earnings of the more advantaged workers. In addition, employment mobility is a myth. Most low-wage jobs are dead-end. Thus, despite the political claims for success, the gains for welfare-to-work recipients are very modest, and often fail to account for the costs of working – transportation, reciprocity in childcare, missed days, and so forth. Most former recipients remain in poverty.

Similar results seem to be true even for the programmes that emphasise education and training. A national evaluation of welfare-to-work strategies in 11 US locations revealed that 81% of participants showed a marked increase in employment and earning rates that equalled or exceeded the results of work-first programmes over the study's two-year follow-up period. Still, these programmes were not able to lift the participants out of poverty. Even though most of the programmes help families rely on their own earnings rather than welfare cheques, reductions in welfare, food stamps and other benefits outweighed this finding. In other words, family net incomes were the same as before. The researchers found that education-focused programmes do not produce added economic benefits relative to job-search-focused programmes. Moreover, the job-search-focused approach is cheaper to operate and moves welfare recipients into jobs more quickly than the education-focused approach (Hamilton, 2002). However, neither job-search-focused nor adult education-focused programmes have typically been successful in helping poor unwed mothers and other low-income parents work steadily and have access to higher-paying jobs (Brauner and Loprest, 1999; Strawn et al, 2001). Thus, mandated work programmes, in general, have little effect on income since they often result in a decline in welfare benefits (Hamilton, 2002). Work programmes did decrease poverty somewhat, but only for families just below the poverty line (Grogger et al, 2002).

Another way to measure the effectiveness of welfare reform is to consider what happens to welfare recipients after they leave the welfare rolls – commonly referred to as 'leavers'. Studies of the employment of leavers are starting to be published, including information on who finds jobs, what kinds of jobs and how much they earn (Loprest, 1999). Between half and two thirds of former recipients find jobs shortly after leaving welfare. Most of the jobs are in sales, food preparation, clerical support and other service jobs. Despite the relatively high number of weekly work hours, there are substantial periods of unemployment (Hamilton, 2002). The pay is between US$5.57 and US$8.42 per hour, and the average reported annual earnings range from US$8,000 to US$16,600, thus leaving many families in poverty (Grogger et al, 2002).[1] Increases in earnings are largely a result of working longer hours rather than a growth in wages. Most employed former welfare recipients do not receive employer-provided health insurance or paid sick or vacation leave. Employment loss is a significant problem (Strawn et al, 2001). In addition, there are sharp declines in Medicaid and food stamps (Grogger et al, 2002). Most do not receive childcare subsidies (Pavetti, 1999).

A recent study of 600 women with a history of welfare receipt living in high-poverty neighbourhoods in Miami, Florida, revealed that they were far from self-sufficient after leaving the welfare rolls. In 2001, 29% of study respondents were neither working nor receiving welfare. Furthermore, 35% of respondents held three or more jobs and only 27% reported having a job that was full time, that paid US$7.50 per hour or more and that offered medical benefits (Brock et al, 2004). Overall, it appears that welfare reform was successful at pushing families off the rolls, but not in lifting them out of poverty.

TANF was scheduled to be reauthorised in 2002, but Congress has only managed to temporarily extend the current policy. The administration of George W. Bush pushed for policies that simply increase the 1996 reforms, including greater work requirements for poor unwed mothers, which are to be increased by 5% per year until they reach 70% in the fiscal year 2007. Moreover, welfare recipients would be required to work a full 40-hour working week and would be further discouraged from participating in education and training programmes. Despite the evidence that prior welfare recipients need supportive services such as childcare to maintain employment, the administration proposed to freeze childcare block grant funding levels for the next five years. Thus far, Congress has failed to enact any of President Bush's proposed reforms. In fact, both the Senate and the House of Representatives have proposed increasing childcare funding.

Prior to the recession in the early 1990s, the states had surpluses from the block grants and significant amounts of money were spent on helping the working poor – childcare, after-school programmes, state Earned Income Tax Credits, transportation assistance, teen-pregnancy prevention programmes, and so on. Now, all this has changed with almost all states experiencing large deficits. Consequently there have been very significant reductions in aid (Greenberg, 2004).

Conclusions

When PRWORA was passed in 1996, lawmakers pledged to 'end welfare as we know it'. They succeeded in making significant reforms to the programme for poor single mothers and their children, including creating mandatory work requirements as well as strict time limits on aid. In a basic sense, the 1996 welfare reform was not new; it mirrored the traditional approach of blaming the victim – poverty and dependency were caused by individual behaviour. What was new was the vigour with which the mandatory work requirements were to be enforced at the state level. Since the passage of welfare reform, there is no consensus about its success. Contrary to the assumption of lawmakers that giving more authority to states would allow them to tailor their programme to local conditions, evidence shows that states form their policies based on national trends, not local needs. Given increased flexibility, most states enacted strict work requirements and sanction policies as well as a work-first approach. Most lawmakers also assumed that welfare offices would be able to change their culture from simply monitoring eligibility to running employment programmes. However, studies reveal that, in most offices, the work programmes have become an add-on component to eligibility determination. Caseworkers routinely ignore the needs of recipients and base their welfare-to-work contracts more on agency needs than on client needs. As for the effects on recipients, while the welfare rolls have been dramatically reduced, studies reveal that families are not better off. Most still live in poverty and many are unemployed.

Note

[1] The current minimum wage in the US is US$5.15 per hour. An individual working full time throughout the year would earn a total of US$9,373, which is far below the poverty level of US$14,348 for a family of three (Rank, 2004). In 2002, the median income for a family of four in the US was US$62,732 (www.census.gov). The poverty threshold for this same family was US$18,104 (http://aspe.hhs.gov/poverty/02poverty.htm). According to the US Bureau of Labor statistics, the unemployment rate in December 2004 was approximately 5.4% (www.bls.gov/cps/home.htm). It is important to note that this percentage is based on workers who are currently seeking employment. Thus, people who are no longer seeking jobs are not included.

References

Aaron, H. (2004) 'Privatize social security? No' (online), *New York Daily News*, available at: www.nydailynews.com

Abromovitz, M. (1988) *Regulating the lives of women: Social welfare policy from colonial times to the present*, Boston, MA: South End.

Brauner, S. and Loprest, P. (1999) 'Where are they now? What states' studies of people who left welfare tell us', *The Urban Institute Series A*, no 32, pp 1-9.

Brito, T. (2000) 'The welfarization of family law', *Kansas Law Review*, vol 48, pp 229-83.

Brock, T., Kwakye, I., Polyne, J., Richborg-Hayes, L., Seith, D., Stepick, A. and Stepick, C. (2004) *Welfare reform in Miami: Implementation, effects, and experiences of poor families and neighborhoods*, New York: Manpower Demonstration Research Corporation.

Brodkin, E. (1997) 'Inside the welfare contract: discretion and accountability in state welfare administration', *Social Service Review*, vol 71, no 1, pp 1-20.

Brodkin, E., Fuqua, C. and Thoren, K. (2002) 'Contracting welfare reform: uncertainties of capacity-building within disjointed federalism', Working Paper of the Project on the Public Economy of Work, Chicago, IL: University of Chicago.

De Parle, J. (1997) 'Lessons learned: welfare reform's first months – a special report: success, frustration, as welfare rules change', *New York Times*, 30 December, A16.

De Parle, J. (2004) *American dream: Three women, ten kids, and a nation's drive to end welfare*, New York, NY: Penguin.

Department of Health and Human Services (DHHS) (1999) *Second Annual Report to Congress*, August, Washington: DHHS.

Diller, M. (2000) 'The revolution in welfare administration: rules, discretion, and entrepreneurial government', *NYU Law Review*, vol 75, no 5, pp 1121-220.

Gais, T., Nathan, R., Lurie, I. and Kaplan, T. (2001) 'The implementation of the Personal Responsibility Act of 1996: commonalities, variations, and the challenge of complexity', paper presented at the conference for The New World of Welfare: Shaping a Post-TANF Agenda for Policy, Washington, DC, February 1-2.

General Accounting Office (1997) 'Poverty measurement: issues in revising and updating the official definition', *GAO/HEHS-97-38*, Washington, DC: United States General Accounting Office.

Gordon, L. (1988) *Heroes of their own lives: The politics and history of family violence, Boston 1880-1960*, New York, NY: Penguin.

Greenberg, M. (2004) 'Welfare reform, phase two: doing less with less', *The American Prospect, Axis of Drivel*, September, vol 15, no 19, www.prospect.org.

Grogger, J., Karoly, L. and Klerman, A. (2002) *Consequences of welfare reform: A research synthesis*, Los Angeles, CA: RAND.

Hacker, J. (2004) 'Privatising risk without privatising the welfare state: the hidden politics of social policy retrenchment in the US', *American Political Science Review*, vol 98, no 2, pp 243-60.

Hamilton, G. (2002) *Moving people from welfare to work: Lessons from the national evaluation of welfare-to-work strategies*, New York, NY: Manpower Demonstration Research Corporation.

Handler, J. (2004) *Social citizenship and workfare in the US and Western Europe: The paradox of inclusion*, Cambridge: Cambridge University Press.

Handler, J. and Hasenfeld, Y. (1997) *We the poor people: Work, poverty and welfare*, New Haven, CT: Yale University Press.

Hartung, W. and Washburn, J. (1998) 'Lockheed Martin: from warfare to welfare', *The Nation*, vol 266, no 7, pp 11-16.

Hasenfeld, Y. (1983) *Human services organisations*, New Jersey, NJ: Upper Saddle River.

Hasenfeld, Y., Ghose, T. and Hillesland-Larson, K. (2001) *Characteristics of sanctioned and non-sanctioned single-parent CalWORKS recipients: Preliminary findings from the first wave survey in four counties: Alameda, Freson, Kern, and San Diego*, Los Angeles, CA: The Lewis Center for Regional and Policy Studies.

Haskins, R. and Blank, R. (2001) *The new world of welfare*, Washington, DC: Brookings Institution Press.

Healy, M. (2000) 'Welfare rolls fall to half of '96 numbers', *Los Angeles Times*, p A12.

Kaiser Commission on Medicaid and the Uninsured (2004) *The continuing Medicaid budget challenge: State Medicaid spending growth and cost containment in fiscal years 2004 and 2005* (online), available at: www.kff.org/medicaid/7190.cfm

Kaiser Family Foundation (2004) *The New Medicare Prescription Drug Benefit* (online), available at: www.kaiseredu.org/IssueModules/Adding/index.cfm

Kaplan, J. (1999) 'The use of sanctions under TANF', *Welfare Information Network: Issue Notes*, vol 3, p 3.

Katz, M. (2001) *The price of citizenship: Redefining the American welfare state*, New York, NY: Metropolitan Books.

Lieberman, R. and Shaw, G. (2000) 'Looking inward, looking outward: the politics of state welfare innovation under devolution', *Political Research Quarterly*, vol 53, no 2, pp 215-40.

Loprest, P. (1999). 'Families who left welfare: who are they and how are they doing?', Urban Institute Discussion Paper No. 10, Washington, DC: The Urban Institute.

Michalopoulos, C. and Schwartz, C. (2000) *National evaluation of welfare-to-work strategies: What works best for whom: Impacts of 20 welfare-to-work programmes by subgroup*, New York, NY: Manpower Demonstration Research Corporation.

Pavetti, L. (1999) 'How much more can welfare mothers work?', *Focus*, vol 20, no 2, pp 16-9.

Pavetti, L. and Bloom, D. (2001) 'Sanctions and time limits: state policies, their implementation, and outcomes for families', paper presented at the conference on 'The new world of welfare: Shaping a post-TANF agenda for policy', Washington, DC, 1-2 February.

Pear, R. (2002) 'House democrats propose making the '96 welfare law an antipoverty weapon', *New York Times*, 24 January, p A24.

Piven, F. and Cloward, R. (1977) *Poor people's movements: Why they succeed, how they fail*, New York, NY: Pantheon Books.

Rank, M. (2004) *One nation underprivileged: Why American poverty affects us all*, New York, NY: Oxford University Press.

Seefeldt, K. and Orzol, S. (2004) 'Watching the clock tick: factors associated with TANF accumulation', National Poverty Center Working Paper Series, Ann Arbor, MI: National Poverty Center.

Strawn, J., Greenberg, M. and Savner, S. (2001) *Improving employment outcomes under TANF*, Washington, DC: Brookings Institution Press.

Wu, C., Cancian, M., Meyer, D. and Wallace, G. (2004) *How do welfare sanctions work?*, Institute for Research on Poverty discussion paper, Madison, WI: Institute for Research on Poverty.

SEVEN

The new governance of Australian welfare: street-level contingencies

Cosmo Howard[1]

Social policy occupies a central position in contemporary theories of governance. It has become commonplace for theorists to describe particular governing paradigms in terms of their specific welfare arrangements and to analyse shifts in governance by making references to changes in social policy. Most readers will be familiar with the distinction that is often drawn between the post-war welfare state, said to be characterised by universal, institutionalised social entitlements, and the newer neo-liberal state, which is distinguished by residual and disciplinary forms of social policy. One of the distinct features of most theories of the new welfare governance is a tendency to promulgate coherent accounts of welfare reform. Neo-liberalism is perhaps the most frequently cited principle underlying current developments, and writers regularly go to considerable lengths to illustrate the ways in which the diverse elements of welfare reform fit together within an 'advanced liberal' logic.

Furthermore, there is also a related tendency in this literature to view the processes of social policy reform in linear terms, meaning that theorists see welfare as becoming progressively more neo-liberal, over time. The result is a largely monolithic story about the significant changes that are currently taking place in the welfare systems of the developed world. These theoretical narratives are elegant and influential, but they give us cause to wonder about the extent to which such simple stories capture the complexity of welfare reform. Perhaps one of the most salient questions concerns the degree to which the linear accounts tally with the experiences of actors at different levels and in different parts of social welfare systems.

This chapter reports on the findings of an ethnographic study of street-level experiences of welfare reform in Centrelink, Australia's national benefits agency. The findings indicate that there is considerably more incoherence and contradiction within welfare reform than is suggested by linear neo-liberal accounts of the process. To demonstrate this point, the focus is on three important aspects of Australian welfare reform. The first is the policy concerning sanctions that are applied to beneficiaries who fail to comply with the rules. I argue that, because of conflicting policy developments in this area, we cannot come to any clear conclusions as to whether sanctions have become more or less stringent. The second area of focus concerns the delivery of a personalised, 'One-to-One Service'. I argue that the initial growth of the One-to-One Service following the creation of Centrelink has been significantly reversed in recent years. Third, I look at the changing role of 'risk management' techniques throughout welfare reform. I suggest that Centrelink's risk management initiatives in the late 1990s, which sought to establish a more entrepreneurial approach to the administration of benefits, have been counteracted by more recent developments, which have moved the agency closer to a traditional bureaucratic mode of operation. In each of these areas I look not only at the policy shifts and street-level experiences, but also at the various staff and beneficiary 'identities' that have been constructed and invoked by policy initiatives. Drawing on developments in street-level implementation, I show how staff and beneficiaries have been asked to assume multiple and contradictory identities in welfare reform.

This chapter begins with a survey of the literature on the new governance of welfare. Following this, I report on the findings from the empirical research into sanctions for non-compliance. I then examine the changing emphasis on the One-to-One Service in Australian welfare administration. After this, I investigate the shifting fortunes of risk management in Centrelink. The conclusion reflects briefly on the implications of my findings for theories of welfare governance.

Theorising the new governance of Australian welfare

There has been much academic commentary about new approaches to the governance of welfare. Disciplinary and theoretical differences exist within this literature, but a common theme is a general tendency to view the patterns within contemporary governance as having a coherent, overarching rationality or logic (Larner and Walters, 2000). In the field of political economy, writers such as Jessop (1999) have sought to chart the evolution of governance paradigms over the 20th century. Jessop's influential formulation contrasts the post-war welfare state model, premised on Keynesian demand management, full employment, social citizenship and Fordist mass production/consumption, with the current neo-liberal 'Schumpetarian' governance paradigm, organised around the imperatives of global competitiveness and featuring residual, coercive welfare policies (1999, pp 349-56). Although Jessop admits that both of these paradigms can take different forms in different jurisdictional contexts, his analysis suggests a basic degree of coherence in the way in which welfare is governed within each paradigm and a significant degree of discontinuity between the two paradigms (Jessop, 1999; Larner and Walters, 2000, p 363). A similar tendency towards monolithic explanations can be found in the increasingly popular 'governmentality' perspective. At the broadest level, the analysis of governmentality writers looks similar to some of the political economy work, in the sense that many place great stress on the central role of neo-liberal or 'advanced liberal' ideas in contemporary governance (Rose, 1996; Dean and Hindess, 1998). However, governmentality writers tend to pay much more attention to the 'micro-level' aspects of the new governance arrangements, including the nature of the interactions between frontline officials and citizens, and the ways in which policies create particular models of how citizens should act and think about themselves (Rose, 1996, pp 37-8).

In governmentality, neo-liberalism is understood as a political rationality that encourages individuals to regulate their behaviour autonomously, as a substitute for state intervention (Hindess, 1996; Rose, 1996). This devolution of responsibility for government is enacted through a myriad of policy instruments or 'technologies', including commercialisation, marketisation and privatisation (Rose, 1996, p 54). Risk management is also a central technology of neo-liberal governance and it has fundamental implications for both state and non-state actors. Within government, it is associated with managerialist critiques of the traditional bureaucrat, who places adherence to the rules ahead of other policy goals. Risk management suggests that public officials should act in an entrepreneurial fashion and give more attention to the achievement of positive outcomes for service users (Du Gay, 2000). For citizens, the rise of risk management as a technique of governance has meant that in policy domains such as employment, health and retirement, individuals are increasingly encouraged and required to take personal responsibility for managing the risks that they face (Dean, 1995; O'Malley, 1996; Rose, 1996).

Australian welfare reform has been a popular subject for governmentality writers. Some have used the theoretical framework to look at the new risk-based governance mechanisms in the Australian system of employment assistance (McDonald et al, 2003; Henman, 2004). According to these researchers, the concept of risk is used in Australia to differentiate between individuals on the basis of their likelihood of long-term welfare dependency. Individualised, actuarial assessments are used to direct intensive support and supervision to those most 'at risk' (Henman, 2004). Central to these processes is the reconstitution of the subjects of social policy, from 'passive' beneficiaries, to active 'job seekers' carrying varying degrees of labour market disadvantage (Rose, 1996; Walters, 1997, 2000; McDonald et al, 2003). For those unwilling to become involved in the management of their own risk, new and more stringent disciplinary strategies and punishments have been implemented (McDonald et al, 2003). Furthermore, neo-liberalism has inspired various 'tutelage' mechanisms, such as case management, contractualism and the 'One-to-One Service', which are aimed at involving jobless individuals in the process of their own treatment and are designed to foster skills required for financial independence, including more 'entrepreneurial' orientations among job seekers (Dean, 1995, 1998; Rose, 1996).

The suggestion that governmentality affirms the coherence of new governance paradigms requires some justification, since many governmentality theorists deny that they propagate a unified account of contemporary public policy. Indeed, one of the frequent claims of the governmentalists is that governance is a product of a multitude of contingent developments and pressures that emerge from different domains to shape policy terrains. The most prominent example of this argument is given by Larner and Walters (2000), who criticise accounts of neo-liberalism that portray it as a monolithic force that has the same effects and implications whenever and wherever it is applied. Using a comparison of privatisation processes in Britain and New Zealand, they show that very different rationales, identities and consequences emerged in the two national contexts. Among other things, they argue that the tendency of authors to view neo-liberalism as a coherent force has the effect of 'occluding' the impact of diverse developments on contemporary governance (Larner and Walters, 2000, p 365). Rather than seeing privatisation as flowing from some central logic or pressure or interest, they suggest that 'it might be more useful and accurate to see neo-liberal initiatives as involving short lived, politically expedient, programmatic experiments' (Larner and Walters, 2000, p 374). They claim that governmentality, which shies away from overarching causal explanations, facilitates an investigation of the contingencies that complicate the nature of neo-liberalism.

While governmentality may permit and encourage a more nuanced perspective on governance, many of the influential writers who use the approach choose to retain a more or less undifferentiated account of contemporary public policy. For instance, Rose (1996, p 53), speaking about the emergence of neo-conservatism in the early 1980s, suggests that although these movements were initially incoherent and did not represent a single objective or perspective, 'gradually, these diverse skirmishes were rationalised within a relatively coherent mentality of government that came to be termed neo-liberalism'. Even Larner and Walters (2000), who downplay the coherence of neo-liberalism, appear not to question the dominance of neo-liberalism *itself* in contemporary governance. A similar line of reasoning is found in Harris's (2003) investigation of recent reforms in Australian social policy. Although she highlights the 'wretched contradictions' of neo-liberalism, she nevertheless believes that the concept is 'useful as a general descriptor', because it captures the salient features of the current policy 'epoch' (Harris, 2003, pp 85-6).

As part of a doctoral research project, I was able to spend time in Centrelink, to observe first-hand the implementation of several Australian welfare reform initiatives. I conducted short ethnographies at three different Centrelink 'Customer Service Centres' and in each case I was located within a team of frontline 'customer service officers' (CSOs) charged with serving welfare beneficiaries. I was able to observe staff in their everyday work, to speak informally with them and also interview the officers about their work. I also observed these staff members interacting with beneficiaries during appointments and I conducted in-depth interviews with recipients. In the first study, conducted in June and July 2000, I spent one month at a Customer Service Centre in Canberra, Australia's capital, and a major city with Australia's highest average income, lowest unemployment rate and lowest proportion of the population relying on government benefits in the country (Australian Statistician, 2000). In the second study, which took place in May and June of 2001, I spent five weeks at a Customer Service Centre in Newcastle, a city in the Hunter Valley of New South Wales that has experienced high levels of structural unemployment since the closure of major manufacturing industries during the 1980s and 1990s (Fincher and

Wulff, 1998). The third case study took place between August and October 2001 at a Customer Service Centre in inner-city Melbourne, where problems of poverty, homelessness and substance abuse are concentrated (Jamieson and Jacobs, 1996). In total I interviewed 26 frontline staff, 31 customers and observed 47 appointments. Fieldnotes were coded and analysed 'inductively' in order to build empirical themes, using the N'Vivo data management software package.[2] In the following sections I will use my field research to demonstrate the complex and contradictory nature of Australian welfare reform.

Welfare police or protectors of the vulnerable?

In Australia, the application of sanctions for non-compliance, or 'breaches' as they are locally called, has generated considerable controversy in recent years. In policy documents and academic commentaries, developments in sanctioning policy have been described in terms of a general and sustained push to 'activate' working-age recipients of social assistance (Carney and Ramia, 1999; Moses and Sharples, 2000). However, despite the growing local interest in these matters, the severity of sanctions in the Australian system has not increased straightforwardly over time. Instead, policy makers have responded to problems with the street-level implementation of breaches by instituting new protocols and invoking new identities, which have had the effect of strengthening certain aspects of the penalty provisions and softening others.

Following their election in 1996, the federal Coalition government pursued a strategy of strengthening the 'activity requirements' in the income support system and toughening the sanctions for non-compliance. These moves were justified on the grounds that employment was available for job seekers and that too many recipients were deliberately languishing on benefits (Newman, 1999; Abbott, 2000). The solution was to stiffen the penalties for those who violated the rules. Importantly, the problem of non-compliance was not just caused by the actions of beneficiaries. It was understood by the government to stem in part from the unwillingness of frontline Centrelink officers to enforce the rules. In 2000, the Minister for Employment Services, Tony Abbott, argued that Australian welfare administrators had been too lenient in the past, and that the government's efforts to tighten administration were meeting bureaucratic resistance:

> Despite ministerial declarations, the practice of officialdom has often been equivocal with widespread winking at beneficiaries who failed to turn up to interviews, participate in training programmes or take jobs. Changing the culture of administration, let alone the attitudes of welfare beneficiaries, to use Weber's words, is like 'slow boring through hard wood.' (Abbott, 2000)

In order to effect a change in the practices of frontline staff and to ensure that they would be less lenient, the government introduced reforms to breaching in July 2000. These streamlined the process of sanctioning in order to make it easier for frontline staff to apply penalties. The reforms also took much of the discretion out of the breaching process, and staff were instructed not to accept certain excuses for non-compliance. Minister Tony Abbott's account of these changes highlights the emphasis on reducing discretion and tightening the administration of sanctions:

> Replacing the old Department of Social Security with Centrelink has helped to produce a more active approach to the administration of welfare. As welfare 'policeman' Centrelink has responsibility for 'breaching' ... job seekers who don't comply with the rules ... Centrelink recently issued staff with new guidelines about acceptable reasons for non-compliance: 'If the customer has failed to attend an interview, is there a history of this sort of behaviour? ... If the customer 'slept in', does he regularly use this excuse? … Reasons such as 'I forgot', 'I won't do it again' or 'I ran out of petrol' are not acceptable ... unless supported by immediate action to put things right. (Abbott, 2000)

Abbott subsequently boasted that, 'under these eminently reasonable guidelines, Centrelink is now enforcing breaches at rates which are 85 per cent higher than those just two years ago' (Abbott, 2000). These accounts suggest that the Coalition government did, in its early years, attempt to tighten the administration of sanctions, with a view to increasing the numbers of individuals sanctioned. The government also constructed and invoked particular identities in this process, including the lenient frontline welfare administrator who bends or disregards the rules as a matter of habit and the calculating welfare recipient intent on defrauding the system. These problematic identities were to be replaced by the 'welfare policeman' and the active, obedient beneficiary.

This early emphasis on tightening the administration of sanctions emerged in my discussions with frontline Centrelink officers. The identities invoked in the early policy rhetoric also found application at the front line. This staff member from the Hunter office reflected on the lenience of staff and its effect on the behaviour of beneficiaries:

> 'I think that [customers] don't take us seriously enough. There is a lot of discretion, so you can breach, or you can decide not to, or to revoke a breach, and I think a lot of [customers] think that they can get away with it.'

During the early stages of this study, staff also spoke of the shift within the agency away from a culture of lenience and towards a strict application of the sanctioning rules. Speaking in July 2000, a staff member from the Canberra office pointed to changes that had removed staff discretion in relation to breaching:

> 'Yeah, up until about a year ago, no one really did the breaches. And a lot of the discretion is being taken out now.... A lot of people used to revoke breaches for not showing up to appointments. It used to be that you didn't get breached for not attending. Now ... because of the system, we have to breach them.'

During this early phase of my research, I also noticed that the majority of staff explained non-compliance by arguing that customers deliberately broke the rules, because they felt they would get away with it:

> 'I think it's also that they still don't expect to be breached. They're still not used to the fact that if you don't turn up, you'll be punished. They're not used to the fact that if you don't show up to an appointment, one, you've got to give a good reason, but you've also got to give proof of the reason.' (Hunter CSO)

> 'The big problem is getting them in for an appointment, them turning up. But I think it's getting better. They're

> starting to realise that they won't just get away with it.' (Canberra CSO)

These quotes reveal the acceptance of certain identities among some of the staff, including the lenient welfare administrator, the 'welfare policeman' and the free-riding beneficiary. Furthermore, they suggest that, on the ground, in 2000, there was a sense that the rules were being tightened, and that lenience was being removed from the system.

These perspectives and approaches attracted considerable criticism. Throughout 2000 and 2001, welfare advocacy groups, academic commentators and independent inquiries pushed the claim that sanctions were falling disproportionately on 'vulnerable' persons, including youths, the homeless, individuals with intellectual and psychiatric disabilities, and those suffering from substance abuse problems (Moses and Sharples, 2000, p 17; Lackner, 2001; ACOSS, 2001a, 2001b). The critics claimed that such individuals were not in a good position to comply with the more stringent rules and requirements. Various 'horror stories' surfaced of vulnerable individuals who had been sanctioned and whose lives had been made significantly more difficult as a result. We can understand these critiques as attempts to redefine the identity of the non-compliant beneficiary by dismissing or downplaying the significance of deliberate rule breaking, while emphasising the problem of vulnerability and the fact of diminished competence. In these counter-narratives, the vulnerable incompetent becomes the salient identity, not the culpable, calculating, work-shy cheat. In 2001, the government responded to these concerns by developing several new policies on breaching and non-compliance. These new policies introduced a number of measures designed to 'protect the vulnerable' from breach penalties (Vanstone, 2002). The first initiative was a 'Third Breach Alert', which required Centrelink staff to seek the opinion of a specialist officer before applying a customer's third consecutive breach penalty. The second initiative involved calling customers facing their second breach in to Centrelink for an appointment to discuss any difficulties they might be having in complying with the requirements, and to investigate 'measures ... to prevent them incurring further breach penalties' (Vanstone, 2002).

One of the effects of this new approach was that it encouraged Centrelink staff to regard non-compliance as a possible consequence of an inability to comply with the rules. Stated in terms of identity, it promoted a splitting up of the singular view of the recipient as a calculating cheat. These individuals continued to present a problem, but, now, a new identity centred on the condition of 'vulnerability' emerged, and the challenge for staff was to distinguish between the cheats and the incompetents. During my interviews at the Melbourne office in late 2001, after these new policies on breaching had been introduced, a very different attitude to non-compliance was in evidence. Not one staff member argued that non-compliance was the result of deliberate cheating. Virtually all explanations for non-compliance now highlighted the role of 'personal issues' beyond the control of beneficiaries. For instance, a Centrelink team leader from the Melbourne office argued that a large proportion of non-compliant customers suffered from personal problems:

> 'I would say that of the customers who are breached ... 70 to 80% of them have readily identifiable issues, which are reflected in the information that already exists on the system.'

This team leader revealed that as part of the new strategy, Centrelink officers were being encouraged to view breaches as a sign that the customer might need specialist help:

> 'We're moving towards looking at breaches as a kind of trigger for looking at other programmes like the Community Support Programme, specialist disability service providers and specialist Job Network services.'

The new strategy also had the effect of increasing the discretion of frontline staff in relation to breaching. This was achieved partly by removing quotas specifying how many customers should be breached. According to a team leader from the Melbourne office in late 2001:

> 'Those targets have been removed from breaching, so we don't have a set proportion that we have to breach. The only target now is a timeliness criterion, where we've got to action the breach within 14 days. It doesn't mean we have to impose it.'

During the same period, another Melbourne officer reflected on the shift towards greater discretion in breaching:

> 'With breaches now I feel that we have a bit more discretion than we used to. Before, the breaches were a really big thing. If they didn't turn up you were supposed to breach them. Now we've been told to back off a bit. We're supposed to look at whether they have homelessness or drug issues and take them into consideration before breaching.'

These accounts suggest that the initial emphasis on the systematic breaching of non-compliant customers has been replaced with a new approach, in which the agency of Centrelink officers is more prominent, and where their judgement is relied upon to a much greater extent in the application of breach penalties. It shows that there has been a shift in the ways in which the identities of the welfare recipient and frontline officer are constructed. Arguably, the latter went through a threefold shift. The move towards tightening administration promoted the 'welfare policeman' identity in place of the lenient administrator. However, the emergence of the 'vulnerability' perspective also posited a new identity for staff, with the demise of the 'welfare policeman' and the rise of the caring, compassionate officer who would protect the beneficiary from the harmful effects of sanctions. In terms of the central argument of this chapter, it is difficult to characterise these changes as a linear progression towards a more neo-liberal set of arrangements. While the early move to tighten penalties and activate beneficiaries is consistent with neo-liberal critiques of passivity and dependency, the later shift to vulnerability and incompetence appears more consistent with paternalistic and welfarist ideas about the need to protect and shelter the disadvantaged.

The rise and demise of the One-to-One Service

Centrelink was created in 1997 as an integrated, quasi-autonomous social service delivery agency, drawing staff from the former Commonwealth Department of Social Security and the now defunct Commonwealth Employment Service. The new organisation was given two important mandates by the government. First, the agency was expected to improve 'customer service' by making service delivery more responsive to the needs of individual users (Australia House of Representatives, 1996). This objective is consistent with aspects of neo-liberalism in the sense that customer service is a key element of contemporary managerialist thinking (Barzelay, 2001) and also because the individualised approach to service delivery is a central part of the neo-liberal model of intensive, personalised welfare administration.[3] Second, Centrelink was asked to reduce the cost of welfare administration (Australia House of Representatives, 1996; Mulgan, 2003, p 170). Centrelink faced an AU$580 million budget cut in its first three years and was forced to shed approximately one sixth of its staff in order to cope with the reduced funding (Mulgan, 2003, p 171). This cost reduction exercise was also clearly consistent with the neo-liberal emphasis on improving productivity and reducing government outlays.

As part of its early attempts to improve customer service, Centrelink management concentrated on shifting the organisational focus away from processing beneficiaries and towards thinking about and responding to the needs of individual 'customers' in 'holistic' terms (Vardon, 2000). Prior to 1999, beneficiaries who wanted to speak to a staff member or who had an appointment with Centrelink were allocated to the next available Centrelink officer. Centrelink's own customer feedback research found that this system was disliked, because recipients felt that they were treated impersonally. In response, Centrelink devised the One-to-One Service initiative. Under this new approach, each recipient was allocated to a specific staff member, who they saw for all appointments. This staff member would act as their 'One Main Contact' and become familiar with their individual needs (Vardon, 2000). The One-to-One Service initiative involved a reconfiguration of the identities of beneficiaries and frontline staff members. In the case of staff, people-processors were to be replaced with dedicated servants who took an interest in the whole customer. Beneficiaries ceased to be nondescript members of broad administrative categories and became demanding customers with unique and complex needs and aspirations, requiring personalised intervention.

Beyond the general claims made in Centrelink publications about the benefits of One-to-One, there is not much publicly available information on the implementation of the model. In my research, I found that the introduction of the One-to-One Service did have some effect on street-level orientations and practices. For instance, when asked to define 'individualised service delivery', the majority of staff referred to elements of the One-to-One Service model (Howard, 2003a, pp 137-8). The majority of staff also supported the principle of one-to-one interaction, and two officers appeared to identify personally and professionally with the model:

> '[One-to-one interaction is] where I get my job satisfaction. Otherwise, it's just processing forms all day. I figure I'm being paid by the community to help the community. I figure I'm actually working for my future employers.' (Melbourne CSO)

> '[One-to-One is] the way I like to operate. I take pride in my work. I put in the extra work, to create rapport with the customer. I explain to them that they're important.' (Hunter CSO)

Some beneficiaries also felt that One-to-One was important because it ensured that their own unique needs were met.[4] This Centrelink customer from Melbourne is a good example:

> '[My One Main Contact] actually helps me a lot .... Like, because he's from an ethnic background too and he understands what people go through most of the times [sic], and yeah. He has more understanding of it than what other people would.... See, he helps me as a person, you know ... and he's been there, and stuff like that.'

Beneficiaries who supported the One-to-One model embraced the notion that they were individuals with specific needs who required the help of a dedicated person. A minority of the officers in the study claimed to have customers who they saw on repeated occasions for One-to-One appointments, and who they had developed a 'rapport' with. To an extent then, at least some of the staff and beneficiaries did embody the identities and practices prescribed by the One-to-One Service initiative.

Interviews with officers and recipients also revealed challenges in relation to the implementation of the One-to-One Service. The most frequently cited difficulty was a lack of staffing resources. This resulted in extremely large caseloads for the Centrelink officers. At the Canberra and Hunter offices, the caseloads of the CSOs interviewed averaged over 1,000. At the Melbourne office, caseloads ranged from approximately 500 for trainee Centrelink officers to almost 1,000 for regular Centrelink officers. Many staff felt that these caseloads were an impediment to individualised service:

> Interviewer: 'Can you provide One-to-One Service?'

> Hunter CSO: 'Not with 900 customers, no, not properly.'

The officer with one of the smallest caseloads in the study felt that it was still too large to facilitate One-to-One Service:

> 'Ideally, it means follow-up. It's getting to know the people you're dealing with.... If you've got 500 people you can't do that.' (Melbourne CSO)

Staff argued that high caseloads meant they would see customers very infrequently, and that many customers would only be seen once in six months, unless they broke the rules. Furthermore, when officers did see customers, they sometimes had very limited time in which to undertake all of their administrative duties, making it difficult to address issues outside the set procedures. These high caseloads occasionally resulted in long waiting times, further reducing the accessibility of staff. For instance, I spoke to a staff member from the Melbourne office who was 'booked out' for three weeks and another officer at the Hunter office who was unavailable for five weeks.

Some staff suggested that customer behaviours also impeded the achievement of One-to-One Service. This was in part due to the difficulty of getting customers to attend appointments. Attendance rates varied with age, appointment type and Centrelink office, but, in some cases, according to staff, up to nine out of 10 appointments were 'no-shows'. This made it hard for staff to keep track of their customers. Furthermore, some of the customers who I interviewed seemed disinterested in the idea of One-to-One Service. One suggested that he tried to avoid appointments by finding a job and going off payments whenever he was called in for a meeting with Centrelink. Another asked to see the next available person, because he was more concerned about being seen quickly than seeing the same officer. In this way, we can see that the universalisation of the identity of the job seeker as a demanding individual requiring intensive personalised service does not always correspond with the orientations of recipients. Some beneficiaries did not regard themselves as unique individuals with particular problems needing holistic support and in-depth intervention.

In 2002, Centrelink introduced the Job Redesign Project, following a review that found that One-to-One Service was inefficient, because individual staff members could not specialise in particular tasks and had to become familiar with many different administrative functions (Centrelink, 2002, pp 113-14). As part of the job redesign process, One-to-One was replaced with a 'streaming' model, in which staff are organised into 'logical groups' that undertake different functions. One team handles enquiries at the reception counter, another takes 'walk-in' (non-booked) appointments and a third group looks after pre-booked appointments. Centrelink argues that the streaming model has resulted in productivity increases, and the agency also believes that staff prefer the new approach over One-to-One Service (Centrelink, 2002, p 113). The rise and demise of One-to-One shows clearly the existence of conflicting pressures and priorities within contemporary welfare reform. It also highlights the conflicts inherent in neo-liberalism. The rise of One-to-One Service reflects (at least in part) the ascendancy of neo-liberal ideas about the need for personalised, intensive interventions into the lives of the disadvantaged, while at the same time the demise of One-to-One is arguably a result of neo-liberal cost-cutting initiatives. These policy shifts support the suggestion that neo-liberalism is best understood as a series of short-lived and potentially contradictory experiments, rather than a coherent and linear reform programme (Larner and Walters, 2000).

From risk management to Getting it Right

The shift towards risk management in contemporary public administration is reflected in some of the early rhetoric of Centrelink's senior management. In 2000, Centrelink's chief executive officer argued that one of the first challenges facing the new agency was to transform the administrative culture and do away with a procedural, risk-averse focus, replacing it with a new mentality in which staff would regard themselves as risk-taking 'entrepreneurs' focused on outcomes (Vardon, 2000). 'Mistakes' would be thought of as a necessary part of the agency's operations and an important aspect of administrative learning (Vardon, 2000). I asked Centrelink officers about the amount of discretion that frontline staff enjoyed, and how this had changed over time. Several of the staff spoke of an early attempt by Centrelink management to increase the discretion of frontline staff and to implement a greater focus on outcomes. This was referred to within the agency as a 'risk management' approach to benefits administration. A staff member from the Hunter office reflected on the move towards risk management with the creation of Centrelink:

> 'When Centrelink became Centrelink, lots changed. At the Customer Service Centre where I was, there was a definite focus on outcomes.... Four years ago, it was all about staff discretion and risk management. You were encouraged to put your own stamp on things, to try new things.'

Another officer from the Hunter office suggested that Centrelink officers had enthusiastically accepted the risk management approach during the early years of Centrelink:

> 'We used to have a lot of discretion, but it's been pulled in.... We used to have a thing called risk management [RM]. They gave the go-ahead for RM, risk management ... early on. We ran with it. We positively embraced it. We galloped with it. We embraced it with all our hearts.'

An officer from the Melbourne office suggested that the early emphasis on risk management was associated with a degree of managerial indifference concerning the specific methods used by officers to achieve outcomes:

> 'It used to be about risk management. That was the term that floated around. We were told to just get the job done.'

These accounts suggest that the rise of risk management in Centrelink involved a change in the identity of frontline staff, from procedural, risk averse, rigid bureaucrats to entrepreneurial, self-directing, outcome-focused officers.

This shift away from proceduralism and the more flexible attitude to the rules may have generated support among staff, but Centrelink's lack of adherence to legislation and policy protocols also came under critical scrutiny. An independent parliamentary body, the Australian National Audit Office (ANAO), undertook audits of Centrelink's administration of the Special Benefit (ANAO, 1999) and Age Pension (ANAO, 2001a), and found high levels of inaccuracies in frontline eligibility determinations. In one audit, the ANAO discovered that payment-granting decisions had been inaccurate in over half of all claims for the Age Pension, within the audit sample. The ANAO argued that this problem was caused by the fact that Centrelink did not have adequate mechanisms in place to detect and prevent frontline decisions that violated the 1991 *Social*

Security Act (ANAO, 2001a, p 20). Importantly, the ANAO drew a direct link between the cultural shift towards risk management within Centrelink and the poor performance in terms of accuracy:

> Centrelink's focus in creating a cultural shift towards customer service has been successful. However, these results also suggest that accuracy per se was not viewed as a priority ... [this] indicates a focus on broad aspects of customer service rather than payment correctness and consistency and accuracy in decision making. (ANAO, 2001b, p 23)

The ANAO concluded that the lack of knowledge of policy and legislative requirements among frontline Centrelink staff constituted a 'risk to effective service delivery' (ANAO, 2001b, p 74). Whatever the validity of these criticisms and casual inferences, there is no doubt that the ANAO's analysis had a substantial effect on Centrelink. In response to the ANAO's recommendations, the agency instituted a new campaign designed to encourage accuracy, called 'Getting it Right', in 2001. As part of this initiative, staff were provided with information about the importance of procedural correctness through specially developed screen savers on agency computers, and they also received printed mouse pads summarising the basic principles of administrative accuracy.

Another important element of the Getting it Right strategy was the introduction of a new computerised auditing instrument known as 'Quality On-Line' (QOL). The QOL system operates by referring the work of CSOs to a 'QOL checker' who uses a computer application to determine whether frontline staff have followed the rules. When work is randomly selected to be 'QOLed', the customer record that the staff member was working on is frozen so that the CSO cannot reverse or modify their action until it has been reviewed (ANAO, 2001a, pp 97-8). Quality On-Line (QOL) checking is normally performed by a select group of CSOs. The QOL checkers' work is itself audited by superior officers from Centrelink's Area Support Offices (ANAO, 2001a, p 104). The QOL system has implications for remuneration, since pay increases require staff to attain a certain amount of accuracy (ANAO, 2001a, p 99).

The introduction of QOL had the effect of reducing the willingness of staff to break the rules. A Hunter officer believed that she might suffer repercussions if QOL picked up her work:

> 'When you've done something on the system, it might come up saying that the action has to be QOLed, and then you can't go back, then it has to be QOLed. And when they check it, I'd say most of the people here would agree with what I've done, but when they QOL it they have to go by the law. Because then the person who checks them up the line will pick it up.'

A staff member from the Melbourne office suggested that QOL would catch staff who broke the rules:

> 'We apply discretion and then we get done for it ... yeah, if you were QOLed, it might be a problem.'

One of the staff members who observed the rise of risk management in Centrelink also argued that, with the introduction of Getting it Right and QOL, there had been a definite shift away from risk management:

> 'I think the amount of discretion that we have has definitely changed over time. Now it's about adhering to the letter of the law.'

A Melbourne officer saw a connection between the problems encountered in risk management and the introduction of QOL:

> 'They realised that [risk management] was a bad idea, and so now we've got QOL.'

Thus we can trace the rise and decline of risk management as a general philosophy of administration in Centrelink. This is not to say that aspects of the risk management approach have not been retained, but there has been a clear shift away from the view that adherence to rules is less important than the achievement of outcomes. The Getting it Right initiative is to some degree hostile to neo-liberalism, in the sense that it appears to promote a kind of social rights or welfare rights perspective, where the principal concern is to minimise arbitrary and inconsistent treatment and ensure that each claimant receives their legislated entitlement. From this standpoint, we can say that the Audit Office, whose criticisms of Centrelink's administrative inaccuracy prompted the Getting it Right initiative, is operating in part with a rationality of 'citizenship rights', which does not easily combine with neo-liberal modes of administrative governance. This case also highlights the role of different institutional actors in Australian welfare reform, and the fact that some of these institutions operate with principles, rationalities and priorities that are not receptive to neo-liberalism.

Conclusions

The experience of Australian welfare reform has been more complicated and contradictory than influential accounts of the new governance of welfare imply. On this matter, I concur with Larner and Walters (2000), who are unwilling to accept a coherent portrait of neo-liberal governance. By looking at the street level, we can extend their logic to determine how new governance initiatives are received, interpreted and implemented at the front line. Just as comparing different jurisdictions provides a more complicated view of neo-liberalism, so too does moving down to the levels at which officers are involved in applying policies. We find that there is not a coherent approach to the sanctioning of clients, or a linear trend towards increased severity in penalties for non-compliance. There have been important changes in the delivery of personalised service, but we cannot conclude that administration has unambiguously become more or less neo-liberal. Advanced liberal ideas about risk management have been tried and replaced with a more traditional procedural emphasis. Rather than promoting a cohesive account, the street-level perspective encourages us to support Larner and Walters' argument that 'governance is a creative process, proceeding by way of experimentation, improvisation and invention' (2000, p 371). As well as calling into question the coherence of neo-liberalism, this research also casts doubt on the idea that all contemporary welfare reforms fit neatly within the rubric of neo-liberalism. The changes to sanctioning policy and the developments around risk management highlight the continuing influence of principles closely associated with the welfare state in contemporary social policy, including the concern to protect the vulnerable and the importance of procedural accuracy and bureaucratic consistency. This research suggests that, in Australia at least, neo-liberal ideas and rationalities are in competition with other principles of governance, and the former do not always triumph (see also Howard, 2003b). A street-level focus, which is attuned to the possibility of conflict and contradiction, encourages this more nuanced perspective on the new governance of welfare.

Notes

[1] The author wishes to thank Michelle Brady, Milena Büchs, Sigrun Kahl and Claus Offe for their comments and suggestions. The author retains responsibility for all errors and omissions.

[2] In the interests of confidentiality, the names of participants are not used in this article, and I have also given each of the Customer Service Centres in this study pseudonyms, which indicate the general regions in which the offices are located.

[3] That is not to say that neo-liberalism is the only political ideology or rationality that promotes or supports individualised forms of service delivery (see, for example, Yeatman, 1998; Yeatman and Owler, 2001).

[4] The majority of beneficiaries in my study (24 out of 31) could not identify a Centrelink 'One Main Contact' who they saw on repeated occasions for appointments.

References

Abbott, T. (2000) 'Motivating job seekers', speech to the Committee for the Economic Development of Australia, Canberra, 31 March.

ACOSS (Australian Council of Social Services) (2001a) *Breaching the safety net: The harsh impact of social security penalties*, Sydney: ACOSS.

ACOSS (2001b) *New research: Hardship intensifies from rise in social security penalties*, (media release), 13 August.

ANAO (Australian National Audit Office) (1999) *Special Benefit*, Canberra: ANAO.

ANAO (2001a), *Assessment of new claims for the Age Pension by Centrelink*, Canberra: ANAO.

ANAO (2001b) *Learning for skills and knowledge: Customer service officers*, Canberra: ANAO.

Australia House of Representatives (1996) 'Commonwealth Services Delivery Agency Bill 1996: Second reading', *House Hansard*, 4 December, pp 7623-4.

Australian Statistician (2000) *Australian social trends 2000*, Canberra: Australian Bureau of Statistics.

Barzelay, M. (2001) *The New Public Management: Improving research and policy dialogue*, Berkeley, CA: University of California Press.

Carney, T. and Ramia, G. (1999) 'From citizenship to contractualism: the transition from unemployment benefits to employment services in Australia', *Australian Journal of Administrative Law*, vol 6, no 3, pp 117-39.

Centrelink (2002) *Annual report 2001-02*, Canberra: Commonwealth of Australia.

Dean, M. (1995) 'Governing the unemployed self in an active society', *Economy and Society*, vol 24, no 4, pp 559-83.

Dean, M. (1998) 'Administering asceticism: reworking the unemployed citizen', in M. Dean and B. Hindess (eds) *Governing Australia: Studies in contemporary rationalities of government*, Melbourne: Cambridge University Press, pp 87-107.

Dean, M. and Hindess, B. (eds) (1998) *Governing Australia: Studies in contemporary rationalities of government*, Melbourne: Cambridge University Press.

Du Gay, P. (2000) *In praise of bureaucracy: Weber/organizaton/ethics*, London: Sage Publications.

Fincher, R. and Wulff, M. (1998) 'The locations of poverty and disadvantage', in R. Fincher and J. Nieuwenhuysen (eds) *Australian poverty: Then and now*, Melbourne: Melbourne University Press.

Harris, P. (2003) 'The neo-liberal era in politics and social policy', in C. Aspalter (ed) *Neo-liberalism and the Australian welfare state*, Hong Kong: Casa Verde, pp 85-104.

Henman, P. (2004) 'Targeted! Population segmentation, electronic surveillance and governing the unemployed in Australia', *International Sociology*, vol 19, no 2, pp 173-91.

Hindess, B. (1996) 'Liberalism, socialism and democracy: variations on a governmental theme', in A. Barry, T. Osborne and N. Rose (eds) *Foucault and political reason: Liberalism, neo-liberalism and rationalities of government*, London: University College London, pp 65-80.

Howard, C. (2003a) 'The promise and performance of mutual obligation', in C. Aspalter (ed) *Neo-liberalism and the Australian welfare state*, Hong Kong: Casa Verde, pp 125-45.

Howard, C. (2003b) 'Civics education in the neo-liberal era', *Curriculum Perspectives*, vol 23, no 1, pp 37-44.

Jamieson, N. and Jacobs, J. (1996) 'The making of marginalisation: highrise living and social polarisation', in K. Gibson, M. Huxley, J. Cameron, L. Costello, R. Fincher, J. Jacobs, N. Janilesen, L. Johnsen and M. Pulvirenti (eds) *Restructuring difference: Social polarisation and the city*, Melbourne: Australian Housing and Urban Research Institute.

Jessop, B. (1999) 'The changing governance of welfare: recent trends in its primary functions, scale, and modes of coordination', *Social Policy and Administration*, vol 33, no 4, pp 348-59.

Lackner, S. (2001) 'The unheard injustice: young people and Centrelink breaches', paper presented at The National Social Policy Conference, University of New South Wales, 4-6 July.

Larner, W. and Walters, W. (2000) 'Privatisation, governance and identity: the United Kingdom and New Zealand compared', *Policy & Politics*, vol 28, no 3, pp 361-77.

McDonald, C., Marston, G. and Buckley, A. (2003) 'Risk technology in Australia: the role of the Job Seeker Classification Instrument in employment services', *Critical Social Policy*, vol 23, no 4, pp 498-525.

Moses, J. and Sharples, I. (2000) 'Breaching – history, trends and issues', paper presented at The 7th National Conference on Unemployment, University of Western Sydney, 30 November-1 December.

Mulgan, R. (2003) 'Centrelink – A new approach to welfare service delivery?', in C. Aspalter (ed) *Neo-liberalism and the Australian welfare state*, Hong Kong: Casa Verde, pp 169-79.

Newman, J. (1999) 'The future of welfare in the 21st century', speech at the National Press Club, Canberra, 29 September.

O'Malley, P. (1996) 'Risk and responsibility', in A. Barry, T. Osborne and N. Rose (eds) *Foucault and political reason: Liberalism, neo-liberalism and rationalities of government*, London: University College London, pp 189-208.

Rose, N. (1996) 'Governing "advanced" liberal democracies', in A. Barry, T. Osborne and N. Rose (eds) *Foucault and political reason: Liberalism, neo-liberalism and rationalities of government*, London: University College London, pp 37-64.

Vanstone, A. (2002) *Breaching rules change to protect the vulnerable*, (media release), Department of Family and Community Services, 4 March.

Vardon, S. (2000) 'One-to-One: the art of personalised service', paper presented at 'Case Management: Fact or Fiction' conference, University of Melbourne, 11 February.

Walters, W. (1997) 'Towards an "active society": new designs for social policy', *Policy & Politics*, vol 25, no 3, pp 221-34.

Walters, W. (2000) *Unemployment and government: Genealogies of the social*, Cambridge: Cambridge University Press.

Yeatman, A. (1998) 'Interpreting contemporary contractualism', in M. Dean and B. Hindess (eds) *Governing Australia: Studies in contemporary rationalities of government*, Cambridge: Cambridge University Press, pp 227-41.

Yeatman, A. and Owler, K. (2001) 'The role of contract in the democratisation of service delivery', *Law in Context*, vol 18, no 2, pp 34-56.

EIGHT

The administration of transformation: a case study of implementing welfare reform in the UK

Sharon Wright

It is relatively uncontroversial to suggest that the delivery of frontline services to the unemployed in the UK has been altered dramatically by a combination of reforms to the substance of policy and changes in the governance arrangements concerning the conditions and mechanisms of implementation. However, the significance and impact of these reforms have tended to be either evaluated at a macro-level or inferred from the preponderance of discourse surrounding change. The aim for this chapter is to provide a micro-level analysis of unemployment policy in practice that assesses the significance of change, along with its extent and character, from the perspectives of frontline staff and unemployed service users. This approach is based on the premise that 'policies cannot be understood in isolation from the means of their execution' (Elmore, 1978, p 185), meaning that policy does not fully exist until the social actors who deliver and receive policy bring it into being. Implementation is not simply a peripheral matter of technicality or practicality, but is central to understanding the constitution of what policies are and what they mean to people. The emphasis is, therefore, on how welfare reform and new governance are accomplished and emerge in street-level practice.

The question that this chapter aims to answer is: what does new governance mean to the frontline workers of employment services and to the users of unemployment benefits and services in the UK? The chapter is divided into two main parts. The first part examines changes to the rules of the game from the perspective of frontline staff. It begins with an overview of key changes in employment services in terms of the style of governance and policy content. The focus is on how changes in the late 1990s affected frontline staff in their everyday work with service users. Several pressures, constraints and tensions are identified, which in some cases led to discrepancies between the official and implemented forms of policy, thereby reducing the impact of reforms. The second part of the chapter considers reform from the perspective of unemployed users, focusing on the alteration of the language of the game through the formal redefinition of welfare subjects as 'customers'. This time the gap between policy and practice was rhetorical, with users being represented formally by a label that they neither recognised nor appreciated.

The reflections presented below are based on empirical evidence from an ethnographic study of a Jobcentre office in the late 1990s.[1] The data was collected during a six-month period of direct observation (74 visits in total, each lasting for between two and six hours) in the main Jobcentre office of a large Scottish town in 1998. This included in-depth qualitative interviews with 48 members of staff and 35 unemployed users. The study formed the basis of a doctoral thesis (Wright, 2003), which was concerned with understanding the implementation of unemployment policy from both staff and user perspectives. In this chapter, the data will be used to assess the impact and implementation of new governance arrangements from the perspectives of both frontline staff and users.

Delivering welfare reform: a street-level perspective

In the UK during the 1990s and early 21st century, policies towards the unemployed and those inactive in the labour market have been transformed in a number of ways. Change in the content of policy has included the individualisation of responsibility and a concerted effort to encourage, compel and enable people without work to enter the labour market. The underlying principles have been characterised by a combination of punitive and enabling elements, driven by an ideological commitment to end welfare dependency. Benefits for unemployed people have been gradually reduced in value while sanctions have been increased in weight and frequency. This 'work-first' strategy appears to have met with some success in the short term, with unemployment dropping and remaining low, although questions remain about how sustainable this welfare-to-work strategy could be in less favourable economic conditions. However, the significance of reform reaches beyond the substantive policy content to the alteration of organisational structures, delivery arrangements and management practices. New governance has been associated with neo-liberalism (Larner and Walters, 2000), privatisation, marketisation and a 'rolling back' of the state. This has been combined with a growing emphasis on performance, incentive management and competition. The focus on new forms of governance implies a shift in power and influence away from the nation state upwards and outwards to international markets and supranational organisations and, simultaneously, downwards in a sub-national regionalisation and localisation (Newman, 2001; Daly, 2003). This latter trend is accompanied by a dilution of direct state authority and control through a greater mix of providers and financiers of welfare, which under New Labour has emphasised partnerships, networks and 'joined-up' approaches (Newman, 2001; compare: Glendinning et al, 2002).

Contrary to such expectations of new governance, the design and administration of social security in the UK remains highly centralised, situated at national level (showing little evidence of direct supranational influence), with control operating vertically downwards through hierarchical structures. Examples of the new steering and coordinating role of central government can be found in the partnership arrangements for the delivery of the New Deal programmes and the contracting out of Employment Zones. However, core employment services such as job matching, advice and benefit processing continue to be provided almost entirely by civil servants, employed directly by the state, subject to and engaged in direct forms of authority and control, operating within a massive hierarchical bureaucracy. Even the creation of devolved forms of government in Scotland (the Scottish Parliament) and Wales (the Welsh Assembly) have failed to bring about fundamental shifts in the locus of power, since social security, job search and support remain matters reserved to the British government.[2]

The frontline administration of welfare benefits and services for unemployed people in the UK has been influenced by major change in the organisational arrangements and management practices of welfare bureaucracies since the 1980s. New governance arrangements have been evident and discourses and practices of new managerialism have saturated organisations and engineered work cultures, leaving few actors unaffected (Clarke and Newman, 1997). The hybrid bureau-professionals who staff frontline services are career civil servants who confront potentially conflicting demands for competitive performance and public service. They are bureaucrats in as much as they are administrators who are required to apply predefined rules within what still remains as enormous hierarchical organisation. They are also part professional by virtue of their specialist training, acquired expertise and ability to exercise discretion. A tension would therefore seem to exist for bureau-professionals in their work with users since the bureaucratic model is based on standardisation and rule-bound activities, while professionalism emphasises decision making based on expert judgement. The following section examines how new governance has impacted upon service delivery.

Towards a new governance of social security?

Changes in the governance of social security and employment services have been evident from the late 20th century. The key moment of decentralisation came in 1990, when the public Employment Service (ES) was given Executive Agency status. As one of the largest semi-autonomous 'Next Steps' agencies (see HM Treasury, 1989), the ES led the way in applying business principles to public service (Horton and Jones, 1996) and 'disrupting traditional civil service practices and values' (Foster and Hoggett, 1999, p 20). These traditional principles and practices of civil service bureaucratic administration had been highly praised, particularly during the post-war period, for efficiency, rationality, fairness and impartiality. By the early 1990s, much had changed internally within the civil service, including a 'white blouse revolution' (Anderson, 1989; Savage and Witz, 1992), involving the feminisation of low-grade, poorly paid, routine clerical work. More generally, the value of bureaucracy as a mode of service delivery had been undermined by a range of critiques from across the political spectrum including neo-Marxists, feminists, anti-racists, the poverty lobby and, most influential of all, the neo-liberals. Bureaucracy was reinterpreted by the Conservative governments (1979-97) as inefficient, wasteful and outmoded. The 'crisis of welfare' was therefore also 'a crisis of the organisational regime' because centralised state bureaucracy was 'an institutional articulation of social democracy' (Clarke and Newman, 1997, p 17; Jessop, 1999). Within the new social, economic, political and ideological settlement, the vogue was for managers and business values (of the particular sort advocated in the excellence literature, see, for example, Peters, 1987, 1993), whose status and legitimacy was lifted above both bureaucrats and professionals (Flynn, 1993; Butcher, 1995; Clarke and Newman, 1997). According to Clarke and Newman (1997), the 'managerial state' was born during the 1980s and 1990s.

New managerialism (Clarke and Newman, 1997), as a key aspect of new governance, has impacted upon the ES in a range of ways, in terms of both rhetoric and reality. During the late 1980s and 1990s the ES came under continuing pressure to reduce its operating costs and obtain better 'value for money', consequently a tier of management was removed (Fletcher, 1997). Market testing, contracting out and cost reviews were among the techniques introduced to help secure efficiency savings. It has been argued that these reforms have created a blurring between public and private spheres (Dunleavy and Hood, 1994), in which power has been dispersed – meaning the 'simultaneous shrinking of the state and the enlargement of its reach into civil society (through its engagement of non-state agents)' (Clarke and Newman, 1997, p 29). When applied to the ES this has meant that 'the delivery of employment and training services [are] being dismantled' (Finn, 2001, p 77). A wider range of organisations and actors have been engaged in the delivery of employment services, particularly through the partnership approaches of the different New Deal programmes. There has been a greater reliance on private and voluntary service providers, eroding the direct training function of the ES, and raising important issues over accountability and quality assurance. It has been noted that:

> A new political consensus seems to be emerging in the UK around the once-controversial principles of compulsion, privatisation and localisation in welfare-to-work programming. (Theodore and Peck, 1999, p 504)

This raises a concern that low-priority user groups, particularly the hardest to place, could become subject to service provision that is distanced from the accountability of democratically elected government.

New managerialism also extended the role of annual performance targets, which became more specific, being set at national, local and even section level (Finn and Taylor, 1990). Pollitt argues that such incentive-based management techniques represent a shift towards 'a neo-Taylorist management process' (1993, p 56), the workers being 'a new generation of front-line employment advisers who have the task of turning abstract incentives and opportunities into real day-to-day choices' (Finn, 2001, p 77). Horton and Jones argue that for staff this has meant increases in 'insecurity of employment, redundancy, job intensification and worsening terms and conditions' (1996, p 34; see also Du Gay and Salaman, 1992; Gagnon, 1996; Foster and Hoggett, 1999; Heery and Salmon, 2000). There is an increased engagement of casual workers, employed on short temporary contracts, with little training, low status and poor pay. Such developments can threaten the core values of service delivery. Those officials who have most face-to-face contact with users are no longer guaranteed the staples that previous generations of bureau-professionals took for granted, for instance in-depth training, expertise, salary and security of contract. It is possible to infer that, under such working conditions, frontline employees as well as managers might be less committed to the public service ideal. Hill argues that these sorts of adjustments in the structure of the delivery of services can transform the policies themselves since 'the rules of the game may change the outcome of the game' (1997, p 136).

These changes in the governance and organisational operation of employment services provide an important context for understanding how reforms are experienced and implemented by frontline workers in practice. However, factors such as explicit cost-cutting, the hiving off of the ES as a Next Steps Agency and the downgrading of bureau-professional civil servants did not seem to hold a great deal of direct significance for the frontline workers in this study. The following section illustrates the key tensions that concerned staff in their everyday work with users.

New governance in practice: balancing tensions

In practice, it seemed to be the content of the policy approach and the emphasis on new managerialism that presented frontline staff in this study with the greatest challenges, rather than the changes in governance that would, from the outside, seem to be most significant to the organisation, for example forming partnerships with non-state providers. In the case study office, there was a noticeable number of staff on temporary contracts, including two who had been employed in the office through the New Deal scheme. The union representative had monitored a general worsening in conditions, which had affected pay and pensions. However, those employed on permanent contracts usually felt that their jobs were relatively secure and that they enjoyed reasonable levels of pay and pensions.

The tension that seemed to most vex frontline staff was in balancing the roles of benefit administration and job matching. At various points during the 20th century, these formal functions have been conjoined, split and spliced together again. When enacted in the staff–user relationship, this tension became centred around whether staff should be primarily concerned with policing benefit claims or assisting and enabling users (whether registered unemployed, non-registered unemployed or already in employment) to find work (Fletcher, 1997). This presented several challenges to staff, who had been afforded greater discretion in their decision making, particularly in relation to the role of personal advisor. Frontline staff were expected to both administer benefits and match a range of clients to job vacancies.

A secondary tension was evident within the realm of job matching. Here, the key dilemma for officials was whether they should match people to jobs in the interests of the employer or in the interests of the user. The problem was that if a matching service is provided on employers' terms then the best-qualified, most-skilled users with the longest and most recent experience should be referred to employers, therefore disadvantaging those users who most need assistance from the service that is meant to be specifically designed to help them. On the other hand, if a job-matching service places users who are least desirable to employers, the risk is that employers will go elsewhere to fill their vacancies. Since the state has accepted a responsibility for ensuring that unemployed people are brought back into the wage relationship, frontline staff therefore occupied a unique space where they were expected to act on behalf of employers *and* the unemployed.

These tensions were increased by the trends that have been identified in unemployment policy. The emphasis on active labour market policies (that is, Jobseeker's Allowance and the New Deal programmes) focused attention on getting the long-term unemployed into work and raising the 'employability' of those furthest from the labour market. Users were expected to prove their engagement in actively seeking work, the conditions for which had become tighter, on threat of sanctions, which had become harsher. This means that high levels of compulsion, paired with a lightly regulated labour market and a growth in part-time precarious and low-paid jobs, created the situation in which unemployed people were forced to take work that they would not otherwise consider, and is unlikely to offer a living wage (Forde and Slater, 2001).[3] Jobcentres have ended up perpetuating this situation by failing to secure an ongoing supply of high-quality vacancies.

These tensions, when combined with a lack of resources and 'a lot of pressure' to meet job placement targets, resulted in a situation that forced staff to neglect job matching for many clients during routine interviews (for instance, fortnightly re-registering) that focused, against policy, almost exclusively on benefit administration. Job placement targets were generally viewed by staff as 'unfair' because they were set at an unrealistically high level. Frontline staff were encouraged and given incentives to concentrate their efforts on getting certain unemployed people into certain jobs, for instance the long-term unemployed people on their caseloads:

> Sarah[4]: 'You've got targets to fill but it's not the best thing for your client. Getting targets filled was the priority, taking away from what they need.'

Even within small caseloads of long-term unemployed people, there was scope for creaming the best candidates and screening out those who were considered to be 'unemployable':

> Zoe: 'If you've got, say, an alcoholic. If they're dirty and smelly and they're not going to look good sending them to an employer, then you might choose somebody else.'

The overwhelming emphasis on targets created a culture of competition between different sections of the office, local offices and service providers. This led to some vacancies not being advertised and to tensions between frontline staff and local recruitment companies and even training companies involved in the employment option of the New Deal, because office staff needed to get the credit for registered unemployed people finding jobs:

> Bob: 'Every year we get some catering vacancies from another area. We wouldn't put them up to compete with our own.'

Although some users benefited from job-search assistance that they might otherwise not have had, many others could be disadvantaged because they were not given access to information about vacancies that did exist. Information about jobs was strictly controlled and regulated and a minority of vacancies were kept secret. Only vacancies 'owned' by the office counted towards meeting targets, so local newspapers and recruitment magazines were not made available.

The introduction of the New Deal for Young People (18-24)

The New Deal for Young People (18-24) provides an example of welfare reform that has involved the design of a new programme and the establishment of new forms of governance. As a discrete policy area, it provides a microcosm for the wider processes of implementation of welfare reform in the field of unemployment policy. The New Deal for Young People was introduced during the period of the case study. The programme benefited from wide support and dedicated funding. The stated intentions were for an initiative that was distinct in targeting assistance at young people to encourage and enable them to actively seek work. The individually tailored services and one-to-one relationships between personal advisors (PAs) and New Deal users were heralded as the key to successful implementation. However, shortly after the programme was launched, aspects of this individual tailoring and one-to-one assistance were eroded. The pressures affecting the success of implementation were clear. As increasing numbers of 18- to 24-year-olds were referred to the programme, caseloads rose and PAs were no longer able to spend the allotted time with each individual. Initial interviews were converted from one-to-one sessions to group-based talks (for approximately 20 people) that allowed little opportunity for open discussion or personal attention. Some of those who attended such interviews said nothing at all during the first session.

The New Deal also brought with it greater discretion, with small funds available for helping people back to work. This gave PAs increased opportunity to operate independently to offer informal rewards and sanctions to users. Decisions, for instance, about who would be permitted access to which of the four options (a job – with or without subsidy, a voluntary sector placement, training or the environmental taskforce), depended on subjective judgements about suitability and moral decisions about a person's value. Getting people into unsubsidised jobs was the main objective. Gaining a subsidised job depended on judgements made by PAs:

> Bob: 'The PAs should know the companies and should know the person. It takes weeks to get to know the

> person. Then they can see if they're "worthy" of a subsidy. A PA could put a lot of effort into contacting an employer and recommending someone, saying take this and you're in for life. But that's not much use if the New Deal person only lasts two days then decides they don't like it and it's not what they want to do.'

Increased discretion therefore seemed to lead to increased selectivity and creaming. Both frontline staff and unemployed people wanted to have the opportunity for more time to be committed to job-searching activities. The New Deal for Young People was seen by PAs as offering better opportunities for young people who had been unemployed for six months or more. However, the selectivity of the scheme could be problematic:

> Mary: 'I think probably that New Deal's unfair. The fact that New Deal people can get all that help when other people can't. If they phone up or they contact you if they're five months and they cannae get it. It makes it more like a two-tier system.'

This section has provided examples of how the combination of new governance and new policy content have impacted upon employment services from the perspective of frontline staff. The next section moves on to consider how unemployed service users have been affected by change.

Redefining the welfare subject: the new language from a user's perspective

It is not only the rules of the game that have been repositioned, but also the language of the game. This section focuses on how a key change in terminology, namely describing 'clients' as 'customers', was perceived by unemployed interviewees. This official redefinition of the welfare subject signified a substantial alteration of the relationship between user and official, and consequently between citizen and state. The question is: what impact did this redefinition have on unemployed service users?

New managerialism has realigned the relationships between citizens and the state. It has reconstructed the public, citizens and users as 'customers' (Clarke and Newman, 1997). Clarke and

Newman (1997, p 14) identify three contrasting representations of citizens within new managerialist discourse:

> While the citizen as taxpayer (and ratepayer) was being subjected to excessive levels of taxation to pay for the welfare state, and the citizen as consumer was being denied effective choice in service provision, the other citizen – the one dependent on welfare services and benefits – was being demonised as a 'scrounger', using public handouts to avoid responsibility.

Business principles are said to offer customers more choice and unemployed people are provided with a Jobseeker's Allowance Charter to guarantee certain levels of service delivery. It could be argued that the main rationale for introducing this new language was to encourage frontline staff to treat unemployed people more respectfully and to provide better customer service. But, from a user's perspective, the newly modelled pseudo-customer is not and cannot be a customer in the purest sense. Customers of unemployment benefits are not voluntary (Lipsky, 1980) because they depend on the essential services and benefits provided by the state to meet their basic needs. In the case of the long-term unemployed, social assistance is paid by the state as a matter of last resort. There are therefore very few alternatives, if any exist at all. In such circumstances the only choice is to take or leave whatever is offered. Furthermore, reforms have been neither customer-led nor customer-focused, explicit cost-cutting has instead formed the rationalisation. If users are represented in the formal policy arena as 'customers', then the logical progression would be for needs to become translated into preferences and rights dissolved down into a residue of choices.

For Jobcentre users in this study, new forms of governance held little direct relevance. What they had noticed was that the tone and content of policy had changed to increase compulsion and job search. Unemployed users continued to deal with Jobcentre staff as their main or only access point to employment services and income maintenance. The redefinition of the welfare subject seems to have been confined largely to 'official' language and discourse, imposed top-down through guidance documents for staff and printed or web-based information for users. The conversion from client to customer was a language that interviewees could not relate to their everyday experience of Jobcentre interaction and customer service did not adequately capture the experience of claiming Jobseeker's Allowance. Users did not recognise the term 'customer' for three main reasons: they did not have choice, they did not have control and they did not have purchasing power.

Choice

Generally, interviewees resisted the market-based customer terminology, primarily because it did not capture their overwhelmingly negative experiences of using the Jobcentre. Most of those interviewed felt uncomfortable and embarrassed when they were inside the Jobcentre office because they were confronting their stigmatised unemployed role in a public way. Users viewed the Jobcentre as 'a last resort' that should be avoided at all costs. Interviewees experienced using the service as a sign of personal and systemic failure. For many users, their interactions with staff were tainted by this sense of enforced dependency. The loss of the previous status associated with being a worker, or having held a particular position of status or respect, increased the psychological costs of being a welfare recipient. This was so keenly felt that some interviewees did not like to be seen coming in or going out of the Jobcentre:

> Tony: 'Degradation ... I hate it. You walk out and you feel people saying, "There's another loser". You're going in and you feel like, "There's another loser". They're not but I think that. It doesnae matter if they're doing that or not doing that. I think that ... I walk up to the top and I sneak in that door as quick as I can and I sneak out as quick as I can. I don't mind being in here because the people in here are in the same boat as me. But I hate coming to it because it just brings me down.'

The interviewees had a clear sense that they did not want to be unemployed. They wanted to work and felt an obligation to earn their income through formal employment. Receiving income from Jobseeker's Allowance also made some users feel like they were begging because the relationship was not reciprocal in the same sense as paid employment. Despite this, users still retained a strong sense of entitlement to benefits because they felt that they had personally and collectively paid into 'the system' through taxes and National Insurance contributions. The low rates of benefit also meant that users were likely to experience poverty while relying on Jobseeker's Allowance as their primary source of income. Users did not consider themselves to be customers because their relationship was to the state. Users felt that this relationship with the state, as mediated through staff–user interactions, was not market based. They did not want to have to come to the Jobcentre and they were deprived of control or choice about the terms, conditions, substance and quality of the service and benefit they received. In this way, the relationship users had to the Jobcentre can be seen almost as the reverse of a customer relationship:

> Lorraine: 'I feel a customer is, you know, you're going in to buy something and like they're there to please you sort of thing. Here it's not. It's almost the other way about.'

Benefits and services for the unemployed were viewed as being controlled by elected and accountable government, which held irreducible meaning and significance. The partial marketisation of sections of service delivery did not separate the state from those services in the minds of recipients. Users held 'the government' responsible for the past and present 'system' that structured the character and funding of benefits, services and sanctions (including the application of new language such as 'customer service') as well as the wider opportunities available to them.

Resisting redefinition

After having approached the Jobcentre, users also lacked control over how they were processed and the opportunities available to them. Benefit recipients were compelled to behave in certain ways according to a complex structure of rules. The following quote is from an unemployed man who resisted the customer label, describing his relationship with the Jobcentre as:

> Sandy: 'More of a, I don't know, sort of "them" and "us" sort of thing, more I'm subject to their rules ... I've got to behave in certain ways obviously to be entitled to my dole cheque. I don't have a sort of customer's right sort of thing. I can't come to them to complain about the system, or at least I feel I can't go and complain about this aspect of the service or that aspect of the service

> 'cause I just don't see how much difference it would make.'

Compulsion was a central defining feature of interactions between staff and registered unemployed users in the Jobcentre. Users knew that staff had 'power to take away the only lifeline I have left at the moment, which is my fortnightly giro'. In order to continue to receive Jobseeker's Allowance, people had to satisfy a series of conditions and participate in a range of activities. To users, this felt like officials 'can pull the strings whatever way', so if 'the government says "jump" and you've got to say "how high?"'.

> Gavin: 'If they want to see you you've got to go and see them. If you don't go and see them you don't get paid. You know. And you've got to get money to live. So it's just a vicious circle. If they ask you to do somersaults you've got to do it 'cause that's what the system declares. So you don't think about it. They say, "Right, you've got to be there on a certain day" ... You go.'

This meant that instead of feeling like customers, interviewees said they felt like 'a problem', 'a loser', 'a waster' or an 'irritant'. Interviewees also had their own alternative descriptions of the relationship they had with staff at the Jobcentre, each emphasising the powerlessness of being subject to official control:

> Ewan: 'I imagine it more as a farm. And you're cattle coming in, you know, and you're going through the process of filling in forms, going back out. Look round, filling out forms, back out. It's like a clock going round and round in circles. But, more of a cow than a customer.'

> Miles: 'It's just an institution feeling. It's like being in a hospital. You don't really feel like you're a customer if you've got a broken arm, just you're in a hospital and you have to get things done. It's like that kind of thing.'

Satisfaction with customer service

There was much criticism of the quality of the service in the Jobcentre and there was a wide gap between the sort of service that users wanted and thought would help them find work and the service that was available. The main issues were insufficient assistance in finding work, inadequate vacancies advertised in the office and a mismatch between notified vacancies and the skills, qualifications and occupational experience of users (borne out in analysis of all vacancies sought by local unemployed people and all vacancies advertised in the office during a three-month period of the ethnography). Very few of the advertised vacancies were for skilled or professional positions. There was a relatively high incidence of low-grade work and part-time and temporary vacancies were not uncommon. This was a magnified reflection of the worst aspects of the flexible labour market, which was inevitable because of the Jobcentre's over-dependence on vacancies from the lower end of the market. The demand from interviewees was overwhelmingly for 'proper jobs' that were paid fairly, fulltime and long term. In some cases the type of service that users wanted was the type of service that they were officially meant to receive.

The powerlessness of being denied choice and being made subject to control was reinforced by regularly being made to wait before accessing services and by a lack of privacy. This waiting reinforced the power relationship between the worker and unemployed person. The great majority of unemployed people who visited the Jobcentre regularly, and especially those who had been unemployed for more than six months, had had to wait for what they considered to be unacceptably long periods of time (usually defined as more than 10 minutes and up to 95 minutes) before they could talk to members of staff, for information about job vacancies (details such as the name of the employer were always omitted from notices and the exact hours and rate of pay were sometimes also absent) and compulsory interviews. There was, therefore, evidence of dissatisfaction, reaching intense levels in some cases.

Users did highlight some instances of good service. Some individual members of staff were singled out for praise because of their local knowledge, length of service or extremely helpful and friendly attitudes. Users seemed to define good service as having been achieved if staff devoted time to their interview (being prepared to 'sit with you for any length of time and try and get you something') and provided a personal service ('a wee personal touch' rather than being 'treated as a number'). This demonstrated that staff were 'interested' and willing to 'try their best' to find vacancies that would be suitable. The individual officials who received most praise were those who worked in the Matching Section, whose role was assistance in finding work and did not involve benefit policing. It could therefore be inferred that the conflicting goals of assisting people to find work and policing benefit claims prevented other frontline staff from offering what users would identify as high-quality customer service.

Although Jobcentre users tended to view staff indifferently, or praised particularly friendly or helpful individuals, the general consensus was that the service offered by the Jobcentre was 'a waste of time', 'useless' or 'a bit of a joke'. One man said he 'hated' coming to the Jobcentre, while another man said that it 'irritated' him. Only four of those interviewed conceived of the Jobcentre in predominantly positive terms. Views of the service provided were linked to how people felt about being unemployed and the enforced dependency implied by that situation. Those who were most optimistic had been unemployed for less than three months and considered their immediate job prospects to be good.

Users often did not receive the service that they needed and wanted, with aspects of service delivery that did not fit within the customer service ideal. One user explicitly criticised the Jobcentre for providing 'poor standards of customer service', in reference to lengthy waits and telephones ringing out unanswered. This shows that despite the new managerialist emphasis on high-quality customer service, the majority of interviewees were not impressed with the service they received.

Some unemployed users had noticed a decline in the quality of services since a private company began to provide the service that replaced the Jobclub:

> Tony: 'A waste of time. I liked to go there. It's worse at the Jobclub because it changed. It used to be good. It's now because of the training company that are running it. They're useless. If they would leave us up there with telephone books, papers, telephone, pencil, our CVs and forget us, we'd get a job. But it's: "Don't use the telephone too long", "Don't use the telephone too much", "Don't do this", "Don't do that".'

Lack of purchasing power

Fundamentally, users felt that they were not customers because they did not have purchasing power. The very nature of a system of income maintenance means that users depended on the service for their income. This lack of purchasing power was combined with feelings of dehumanisation, for instance being 'shunted about' between different sections of the office, or between different types of offices.

As Jobseeker's Allowance claimants, their income was regulated, the prevalence of means testing meaning that many short-term and almost all long-term Jobseeker's Allowance users were living below poverty levels. Users had very little control over their income and had to accept the level of benefit that was set by law. The legacy of the low levels of benefit available in the UK can be traced back to the 19th-century principle of 'less eligibility' associated with the Poor Laws (Veit-Wilson, 1998). During the interaction between frontline staff and users there is a clash between the type of policy that is to be implemented and the experiences and needs of the people using the service. In many cases, policy simply did not fit those it was meant to be designed for.

Interviewees, with few exceptions, felt that the levels of benefit were insufficient to cover the costs of living during periods of unemployment. Interaction with staff was part of the 'necessity' of claiming benefit. They saw the determination of benefit levels as something that was outside of their control and were aware that there were therefore limits to what they could expect:

> Paul: 'I'm totally skint. I can't get access to a computer. Ehm, Jobseeker's Allowance, it's yeah, ehm, not a lot to live on.'

Low benefits had greater effects for those who lived a further distance from the Jobcentre, but did not qualify as postal claimants. The cost of using local public transport made it very difficult for them to attend the office to look for jobs. A lack of money meant that some users had to borrow money from friends and family, the repayment of which left them short on the next fortnight's worth of benefit. Living in poverty made life difficult for unemployed users. One interviewee spoke of the difficulty of living on the amount of Jobseeker's Allowance money he received and the cumulative effect of having to miss one bill to pay another, driving him further and further into debt. Certain circumstances presented people with dilemmas. Denis, for instance, owned a car, which he considered gave him a better chance of finding and keeping work. Without the money to run it and with the expense of public transport he did not know whether to sell it or keep it. Similar problems of poverty and unemployment have been well documented for many years.

They are also denied information about the financial 'product' they receive. Jobseeker's Allowance can only be accessed by completing long and complex forms, which were a source of irritation to many users. Precise information about how the final amount of benefit is calculated can be difficult to obtain. For instance, one man reported difficulties when he wanted to know how his means-tested benefit had been calculated because he had received less than he had expected:

> Simon: 'My benefit was like, they said you'll get this much each week. And I was saying to them, "Well how do you work that out", you know. "Come on, why am I getting so little when it says in the booklet I should get this." And they weren't willing to tell me at first and I was saying, "Look I don't want to create a fuss I just want to know how you've come to this thing". So finally after about sort of quarter of an hour arguing and them on the phone to people upstairs I was allowed upstairs to talk to somebody to tell me how they calculated it! Which was great 'cause then you knew.'

Aside from superficial improvements to the physical space in which interactions occur, new managerialism had not made noticeable changes to the conditions under which people received policy. While the introduction of the term 'customer' might signal an aspiration for improvements to service delivery, the reality of visiting the Jobcentre did not match up. The fundamental basis of service provision was experienced as involving compulsion, conditionality and punitive measures that restricted and dictated behaviour. This means that users were represented in the official policy arena by a label that did not depict the existing relationship. The continued use of the term 'customer' therefore reinforces the multiple levels of powerlessness that leave unemployed people at the bottom of the policy-making hierarchy, despite the fact that the service is said to exist for them.

Conclusions

Despite the introduction of complex discourses and practices of policy reform, new governance and new managerialism, the design and delivery of social security benefits and job-matching services for the unemployed has remained highly centralised and is implemented almost entirely by frontline workers employed directly by the state. The late 1990s and early 21st century have seen a greater variety of actors involved in providing employment services through partnership arrangements, especially in the New Deal programmes. However, the reach of marketisation and privatisation have been limited, evident in certain targeted geographical areas, for only parts of new services, for example Employment Zones. While these formal changes are significant, they are not wholesale.

This chapter has moved the assessment of the impact of new governance beyond these formal concerns, to explore the dynamics of implementing welfare reform at street level. For frontline staff, tensions exist in both the content and style of reforms. The key challenge is to balance the roles of benefit administration with job matching, under time and resource constraints and in response to performance management. Job placement targets focus attention on job-matching activities that might otherwise be neglected, but also lead to creaming and churning effects. In fact, those working in public employment services are cognisant of the potentially conflicting needs of both sets of 'customers' – employers and the unemployed.

The effects of new governance and new managerialism did not seem to have filtered through to the set of service users interviewed in this study. The unemployed interviewees did not seem to identify any major changes in the way they claimed and received Jobseeker's Allowance. The major issue for Jobcentre users more generally was the incongruity between how they perceived their relationship with benefits and services for the unemployed and the label that represented them in the public arena of policy discourse. From a user's perspective, the language of the customer was entirely inappropriate in describing or explaining their relationship with frontline staff and the social security system in general. In their view, a customer relationship would involve more equal power relations with service providers, choice and purchasing power. In contrast, unemployed people felt very negatively towards being unemployed, they found the level of benefits inadequate and the services did not meet their needs. The term 'customer' was so alien to their experience that it amounted to an inversion that essentially misrepresented what happened in the everyday life of a Jobcentre office and compounded feelings of powerlessness. While policy makers might argue that the intension of using the term 'customer' is to bring about change in the way frontline staff perceive and interact with their clients, this alteration was not apparent to users.

It is, therefore, unclear what purpose the use of customer terminology fulfils.

Notes

[1] There have been significant policy changes since this research was conducted.

[2] Concordats exist between the Department for Work and Pensions (DWP) and the Scottish Executive and the Welsh Assembly, to establish a framework of cooperation on matters of social security. Northern Ireland is different, in that its Department for Employment and Learning has power to change social security policy, although this must be done in 'close relationship' with the DWP to maintain parity. It is the UK government that holds the purse strings for social security in all parts of the country.

[3] Particularly since interviews were conducted before the introduction of the National Minimum Wage or Working Tax Credit.

[4] The names of research participants have been changed to protect their anonymity.

References

Anderson, G. (ed) (1989) *The white blouse revolution*, Manchester: Manchester University Press.

Butcher, T. (1995) *Delivering welfare services*, Buckingham: Open University Press.

Clarke, J. and Newman, J. (1997) *The managerial state*, London: Sage Publications.

Daly, M. (2003) 'Governance and social policy', *Journal of Social Policy*, vol 32, no 1, pp 113-28.

Du Gay, P. and Salaman, G. (1992) 'The cult(ure) of the customer', *Journal of Management Studies*, vol 29, no 5, pp 615-33.

Dunleavy, P. and Hood, C. (1994) 'From old public administration to New Public Management', *Public Money and Management*, July–September, pp 9-16.

Elmore, R. (1978) 'Organisational models of social program implementation', *Public Policy*, vol 26, pp 185-228.

Finn, D. (2001) 'Welfare to work? New Labour and the unemployed', in S. Savage and R. Atkinson (eds) *Public policy under Blair*, Basingstoke: Palgrave.

Finn, D. and Taylor, D. (1990) *The future of Jobcentres: Labour market policy and the Employment Service*, Employment Paper No. 1, London: Institute of Public Policy Research.

Fletcher, D.R. (1997) 'Evaluating special measures for the unemployed: some reflections on the UK experience', *Policy & Politics*, vol 25, no 2, pp 173-84.

Flynn, N. (1993) *Public sector management* (2nd edn), Hemel Hempstead: Harvester Wheatsheaf.

Forde, C. and Slater, G. (2001) 'A temporary solution to unemployment?', paper presented to the 'Labour Market Change, Unemployment and Citizenship in Europe' conference, Helsinki, 20-25 April.

Foster, D. and Hoggett, P. (1999) 'Change in the Benefits Agency: empowering the exhausted worker?', *Work, Employment & Society*, vol 13, no 1, pp 19-39.

Gagnon, S. (1996) 'Promises vs performance: pay devolution to "Next Steps" Executive Agencies in the British Civil Service', *Employee Relations*, vol 18, no 3, pp 25-47.

Glendinning, C., Powell, M. and Rummery, K. (eds) (2002) *Partnerships, New Labour and the governance of welfare*, Bristol: The Policy Press.

Heery, E. and Salmon, J. (eds) (2000) *The insecure workforce*, London: Routledge.

Hill, M. (1997) *The policy process in the modern state* (3rd edn), London: Prentice Hall.

HM Treasury (1989) *The financing and accountability of Next Step Agencies*, Cmnd 914, London: HMSO.

Horton, S. and Jones, J. (1996) 'Who are the new public managers? An initial analysis of "Next Steps" chief executives and their management role', *Public Policy and Administration*, vol 11, no 4, pp 18-44.

Jessop, B. (1999) 'The changing governance of welfare: recent trends in its primary functions, scale, and modes of coordination', *Social Policy & Administration*, vol 33, no 4, pp 348-59.

Larner, W. and Walters, W. (2000) 'Privatisation, governance and identity: the United Kingdom and New Zealand compared', *Policy & Politics*, vol 28, no 3, pp 361-77.

Lipsky, M. (1980) *Street-level bureaucracy: Dilemmas of the individual in public services*, London: Harvester Wheatsheaf.

Newman, J. (2001) *Modernising governance: New Labour, policy and society*, London: Sage Publications.

Peters, T. (1987) *Thriving on chaos: Handbook for a management revolution*, London: Pan.

Peters, T. (1993) *Liberation management*, New York, NY: Knopf.

Pollitt, C. (1993) *Managerialism and the public services* (2nd edn), Oxford: Basil Blackwell.

Savage, M. and Witz, A. (eds) (1992) *Gender and bureaucracy*, Oxford: Blackwell.

Theodore, N. and Peck, J. (1999) 'Welfare-to-work: national problems, local solutions?', *Critical Social Policy*, vol 19, no 4, pp 485-510.

Veit-Wilson, J. (1998) *Setting adequacy standards: How governments define minimum incomes*, Bristol: The Policy Press.

Wright, S. (2003) *Confronting unemployment in a street-level bureaucracy: Jobcentre staff and client perspectives*, Stirling: University of Stirling, unpublished doctoral thesis.

Part Three: Processes: the changing spaces of welfare governance

NINE

Administering global welfare: public management, governance and the new role of INGOs

Gaby Ramia[1]

Global governance institutions and scholars of global civil society are acutely aware of the importance of international non-governmental organisations (INGOs) to transnational welfare arrangements (UN, 2004). Yet within these arrangements the role of INGO organisational management principles in determining the effectiveness of transnational welfare is less well understood. Coming to terms with the significance of management calls for a renewed understanding of New Public Management (NPM) and its place within global governance.

The impact of NPM on national-level non-governmental organisations (NGOs), particularly service-based NGOs, has been subject to significant scrutiny (for example, Ryan, 1999; Alexander, 2000; Considine, 2001; Ramia and Carney, 2003). As part of the NPM agenda, many national governments, particularly those of the Anglo-Saxon countries, have contracted out and put up for competitive tender the majority of welfare functions traditionally carried out in a non-competitive environment by organisations in the public and non-profit sectors. Today, services can be and are delivered not only by public sector and non-profit organisations, but also by profit-seekers. Non-profits have accordingly been forced to be 'competitive' in their outlook, often emulating the strategic management techniques of their for-profit counterparts. These trends have been examined cross-nationally (Polidano, 1999; Pollitt and Bouckaert, 2000; Considine, 2001; Pollitt and Talbot, 2003), but the adaptation of NPM changes to the *global* sphere has not attracted a great deal of attention in governance debates.

This is not surprising. At least from one view, governmental change can be deemed nebulous as a global concept, given the lack of a global 'government'. In contrast to this view, however, this chapter argues that supranational governmental change is conceivable, and it is amenable to global governance analysis. This makes the search for 'good governance' more elusive and more complex than it has been in times past.

The adaptation of NPM principles to the global arena can be seen mainly in changes to multilateralism, particularly since the mid-1990s, which present those seeking global democracy with added complexities. In particular, multilateral governance patterns have partially disempowered nation states in their policy-making capacities, and, in so doing, they afford a more prominent part to be played by INGOs in governance processes; particularly in relation to consultation and hands-on input on governance alongside intergovernmental organisations (IGOs) such as the United Nations (UN) and the World Bank (Held, 1995; O'Brien et al, 2000; Ottaway, 2001; Baker, 2002; UN, 2004). In particular, for better or for worse, the role of INGOs in delivering and implementing *contracted* anti-poverty services has become a prominent reality. As the chapter outlines, this mirrors the trend at the national level under NPM.

Although the activities and status of INGOs in global governance have been common focal points within the field of international relations (Deacon, 1995; Weiss and Gordenker, 1996; Cox, 1997; Deacon et al, 1997), analysts have not often paid systematic attention to the role of INGO management strategies and organisational structures in their attempts to gain a greater share of world development resources. This chapter is a conceptual analysis seeking to contribute to the narrowing of this gap in understanding, which resides primarily in a cleavage between the literatures of welfare and global governance on the one hand, and INGO management on the other. The central objective is neither to support nor challenge current change programmes, but to seek a greater comprehension of them and to raise awareness of them. The developments that have changed the INGO sector's strategic landscape are outlined, concentrating on the strategy–structure configurations of world-focused INGOs in poverty relief and development.

The chapter locates the key organisational environment changes for the sector mainly within the globalisation of governance institutions in two interrelated areas: social policy and public management. The central argument of this chapter is that globalisation and the ever-increasing urgency of humanitarian development have forced INGOs to recognise the importance of their 'strategy–structure configurations' as they pursue transnational service efficiency. Yet this recognition poses a problem for INGOs, in that a focus on efficiency in the struggle for resources represents an emulation of multinational corporations (MNCs). In this way INGOs face similar pressures to national NGOs operating under NPM conditions. This factor has not often been examined in the literatures of public management, global governance and international business. The chapter further argues that understanding this phenomenon calls for an analysis of the link between INGO management strategies and the broader global governance arrangements underpinning multilateralism. In fleshing out the argument it is demonstrated that there are important conceptual connections and parallels between global governance theory and NPM analysis.

In linking global governance and NPM to understand contemporary INGOs, the starting point is the impact of globalisation on social policy. This is the focus of the first section. The second section turns attention to the importance of the link between NPM and multilateralism. The third and final section examines the implications of global governance change for INGO management, focusing on the factors pushing INGOs towards a greater focus on management strategy and organisational structure.

The social policy context and globalisation

Traditionally, social protection institutions – and the social policy literature – did not easily grapple with the existence of international and world-focused organisations such as INGOs. Far from being global in focus, traditional social policy researchers were largely preoccupied with the nation state. More specifically the field had its home in the western nation state, springing mainly from social protection measures that had their birth in the mid to late 19th century (compare: Webb and Webb, 1897, 1911; Polanyi, 1944) but which had their high point in the middle of the 20th century with the institutionalisation of the welfare state (compare: Titmuss, 1958; Baldwin, 1990). Despite a move towards policy internationalisation from the end of the Second World War through the creation of the League of Nations, and then again after the Second World War – seen most clearly in the beginnings of European integration – the 'post-Second World War settlement' in social policy entrenched welfare measures supporting an almost entirely *national* set of institutions. The inherently national focus of research in the field, for the most part, lives to this day.

However, social policy researchers have long been curious about policies and policy regimes in countries outside their own. This tradition is most clearly represented by cross-national comparative and regime-type research, which has its roots mainly in the 1960s but which has seen its major growth since the early 1980s (Esping-Andersen, 1990; Castles and Mitchell, 1993; Ginsburg, 1994). Although comparativism can be viewed as part of the much broader theoretical project of understanding the strength and reach of globalisation (Held and McGrew, 2000), cross-national research by its nature must emphasise national (regime) and regional (regime-type) institutional and policy distinctiveness. In addition it has been characterised by a western focus, and in this way does not truly embrace the *global* aspects of policy.

International social policy as a distinct area of analysis has formed the focus of some research (for example, Townsend, 1993; Gough, 2000; Townsend and Gordon, 2002). Townsend (1993), for instance, who has been one of the leading advocates of international welfare scholarship, focuses on the general possibilities for international social policy responses to poverty. The work of other scholars in this area deals with the issue of a 'race to the bottom' in regard to social labour standards (see Strange, 1996; Rodrik, 1997). The focal problem here is that as nations and regions search for international competitive advantage, they are pushed by the logic of capitalist competition to commodify workers, constructing them as resources analogous to non-human means of production. The danger then is that capitalists can lower standards of employment in the ongoing quest to minimise production costs (for example, OECD, 1994, ch 4; Sengenberger and Campbell, 1994; Standing, 1999). Although the production costs thesis has been widely contested, the original basis of protection within western industrial relations systems lies in this very line of thinking (for example, Webb and Webb, 1897; Higgins, 1915).

Yet, despite the impact of international competition for welfare and social protection, both inside and outside the world of employment, there is a dearth of literature that explores in depth the role of *world*-focused institutions and organisations as they affect social policy (see especially Deacon, 1995; Deacon et al, 1997; Langmore, 1998; Yeates, 2001). Global social policy stems from what are now well-established trends towards the empowerment of supranational and global institutions in the formulation and delivery of policy programmes. This encompasses a focus that is different to – and arguably transcends – Mishra's (1995, 1999) and Scharpf's (2000) analyses of the implications of economic globalisation for the downfall of the 'golden age' of the welfare state. The analytical project seeking an understanding of *global* social policy is inherently problematic in its complexity. It involves establishing the links between globalisation theory and social policy, where globalisation invokes a generalised 'widening, deepening and speeding up of worldwide interconnectedness in all aspects of contemporary social life' (Held et al, 1999, p 2).

Despite globalisation's vague character, social policy analysts are compelled to grapple seriously with it if they are to uncover more effective ways to formulate and deliver international social development programmes. As Yeates (2001, p 2) argues, globalisation urges the analyst 'to bring globalization into the study of social policy and social policy into the study of globalization'. In Deacon's perspective (1995; Deacon et al, 1997), the researcher on global social policy must examine not just the globalisation of social policy, but its companion phenomenon, 'the socialisation of global politics'. This refers to the basis of social policy in the globalisation of political and policy processes more broadly (globally) conceived. Thus globalisation has meant that organisations such as the Bretton Woods institutions – the World Bank and the International Monetary Fund (IMF) – are afforded a greater role than was hitherto the case in determining the international distribution of income, resources and life opportunities. As was argued in the previous section of the chapter, the role of the UN – although always highly significant since its inception – has been recast in the light of more complex cross-sectoral alliances and shifting global governance patterns.

Globalisation and national institutions

For Yeates (2001) the relationship between globalisation and social policy is a dialectical one, such that nation states and national institutions are not merely passive receptors of global trends. To the contrary, as well as reacting to globalisation, national institutions contribute to and help to shape globalisation. This supports the overriding conclusion of the so-called globalisation 'sceptics' (a term coined by Held and McGrew, 2000), who reject the 'convergence' thesis (see Weiss, 1997; Geyer, 1998; Mishra, 1999). Convergence theory constructs nation states and national policy regimes as becoming more similar over time in the face of the neo-liberalism inherent to globalisation. Sceptics, on the other hand, highlight the impact of agency on the part of the nation state and its institutions and political and economic interests; thus, more so than in the estimations of some theorists (for example, Pontusson and Swenson, 1996; Iversen and Cusack, 2000), politics and institutions still 'matter' in determining the power of global political-economic trends. Sceptics also argue that 'regionalisation' is a somewhat separate phenomenon to globalisation, but one that is just as important, if not more so. Thus the expanding scope of the European Union (EU), for example, need not be seen as an instance of globalisation, for it can be conceived as internationally important in and of itself.

Supranational global governance

For Deacon et al (1997) the relationship between social policy and globalisation is best examined by specific reference to the growing importance and influence of supranationally and globally based organisations and institutions. They view the supranationalisation of social policy as taking three forms: supranational regulation; supranational redistribution; and supranational provision (Deacon et al, 1997, p 2). *Regulation* refers to supranational and global mechanisms, instruments and policies that govern trade and the operation of capitalist firms. It is noteworthy, however, that Deacon et al do not enter deeply into the *management* of the operations of either capitalist firms, INGOs or supranational political institutions. *Redistribution*, which they view as centrally important, pertains to the extent to which the economic and social protection efforts of poorer countries can be subsidised by richer ones. Deacon et al's third category relates to supranational welfare *provision*, which includes services, benefits or citizenship rights dispensed by supranational agencies such as the United Nations High Commission for Refugees (UNHCR) and the Council for Europe. It may also include IMF loans and World Bank development programmes. Interestingly, however, although the authors deal extensively with INGOs, the role of the latter in relation to supranational provision is not mentioned in their initial discussion of the three dimensions of supranationalism (see Deacon et al, 1997, p 3).

Both Yeates and Deacon et al acknowledge appropriately that the study of global social policy must take into account that different supranational and global bodies have different aspirations, orientations and objectives; and they do not follow the same path towards globalisation, nor even the same understanding of the phenomenon. For instance, in leaning slightly on the comparative welfare regime-types framework of Esping-Andersen's (1990) and Titmuss's (1974) models of welfare capitalism, Deacon et al begin the process of attaching 'conservative corporatism'/'social liberalism' to the World Bank's approach to global policy programmes (welfare as social cohesion/safety net), 'classical liberalism' to the IMF (welfare as burden/workfare) and 'citizenship entitlement/income' to the International Labour Organisation (ILO) (welfare as rights) (Deacon, 1995, 2001; Deacon et al, 1997). This runs contrary to the work of those such as Ohmae who proclaimed *The end of the nation state* (Ohmae, 1995). Under this framework, national politics and economics are rendered virtually powerless in the face of a *Borderless world* (Ohmae, 1990), which supports increasingly streamlined, integrated and all-powerful global economic forces.

Ohmae's extremist position on globalisation would be profound, if it were accurate; implying as it does that INGOs must follow an almost uniformly global strategic orientation to their activities. The more reliable and more nuanced view has different ramifications, although just as profound and arguably more complex. It is this latter view that informs INGO management.

The INGO sector, NPM and multilateralism

INGOs constitute a highly significant organisational sector on the global stage. Part of this significance stems from the sector's consolidation. This consolidation manifests itself through the creation of an oligopoly-type structure in each of the major sub-sectors: the natural environment, development and poverty alleviation, and health (Donini, 1996, p 91; Gordenker and Weiss, 1996). Given that the largest organisations are therefore dominant, a focus on the relatively few world-focused INGOs is justified despite the existence of hundreds of thousands of smaller NGOs worldwide. More will be said on the structure of the sector later.

To be sure, it is possible to overstate the importance of the INGO sector as a whole to global governance. In particular there has been a well-acknowledged, steady growth in corporate foreign direct investment (FDI) by MNCs since the early 1990s (UNCTAD, 2002, pp 11-12). This raises questions about the extensiveness of the social investment role of INGOs as compared with that of big business. Of equal significance is the more recent growth – since the mid-

1990s – of bilateral aid, and the increase within this of aid for emergency assistance and debt relief, 'constituting 25 percent of total aid commitments by DAC [the OECD's Development Assistance Committee] member countries in 1998-2000' (UNCTAD, 2002, p 11). As important as these indicators are, however, at present there are 20,000 or more major INGOs. Although only a small proportion of these organisations are agencies providing social services, from the management strategy and global governance perspectives the INGO sector's significance is reflected in the 'privatisation of both development and relief'. This is indicated by INGOs 'relying on NGOs [for social programme implementation] so much that now the total share of development aid transferred through NGOs outweighs that distributed by the UN system, excluding the Washington-based financial institutions (The World Bank and the International Monetary Fund)' (Weiss, 1999, p 13). As Weiss outlines:

> In the mid-1990s NGOs dispersed annually almost 15 percent of total public development aid – some $10-12 billion and probably much more since neither food aid nor military help figures accurately in statistics; an ever-growing share (approaching half) was emergency relief. With a six-fold increase in emergency spending over the last decade, NGO humanitarian relief has become substantial. Even in relationship to the dramatic change by the UN system in devolving responsibilities to NGOs, the European Union's switch away from funding for emergencies channelled through governments toward NGOs has been remarkable – for governments from over 95 percent in 1976 to only 6 percent in 1990, and for NGOs from nothing to 37 percent. In the first 5 years of the 1990s, between half and two-thirds of European Commission Humanitarian Organisation's (ECHO) emergency funding was channelled through NGOs. (Weiss, 1999, p 14)

While bearing in mind the growth in bilateral aid for emergency relief (de la Porte and Deacon, 2002) and the increasing bilateralism and regionalism in trade (Findlay, 2002; Mansfield and Reinhardt, 2003), the trends identified by Weiss are more significant when it is considered that in the area of humanitarian relief, in the mid-1990s the eight largest NGOs that dominated the sector 'account[ed] for what may be 80% of the financial value of assistance in complex emergencies' (Gordenker and Weiss, 1996). These 'super' NGOs include: the Co-operative for American Relief Everywhere (CARE); World Vision International; Oxfam International; and the Save the Children Federation (Donini, 1996, p 91; CARE Australia, 2002; Oxfam International, 2002; World Vision, 2002).

International trends

Given that the 'industry' for INGO services displays oligopolistic structural characteristics, pushing the organisations into strategies resembling non-price competition, INGOs have been forced to emulate organisations that are well accustomed to competing internationally: multinational corporations (Smillie, 1995; Ramia, 2003). This induces organisational change, both in terms of *organisational structure* (how organisational tasks, units [offices] and members are linked for perceived maximal efficiency and effectiveness), and *management strategy* (the plans and courses of action perceived by management to be performance enhancing, for utilisation in search of sustained competitive advantage). More will be said on the link between INGO strategy–structure patterns and global governance in the final section of the chapter.

One of the primary imperatives for an analysis of the link between INGO strategy and structure, however, is first to closely examine the proposition that the shifts in global governance associated with multilateralism have substantively affected INGOs; and that the changed governance environment has prompted INGOs to take on organisational structures and management strategies similar to those of MNCs. In order to generate an effective understanding of the global governance factors that have fed INGOs' greater awareness of their strategies and structures, it is important to outline the roots of the issue in what was called the 'new multilateralism' (for example, Cox, 1997; O'Brien et al, 2000). This has parallels with NPM in the late 1980s and 1990s at the national level.

The trajectory of public administration through the 20th century, which was strengthened in the post-Second World War period up to the 1970s, was highly consistent with Weberian bureaucracy theory. This environment formed the institutional basis for the traditional public or civil service and public sector (see, for example, Newman, 1998). This settlement has undergone a major transformation since the early 1980s, however, public administration having gradually given way to ever-greater reliance on market imperatives in the management and governance of the public sector and in the mix between public and private (see especially Aucoin, 1990; Hood, 1991; Pollitt and Talbot, 2003). The NPM agenda has seen the introduction of measures that alter the public sector's structure, elevate the importance of 'strategic management' and recast the notion of public ownership (Hughes, 1998). Included among the important changes are: a sharper focus on (most often quantifiable) results or outcomes as opposed to (qualitative) processes; an elevation in cost management and (economic) efficiency enhancement in the use of public resources; the devolution of management control, so as to 'let public sector organisational managers manage'; the separation of commercial from non-commercial activities; a significant stepping up of market-style contestability and the increased use of contracting out of traditionally publicly provided services; and more emphasis on monetary incentive schemes (Hood and Jackson, 1992, pp 182-3; Boston et al, 1996, p 26).

Although the dictates of NPM have only relatively recently been applied extensively to the domain of national social service activities provided by NGOs (Ryan, 1999; Alexander, 2000; Ramia and Carney, 2003), its effects have now been clearly felt in the governance of most areas of the welfare state. As a result, the traditional 'social division of welfare' (Adler, 1997; Walker, 1997), which had relatively rigid definitions of which sector should provide which services, has been recast. This is seen in the allowance of more discretion to public sector welfare officials than was previously the case. This is part of the NPM push to allow managers of all sorts of organisations to lead their organisations 'unencumbered' by outside intervention from policy makers. In addition, the managers of the organisations contracted to deliver services – often private sector, profit-seeking organisations – have been given new-found discretion over the lives and living standards of welfare recipients; indeed in some cases usurping the authority of public officials and blurring lines of public interest accountability (Considine, 2001; Carney and Ramia, 2002). Considine (2001), for instance, points to key shifts in the governance of employment services, raising questions about accountability in light of the de-legalisation and fragmentation of service provision. In a similar tradition, Carney and Ramia (2002) analyse the effects of service marketisation on *client understandings* of their legal and social rights before the law. Frameworks used to capture changes such as these include those of 'quasi-markets' (Bartlett et al, 1998), 'enterprising states' (Considine, 2001) and 'contractualism' and 'managerialism' (Clarke and Newman, 1993; Boston, 1995; Clarke, 1998; Yeatman, 1998; Carney and Ramia, 2002; Pollitt and Talbot, 2003).

NPM and national NGOs

But management change resulting from the NPM agenda does not stop with the public sector. Service organisations within the non-profit sector have been given little choice but to respond to the imperatives of competition set by government policy, and, as will be seen, the management dimension of the NGO response has been decidedly 'strategic' in focus. As the work of non-profit sector specialist William Ryan (1999) demonstrates, the line between profit-seeking corporations and non-profit organisations has been blurred. This has occurred principally because of significantly increased recourse by national governments to competitive tendering and contracting, a key tenet of NPM. Services once traditionally only provided on a largely uncontested basis by either the public sector or the non-profit sector – both previously having a higher certainty of funding and thus viability of existence – are now subject to competition. Competition now encompasses the corporate sector, corporations in some countries having lined up to answer governments' pleas for efficiency in service delivery. Instances of this at the global level will be discussed below. At the national level, US-based defence manufacturer and private corporation Lockheed Martin provides a good example. It has won a plethora of contracts to provide welfare-to-work services in the US, including case management, skills training and job placement assistance (Ryan, 1999, pp 127-8). Similar developments, although more systematically applied, have been seen under Australia's so-called Job Network, under which over half of the total 300 or so employment service organisations contracted to government are private sector profit-seekers (for example, Kellie, 1998; Considine, 2001, ch 6; Ramia and Carney, 2001; Carney and Ramia, 2002, ch 3).

Stemming from the NPM agenda in general and contracting out and contestability in particular, non-profit service organisations are presented with four possible strategic choices (Ryan, 1999). First, they can stand on their own as non-profit organisations and compete with the government and for-profit sectors. Second, they can make themselves available for acquisition by a corporation; and in this matter they may have little genuine choice. Third, they can become a corporation. And fourth and finally, the non-profit organisation can engage in strategic alliances, thus often becoming part of inter-organisational and/or inter-sectoral organisational networks.

Tangible analogies are contained in this strategic choice framework for NGOs at the global level. To be sure, adapting the framework to the global arena has its problems. First, although the NPM concept has been used explicitly by some authors for general public policy analysis (Aucoin, 1990; Hood, 1991; Pollitt, 1993; Hughes, 1998; Minogue et al, 1998), the application of *comparativism* to NPM in social policy has been somewhat less common (exceptions include Polidano, 1999; Pollitt and Bouckaert, 2000; Considine, 2001; Pollitt and Talbot, 2003). Second, there is an obvious absence of an adequate global equivalent for the government of a nation state. That is, NPM assumes a governing authority with an ultimate monopoly over the recourse to legitimised violence in order to enforce change.

Yet, as will be seen in the next section, globalisation implies that governance in the global arena has been increasing in focus. With the importance of multilateralism, strong lessons – negative though many of them may be – are available for globally focused NGOs stemming from the experience of smaller NGOs at the national and sub-national levels. As it is painted in global governance analysis (for example, NGLS, 1995; Jayasuriya, 1999; UNDP, 1999; O'Brien et al, 2000), whereas the 'old multilateralism' was largely a 'top-down' affair and nation states were still powerful actors in the global governance system through their membership to multilateral agencies, the new multilateralism is more 'bottom-up', allowing greater engagement with international social movements, civil society and INGOs. Of course, within this trend, different types and intensities of engagement are evident across the various multilateral institutions; particularly the UN, the World Bank, the IMF and the World Trade Organisation (WTO) (see especially O'Brien et al, 2000). Regardless of the important need for comparing the generosity and genuineness of engagement between these institutions, in allowing democracy at all, multilateralism 'opens the question as to the normative basis of an alternative world order' (Cox, 1997, pp xv-xvii) and celebrates the *possibility* of a more genuinely pluralist and democratic form of global governance.

NPM and INGOs

This does not mean that 'good global governance' is necessarily any closer to hand. In the welfare sphere, and as discussed further in the next section of the chapter, multilateralism has ushered in 'global welfare markets', where INGOs play a fundamental role (Deacon et al, 1997; Yeates, 2001). Yeates (2001, pp 43-5), for instance, outlines four forms which international trade in welfare services may take. First, there can be consumption of welfare services abroad, as in the case of school and higher-education exchanges. Second, professionals such as doctors, nurses and consultants in public health systems can move abroad, thus constituting cross-national trade in welfare services. Third, some service organisations may set up greenfield or brownfield operations overseas, as is common in higher-education institutions that establish or purchase campuses abroad. Fourth, cross-border services can be supplied remotely through tools such as distance learning in higher-education institutions and telediagnosis in the health area. All of these involve contestability in regard to service provision, providing some analogy with the strategic choices faced by service-based (as opposed to advocacy) NGOs at the national level under NPM.

Other imperatives associated with multilateralism have pushed INGOs into competitive strategies. Weiss (1999) points out that with the elevation in the role of INGOs within governance, Organisation for Economic Co-operation and Deveopment (OECD) countries have become more favourable to NGO involvement in the implementation of projects, but that increasingly these projects are of a 'retail' rather than a 'wholesale' nature. This implies that INGOs are often at the client or consumer end of the value chain, being intimately engaged in programme delivery and execution. Weiss (1999, p 13) also points to a 'privatization of both relief and development'. When combined with the increasing tendency for the UN to 'devolve its responsibilities to INGOs', it becomes clear that we have witnessed the creation of a 'market-driven aid system'; one that shares a great deal with the welfare services provided by NGOs at the national level as they respond to pressures in their own immediate economic and governance environment.

These pressures are evident in global governance generally. Multinational corporations have entered what they see as the 'business' of aid (for example, Shawcross, 1996; Wagle, 1996). Wagle (1996), for instance, uses the example of the (now disgraced) corporation Enron in its combination of economic and social investment in India in the mid-1990s when it established a power plant concurrently with health facilities and other infrastructure for the Dahbol community. Enron argued that, like other multinationals, it was effectively acting as a replacement for traditional aid agencies. As part of a trend in the same general direction, privatisation inducing competition can also be seen in the UN system. Lee et al (1997), for instance, demonstrate convincingly using the cases of governance in the global telecommunications, transportation and natural resources sectors that multinational corporate interests have become prominent in the way those sectors articulate with UN interests. In their unique perspective, 'a transnational managerial class of core public–private interests can be observed' (Lee et al, 1997, p 341).

The tendency to contract on a competitive basis for services, in a manner very similar to that which occurs at the national level under NPM, is alive and well in supranational programmes (Wedel, 2000; de la Porte and Deacon, 2002). As de la Porte and Deacon (2002) demonstrate in their analysis of EU governance in relation to accession countries, private sector consultants, contracting companies and even key individuals have major influence over the policy formulation process. In particular they highlight the vital point that contracting 'through competitive tendering favours private sector players' (de la Porte and Deacon, 2002, p 94). The impact on INGOs, as Stubbs (2000, p 30) makes clear in his analysis of aid agencies and local NGOs, is that 'the dominant mode of assistance has reinforced "projectisation" at all levels in which longer-term visions, wider objectives, much less any kind of coherent articulation of need, are subsumed within discrete "project proposals which identify particular, narrow objective".

Projectisation is consistent with the economic dimension of multilateralism: the consolidation of the INGO sector as previously mentioned. As Donini (1996, p 91) outlines, 'eight major families or federations of international NGOs have come to control almost half [of] an $8 billion market'. This raises not only significant international relations and global governance issues, but also important questions regarding the strategic choice frameworks facing global INGOs in managing their organisations for maximal performance; however performance is measured. Smillie's (1995) position sums up the need for an analysis of the relationship between governance and management strategy in large NGOs by arguing that the world-focused NGOs:

> have traded long-term development impact for growth, short-term child sponsorship and emergency donors.... At corporate level many actually do bear an uncanny resemblance to transnational corporations in their opportunistic behaviour. Like many transnationals, they

> have maximized growth through the successful international manipulation of pricing, marketing and product. (Smillie, 1995, p 212)

Although Smillie's comments are not the final word on the changing nature of strategy in INGOs, he does provide a justification for an assessment of the significance for global governance and global social policy of the increasingly competitive global environment.

Global governance and strategic configuration

When the changing structure of the INGO sector (or 'industry') is considered alongside changes in the conduct of INGO activities, the place of organisational management strategy has an important place in analysis. The debate between convergence and continuing significant differences among policy regimes in the face of globalisation – as well as differences between the global multilateral institutions in regard to social policy approach – resonate strongly with issues currently being faced by organisations in the INGO sector. There is a need to explore, as an extension of the multilateralist framework, one that includes strategic management, whether and in what ways different approaches to management strategy and organisational structure differ between organisations within the sector. An associated question relates to how effective INGOs can be in contributing to the broader goals of global social policy and governance. This analysis can take the form of explicating in detail the strategies and structures of each organisation in focus. This would be cumbersome and relatively unhelpful, however, since an understanding of the sector as a whole is required before the impact of multilateralism on strategy and structure can be unearthed.

The most appropriate way is to use a framework that simultaneously applies to the *patterns* of strategy and the *patterns* of structure consistent with them. This is captured in the concept that has been used within the international business/management literature in regard to MNCs; 'strategy–structure configuration'. Such an approach is consistent with Miller (1986; see also Miller and Mintzberg, 1984) in relating business (or competitive) strategy to organisational structure. His conception of 'configurations' is based on the premise that 'strategy, structure and environment coalesce or configure into a manageable number of common, predictively useful types [of world-focused corporation]' (Miller, 1984, p 236). In a similar vain, Birkinshaw and Morrison (1995) draw associations between the strategies of MNC subsidiaries and their 'structural context'. Many other authors have sought to explore the relationship between strategy and structure, which is so central to strategic management as to be viewed as one of the field's 'cornerstones' (Birkinshaw and Morrison, 1995, p 730), with a history of scholarship dating back to the 1960s (see Chandler, 1962; Perlmutter, 1969; Stopford and Wells, 1972; Amburgey and Dacin, 1994; Birkinshaw and Morrison, 1995).

The conceptual approach taken in this chapter, however, is consistent with the broadest analysis in this general literature. It examines the patterns characterising the entirety of a multinational corporation *and* its approach or orientation to international expansion in the context of environmental pressures consistent with globalisation. This framework in relation to multinational corporations is typified by Bartlett and Ghoshal's germinal analysis (1989/98; see also Leong and Tan, 1993; Harzing, 2000). According to these authors, MNCs can take one of four ideal-typical configurations. First, they can be *international* in focus, whereby they are global in orientation but operations tend to be concentrated in the home office, hence emphasising and leveraging parent company 'knowledge' worldwide. McDonald's provides an example of such a corporation. Second, an organisation can be *multinational* (or *multidomestic*), typified by car manufacturers, where the organisation seeks to maximise its responsiveness to local conditions in all of the countries and regions it has activities in. In the process the benefits of economies of scale are not foregone. Third is the *global* corporation, which purposefully does not vigorously pursue localisation as this induces extra costs implied by duplication of effort and knowledge in each country and/or regional market. Instead, the global company seeks to maximise its economies of scale and hence mass markets 'homogenised' products worldwide. High-fashion garment manufacturers tend to fit the global pattern as they tend to make merchandise that is deemed to be of the highest quality, which should not be compromised in any of the organisation's markets worldwide. Finally, the strategy–structure configuration, which Bartlett and Ghoshal argue is inevitable, is that striving for the '*transnational* solution'. The transnational mindset attempts to combine two desirable yet conflicting characteristics: economies of scale and associated cost reductions on the one hand, and localisation to different markets on the other.

Possible consequences for INGOs

One major proposition for empirical testing is that the tension between the standardisation consistent with globalisation in the policy and governance environment, is attractive to INGOs as a strategy for operating within the confines set for them by the multilateral order. This may depend on the conception of the new multilateralism taken by the individual organisation. The new multilateralism offers the *possibility* of greater INGO choice in the sense of offering *new* strategies (Cox, 1997), but it may be seen by an INGO as prohibiting choice because it narrows the *range* of realistic options available. It can be seen to be desirable that INGOs follow transnationalism because it helps them to be adaptable to both emergencies and ongoing routine projects at the same time. In this way they might more effectively mitigate their 'projectisation', as de la Porte and Deacon (2002) identify. After all, INGOs are called upon to have an eye both for global efficiencies and cost savings, as well as on local responsiveness.

Rather than being pushed in the same direction, the alternate proposition would be that different INGOs have been led to adopt radically different strategy–structure configurations. This is in essence an assessment of the possibility that strategic management in the current environment – dominated by complexity as it is – calls for less complex approaches to the pursuit of organisational goals; or as Eisenhardt and Sull (2002) label it, 'strategy as simple rules'. As these authors argue, elaborate strategic planning and restructuring frameworks may be seen as luxuries when the time, resource and cost pressures associated with the intensification of international competition are considered. Arguably, for better or for worse, the same pressures can be said to bear upon the service-provision environment faced by INGOs. This was implied by civil society analysts such as Donini (1996) and Gordenker and Weiss (1996), although neither of these identified strategic management frameworks as ways INGOs are adapting to globalisation; whether in similar ways across the board or with significant variation. Donini (1996, p 19), however, implies – albeit in an indirect fashion – that the main global anti-poverty service organisations adhere to different models:

> In most cases these groupings [of offices within individual global NGOs] do not affect the individuality of their constituent members, who retain their *operational and*

> *financial independence*, except for World Vision, which is *managed centrally*. They do, however, engage in some co-ordination and organised division of labour within groupings, which greatly facilitates fundraising and helps in particular with *access to European Union and UN funds*. CARE, for example, has a *lead agency approach* whereby one if its branches is the principal partner in specific countries. The groupings are thus in a position to better co-ordinate policies on specific situations and to shape the market by their sheer presence in *particular sectors or geographical areas*. (emphasis added)

Donini's discussion implies that there are differences between the individual NGOs in regard to strategy–structure patterns. For instance, one implication is that World Vision comes closer than the others to a global strategy model. Regardless of the uncertainty, the common thread in the case of World Vision is the perceived imperative to reduce costs. CARE, on the other hand, appears to be following a multidomestic strategy and structure, seeking to maximise responsiveness to local needs and allowing regional and national offices significant autonomy. Analysis is needed, however, on the relationship between INGO donors, other constituencies and INGO organisational management structures so as to inquire into the governance of the sector, and then to examine the implications of these for global governance through criteria associated with programme effectiveness. More sophisticated frameworks will allow the analysis of the links between corporate (or internal INGO) governance and global governance. Deacon's (2000; also Deacon et al, 1997) classification of the approaches of key multilateral agencies engaged in the global social policy arena as discussed above, can be brought fruitfully to bear in examining the contours of key strategic relationships between global INGOs and bodies such as the UN, the World Bank, the WTO and the IMF. Analysis of these contours can go some way to interrogating the suggestion that, by forming strategic contractual relationships and strategic alliances with multilateral institutions such as the World Bank and the IMF as part of multilateralism, INGOs compromise their inherently 'social' mission. There is a need to examine the extent to which cross-sectoral relationships put pressure on INGOs to be more focused on the financial, efficiency-based imperatives of service delivery. This issue is problematic, not only because it is difficult to weight the relative importance of efficiency and effectiveness, but also because different INGO managers have different levels of discretion based on differently constituted cross-sectoral relationships as part of changed governance arrangements. These relationships in turn are continually reinvented as world development policy unfolds.

Conclusions

At the level of the nation state, frameworks examining non-profit strategy have drawn links between various elements of NPM and the need for commercially inspired strategic management in (national-level) NGOs. It is widely agreed that contractualism in the public sector in particular has had major impacts on the non-profit sector, inducing national NGOs to compete on a nominally 'level playing field', not only with public sector organisations but with profit-seekers as well. This chapter has argued that similar trends are identifiable in INGOs. However, the plight of the INGO sector is more mysterious. The complexity of governance at the global level, given its multilateral character, and the absence of global equivalents to national government and the public sector, provides a major barrier to understanding the impact of global governance change on the INGO sector. The analysis sought to contribute to a narrowing of the conceptual gap between global governance theory and INGO management analysis. More precisely, under consideration were the key developments that have altered the strategic landscape within which the INGO sector operates, principally by examining relevant trends within multilateralism. Although multilateralism has been subjected to extensive analysis by international relations theorists, its implications for INGO sector strategies and structures have been largely excluded from the debate. Neither have the connections and parallels between NPM at the national level – governance at the national level – and global governance been explored in great depth.

By reviewing the frameworks underpinning global governance, NPM and global social policy, and by searching for conceptual connections between these theoretical concepts and strategy–structure patterns as discussed in the international business/management literature, this chapter has argued that globalisation and the increasing urgency of world development have elevated INGOs' recognition of the importance of their strategy–structure configurations. Understanding this phenomenon adequately, however, calls for an extensive analysis, more searching than the present literature affords, of the conceptual link between INGO management strategies and structures and broader global governance arrangements. By concentrating on the oligopolised development of the INGO sector, rather than verifying or discrediting key propositions on this link, the chapter left open the possibility that these organisations find the *transnational* strategies desirable in the way that multinational corporations do. Because their criteria are significantly broader than those of MNCs, and because they do not prioritise the pursuit of profit, INGOs seem to differ widely, both from MNCs and from each other. This is despite belonging to the same sector and being driven by very similar pressures emanating particularly from globalisation and multilateralism. Although uncertainty remains on precise classifications of strategic response-types, and although there is doubt about whether or not democracy is enhanced by multilateral change, the chapter leaves little doubt as to the proposition that the new regime of global governance is a force driving unprecedented change in the INGO sector. The contours of this change tell us much about the changing character of globalisation and its impact on the search for good governance.

Note

[1] An earlier version of this analysis was presented at the Academy of Management Conference, Seattle, Washington, 1-7 August 2003.

References

Adler, M. (1997) 'Welfare rights, rules and discretion: all for one or one for all?', Richard M. Titmuss Memorial Lecture, Department of Social Policy, University of Edinburgh.

Alexander, J. (2000) 'Adaptive strategies of nonprofit human service organisations in an era of New Public Management', *Nonprofit Management and Leadership*, vol 10, pp 287-303.

Amburgey, T.L. and Dacin, T. (1994) 'As the left foot follows the right? The dynamics of strategic and structural change', *Academy of Management Journal*, vol 37, pp 1427-52.

Aucoin, P. (1990) 'Administrative reform in public management: paradigms, principles, paradoxes and pendulums', *Governance*, vol 3, pp 115-37.

Baker, G. (2002) 'Problems in the theorisation of global civil society', *Political Studies*, vol 50, pp 928-43.

Baldwin, P. (1990) *The politics of social solidarity: Class bases of the European welfare state 1875-1975*, Cambridge: Cambridge University Press.

Bartlett, C.A. and Ghoshal, S. (1989/1998) *Managing across borders: The transnational solution* (2nd edn), Boston, MA: Harvard Business School Press.

Bartlett, W., Roberts, J.A. and Le Grand, J. (eds) (1998) *A revolution in social policy: Quasi-market reforms in the 1990s*, Bristol: The Policy Press.

Birkinshaw, J. and Morrison, A.J. (1995) 'Configurations of strategy and structure in subsidiaries of multinational corporations', *Journal of International Business Studies*, vol 26, no 4, pp 729-53.

Boston, J. (ed) (1995) *The state under contract*, Wellington: Bridget Williams Books.

Boston, J., Martin, J., Pallot, J. and Walsh, P. (1996) *Public management: The New Zealand model*, Oxford: Oxford University Press.

CARE Australia (2002) *About CARE Australia* (online), available at: www.careaustralia.com.au/about.htm

Carney, T. and Ramia, G. (2002) *From rights to management: Contract, New Public Management and employment services*, The Hague: Kluwer.

Castles, F.G. and Mitchell, D. (1993) 'World of welfare and families of nations', in F.G. Castles (ed) *Families of nations: Patterns of public policy in western democracies*, Aldershot: Dartmouth, pp 93-128.

Chandler, A.D. (1962) *Strategy and structure: Chapters in the history of the industrial enterprise*, Cambridge, MA: MIT Press.

Clarke, J. (1998) 'Thriving on chaos? Managerialism and social welfare', in J. Carter (ed) *Postmodernity and the fragmentation of welfare*, London: Routledge, pp 117-86.

Clarke, J. and Newman, J. (1993) 'The right to manage: a second managerial revolution?', *Cultural Studies*, vol 7, pp 427-41.

Considine, M. (2001) *Enterprising states: The public management of welfare-to-work*, Cambridge: Cambridge University Press.

Cox, R.W. (ed) (1997) *The new realism: Perspectives on multilateralism and world order*, Tokyo/New York/Paris: United Nations University Press.

de la Porte, C. and Deacon, B. (2002) 'Contracting companies and consultants: the EU and the social policy of accession countries', *GASPP (Globalism and Social Policy Program) Occasional Papers No. 9/2002*, Helsinki: STAKES.

Deacon, B. (1995) 'The globalisation of social policy and the socialisation of global politics', in J. Baldock and M. May (eds) *Social policy review* 7, Canterbury/Kent: Social Policy Association, pp 55-76.

Deacon, B. (2000) 'Globalisation: a threat to equitable social provision?', in H. Dean, R. Sykes and R. Woods (eds) *Social policy review 12*, London: Social Policy Association, pp 250-71.

Deacon, B. (2001) 'International organizations, the EU and global social policy', in R. Sykes, B. Palier and P.M. Prior (eds) *Globalization and European welfare states: Challenges and change*, Basingstoke: Palgrave, pp 59-76.

Deacon, B. with Hulse, M. and Stubbs, P. (1997) *Global social policy: International organizations and the future of the welfare state*, London: Sage Publications.

Donini, A. (1996) 'The bureaucracy and the free spirits: stagnation and innovation in the relationship between the UN and NGOs', in T.G. Weiss and L. Gordenker (eds) *NGOs, the UN, and global governance*, Boulder, CO, and London: Lynne Rienner Publishers, pp 83-101.

Duysters, G. and Hagedoorn, J. (2001) 'Do company strategies and structures converge in global markets? Evidence from the computer industry', *Journal of International Business Studies*, vol 32, no 2, pp 347-56.

Eisenhardt, K.M and Sull, D.N. (2001) 'Strategy as simple rules', *Harvard Business Review*, vol 79, pp 106-22.

Esping-Andersen, G. (1990) *The three worlds of welfare capitalism*, Cambridge: Polity Press.

Findlay, C. (2002) 'Walking and chewing gum at the same time: Australia's free trade areas strategy', *Australian Journal of Agricultural and Resource Economics*, vol 46, pp 605-17.

Geyer, R. (1998) 'Globalisation and the (non-)defence of the welfare state', *West European politics*, vol 21, no 3, pp 77-102.

Ginsburg, N. (1994) 'Comparative social policy: a review', *International Review of Policy*, vol XXV, no 2, pp 18-33.

Gordenker, L. and Weiss, T.G. (1996) 'Pluralizing global governance: analytical approaches and dimensions', in T.G. Weiss and L. Gordenker (eds) *NGOs, the UN, and global governance*, Boulder, CO, and London: Lynne Rienner Publishers, pp 17-47.

Gough, I. (2000) *Global capital, human needs and social policies: Selected essays, 1994-99*, Basingstoke: Palgrave.

Harzing, A. (2000) 'An empirical analysis of the Bartlett and Ghoshal typology of multinational companies', *Journal of International Business Studies*, vol 31, no 1, pp 101-20.

Held, D. (1995) *Democracy and the global order: From the modern state to cosmopolitan governance*, Cambridge: Polity Press.

Held, D. and McGrew, A. (2000) 'The great globalization debate: an introduction', in D. Held and A. McGrew (eds) *The global transformations reader: An introduction to the globalization debate*, Cambridge: Polity Press, pp 1-45.

Held, D., McGrew, A., Goldblatt, A. and Perraton, J. (1999) *Global transformations: Politics, economics and culture*, Cambridge: Polity Press.

Higgins, H.B. (1915) 'A new province for law and order: industrial peace through minimum wage and arbitration', *Harvard Law Review*, vol XXIX, pp 13-39.

Hood, C. (1991) 'A public management for all seasons', *Public Administration*, vol 69, pp 3-19.

Hughes, O. (1998) *Public management and administration* (2nd edn), London: Macmillan.

Iversen, T. and Cusack, T.R. (2000) 'The causes of welfare state expansion: deindustrialisation or globalisation?', *World Politics*, vol 52, pp 313-49.

Jayasuriya, K. (1999) 'Globalization, law, and the transformation of sovereignty: the emergence of global regulatory governance' (unpublished mimeo).

Kellie, D. (1998) 'Unemployed? Board the enterprise for a brave new world and a "real" job: a critique of the new strategy for reducing unemployment', *Australian Journal of Social Issues*, vol 33, no 3, pp 285-302.

Langmore, J. (1998) 'Globalisation and social policy', in G. Jungwirth (ed) *New visions for government*, Sydney: Pluto Press, pp 171-86.

Lee, K., Humphreys, D. and Pugh, M. (1997) ' "Privatisation" in the United Nations system: patterns of influence in three intergovernmental organisations', *Global Society*, vol 11, pp 339-57.

Leong, S.M. and Tan, C.T. (1993) 'Managing across borders: an empirical test of the Bartlett and Ghoshal [1989] organizational typology', *Journal of International Business Studies*, vol 24, pp 449-64.

Mansfield, E.D. and Reinhardt, E. (2003) 'Multilateral determinants of regionalism: the effects of GATT/WTO on the formation of preferential trading agreements', *International Organization*, vol 57, pp 829-62.

Miller, D. (1986) 'Configurations of strategy and structure: towards a synthesis', *Strategic Management Journal*, vol 7, pp 233-49.

Miller, D. and Mintzberg, H. (1984) 'The case for configuration', in D. Miller and P. Friesen (eds) *Organizations: A quantum view*, Eaglewood Cliffs, NJ: Prentice Hall, pp 10-30.

Minogue, M., Polidano, C. and Hulme, D. (eds) (1998) *Beyond the New Public Management: Changing ideas and practices in government*, Cheltenham: Edward Elgar.

Mishra, R. (1995) 'Social policy and the challenge of globalisation', in P. Saunders and S. Shaver (eds) *Social policy and the challenges of social change: Proceedings of the national social policy conference*, Sydney, 5-7 July, Vol. I, Sydney: Social Policy Research Centre, University of New South Wales, pp 15-34.

Mishra, R. (1999) *Globalization and the welfare state*, Cheltenham: Edward Elgar.

Newman, J. (1998) 'Managerialism and social welfare', in G. Hughes and G. Lewis (eds) *Unsettling welfare: The reconstruction of social policy*, London: Routledge, pp 333-74.

NGLS (Non-Governmental Liaison Service) (1995) *Social priorities of civil society: Speeches by non-governmental organizations at the world summit for social development*, Geneva: UN NGLS.

O'Brien, R., Goetz, A.M, Scholte, J.A. and Williams, M. (2000) *Contesting global governance: Multilateral economic institutions and global social movements*, Cambridge: Cambridge University Press.

OECD (Organisation for Economic Co-operation and Development) (1994) *Employment outlook*, Paris: OECD.

Ohmae, K. (1990) *The borderless world*, London: Collins.

Ohmae, K. (1995) *The end of the nation state*, New York, NY: Free Press.

Ottaway, M. (2001) 'Corporatism goes global: international organizations, nongovernmental organization networks, and transnational business', *Global Governance*, vol 7, pp 265-92.

Oxfam International (2002) *About OI* (online), available at: http://oxfam.org/intouch/default.htm

Perlmutter, H.V. (1969) 'The tortuous evolution of the multinational corporation', *Columbia Journal of World Business*, Jan-Feb, pp 9-18.

Polanyi, K. (1944) *The great transformation: The political and economic origins of our time*, Boston, MA: Beacon Press.

Polidano, C. (1999) 'The New Public Management in developing countries', *Public policy and management working papers series no. 13*, University of Manchester: Institute for Development Policy and Management.

Pollitt, C. (1993) *Managerialism in the public services: Cuts or cultural change in the 1990s?* (2nd edn), Oxford: Blackwell.

Pollitt, C. and Bouckaert, G. (2000) *Public management reform: A comparative analysis*, Oxford: Oxford University Press.

Pollitt, C. and Talbot, C. (eds) (2003) *Unbundled government: A critical analysis of the global trend to agencies, quangos and contractualisation*, London/New York: Routledge.

Pontusson, J. and Swenson, P. (1996) 'Labor markets, production strategies, and wage bargaining institutions: the Swedish employer offensive in comparative perspective', *Comparative Political Studies*, vol 29, pp 223-50.

Ramia, G. (2003) 'Global social policy, INGOs and strategic management: an emerging research agenda', *Global Social Policy*, vol 3, pp 79-102.

Ramia, G. and Carney, T. (2001) 'Contractualism, managerialism and welfare: the Australian experiment with a marketised employment services network', *Policy & Politics*, vol 29, pp 59-80.

Ramia, G. and Carney, T. (2003) 'New Public Management, the Job Network and non-profit strategy', *Australian Journal of Labour Economics*, vol 6, pp 253-76.

Rodrik, D. (1997) *Has globalization gone too far?*, Washington, DC: Institute of International Economics.

Ryan, W.P. (1999) 'The new landscape for nonprofits', *Harvard Business Review*, Jan-Feb, vol 77, no 1, pp 127-36.

Salamon, L.M., Anheier, H.K., List, R., Toepler, S. and Sokolowski, S.W. (1999) *Global civil society: Dimensions of the nonprofit sector*, Baltimore, MD: Johns Hopkins Center for Civil Society Studies.

Scharpf, F. (2000) 'Globalization and the welfare state: constraints, challenges and vulnerabilities', paper given at the International Social Security Association's 'The year 2000 international research conference on social security', Helsinki, 25-27 September.

Sengenberger, W. and Campbell, D. (eds) (1994) *Creating economic opportunities: The role of labour standards in industrial restructuring*, Geneva: International Institute of Labour Studies.

Shawcross, W. (1996) 'Never mind Oxfam, DHL can deliver', *The Independent*, 10 October, p 21.

Smillie, I. (1995) *The alms bazaar: Altrusim under fire: Non-profit organizations and international development*, London: IT Publications.

Standing, G. (1999) *Global labour flexibility: Seeking distributive justice*, London: Macmillan.

Stopford, J.M. and Wells, L.T. (1972) *Managing the multinational enterprise: Organization of the firm and ownership of the subsidiaries*, New York, NY: Basic Books.

Strange, S. (1996) *The retreat of the state: The diffusion of power in the world economy*, Cambridge: Cambridge University Press.

Stubbs, P. (2000) 'Partnership or colonisation? The relationship between international agencies and local non-governmental organisations in Bosnia-Herzegovina', in B. Deacon (ed) *Civil society, NGOs and global governance*, GASPP (Globalism and Social Policy Programme) Occasional Papers, No. 7/2000, Helsinki: STAKES, pp 23-32.

Titmuss, R.M. (1958) 'The social division of welfare: some reflections on the search for equity', in R.M. Titmuss (ed) *Essays on the welfare state*, London: Unwin University Books, pp 34-55.

Titmuss, R.M. (1974) *Social policy: An introduction*, edited by B. Abel-Smith and K. Titmuss, London: George Allen and Unwin.

Townsend, P. (1993) *An international analysis of poverty*, Hemel Hempstead: Wheatsheaf.

Townsend, P. and Gordon, D. (2002) *World poverty: New policies to defeat an old enemy*, Bristol: The Policy Press.

UN (United Nations) (2004) *We the peoples: Civil society, the United Nations and global governance: Report of the Panel of Eminent Persons on United Nations–Civil Society Relations*, New York, NY: UN.

UNCTAD (United Nations Conference on Trade and Development) (2002) *The least developed countries report 2002*, New York and Geneva: UN.

UNDP (United Nations Development Programme) (1999) *Globalization with a human face* (online), Human development report 1999, available at: www.undp.org/hdro/99.htm

Wagle, S. (1996) 'TNCs as aid agencies? Enron and the Dahbol power plant', *The Ecologist*, vol 26, pp 179-84.

Walker, A. (1997) 'The social division of welfare revisited', in A. Robertson (ed) *Unemployment, social security and the social division of welfare: A festschrift in honour of Adrian Sinfield*, Edinburgh: Department of Social Policy, University of Edinburgh, pp 1-15.

Webb, S. and Webb, B. (1897) *Industrial democracy*, London: Longmans, Green and Co.

Webb, S. and Webb, B. (1911) *The prevention of destitution*, London: Longmans, Green and Co.

Wedel, J. (2000) 'USA economic aid to Russia: a case study in subcontracting governance', in B. Deacon (ed) *Civil society, NGOs and global governance*, GASPP (Globalism and Social Policy Programme) Occasional Papers, No. 7/2000, Helsinki: STAKES, pp 33-44.

Weiss, L. (1997) 'Globalization and the myth of the powerless state', *New Left Review*, no 225, p 3-27.

Weiss, T.G. (1999) *International NGOs, global governance, and social policy in the UN system*, in B. Deacon (ed) *Civil society, NGOs and global governance*, GASPP (Globalism and Social Policy Programme) Occasional Papers, No. 3/1999, Helsinki: STAKES.

Weiss, T.G. and Gordenker, L. (eds) (1996) *NGOs, the UN, and global governance*, Boulder, CO, and London: Lynne Rienner Publishers.

Willetts, P. (2002) *What is a non-governmental organization?* (online), output from the research project on civil society networks in global governance, available at: http://staff.city.a.u/CS—NTWKS-ART.HTM

World Vision (2002) *World Vision Australia* (online), available at: www.wva.org.au/contact/

Yeates, N. (2001) *Globalization and social policy*, London: Sage Publications.

Yeatman, A. (1998) 'Interpreting contemporary contractualism', in M. Dean and B. Hindess (eds) *Governing Australia: Studies in contemporary rationalities of government*, Cambridge: Cambridge University Press, pp 227-41.

TEN

The fight against unemployment as a main concern of European social policy: the implications of a new, local-level approach

Carla Valadas

Since the beginning of the 1990s, the promotion of employment has been recognised as one of the necessary conditions for a stable European Union (EU) economy. Subsequently, EU member states have been trying to define an integrated and innovative approach in the fight against unemployment. The perceived need for such an approach arises from two sources. First, member states have increasingly recognised the structural nature of unemployment. Second, member states' national policies have failed to overcome the evolving but persistent problem of unemployment and respond to new social demands.

The European Employment Strategy comprises initiatives and events promoting efforts to decrease or even eradicate the causes of unemployment as well as its negative consequences (Hespanha and Valadas, 2001). This chapter concentrates on one of these initiatives, called Territorial Employment Pacts (TEPs). Territorial Employment Pacts form a pilot measure developed in specific geographical areas and their main objective is to solve problems of unemployment by utilising and enhancing the social, political and economic resources of a given area. The initiative recognises the complex and problematic character of employment and unemployment situations in European countries. Significantly, it seeks to highlight the usefulness of a local/regional intervention as a particular method of solving problems (in this case unemployment) that have a global/international dimension. As demonstrated in this chapter, TEPs have the potential to reconstruct national and international initiatives into plans of action at the local level, according to the specificities of local conditions (Greffe, 1998).

It is argued here that the importance accorded to this (local) level of intervention is stimulated by a broader context characterised by profound changes in the role of the state. At the same time that the state, a central actor, seems less capable of effectively responding to the fast and unexpected transformations in the economic and social spheres of our lives, the benefits of local and regional approaches are stressed.

Since the mid-1970s, the role played by the state in the achievement of social rights has changed. Facing new internal and external pressures, the state has increasingly had to negotiate and articulate its actions with other international organisations, such as the EU, the Organisation for Economic Co-operation and Development and the World Trade Organisation. Some authors (for example, Deacon et al, 1997) subsequently emphasise the supranational and transnational character of social policies. We agree that national social policies are influenced by international agreements and standards established in the field of social protection, but we disagree with these authors' contention that the national level of intervention is less central. Our view is that nation states maintain a crucial role in forming and implementing social policies, although this happens in a more dense and complex institutional context.

This chapter is organised as follows: first, we argue that welfare state variations (in terms of size, bases of funding, patterns of entitlement, forms of delivery and redistributive capacity) must be (re)considered if we want to understand how welfare states are exposed to and react to international pressures. Then we analyse TEPs as an example of the application of the EU's Open Method of Coordination (OMC). In our opinion, despite the mechanisms and principles underlined in the new form of governance evident in TEPs, the nation state retains a central role. To support our argument we provide empirical evidence from a case study of one of the Portuguese TEPs.[1] Finally, we draw some conclusions about the role and impact of the OMC on welfare state reform, and more specifically on the Portuguese welfare state and power relations within Portugal.

Welfare state regimes: different answers to unemployment

In Europe, national social protection systems are characterised by profound differences. Considering several criteria (for example, level of social expenditure and decommodification), various authors (Castles and Mitchell, 1990; Esping-Andersen, 1990; Leibfried, 1993; Ferrera, 1996) have established different regime types (or models) around which welfare states are seen to cluster. Remarkable differences between countries have been observed in welfare state intervention into unemployment. We briefly examine these differences to help us appreciate how they can obstruct the construction of a uniform European Employment Strategy.

Gallie and Paugam (2000) developed a typology on the basis of three criteria: coverage; level of financial compensation; and extent of active employment policies. This theoretical approach complements Esping-Andersen's original proposal but addresses a specific domain of welfare state intervention, namely instability and precariousness associated with the labour market. Gallie and Paugam's typology consists of four unemployment welfare regimes: the sub-protective regime; the liberal/minimal regime; the employment-centred regime; and the universalistic regime.[2] As with other typologies, the four regimes should be considered 'ideal types'; in practice, most welfare states embrace elements of more than one model, however, 'they approximate *more closely* to one type of welfare model than another' (Gallie and Paugam, 2000, p 7; emphasis in original).

Besides the role played by the state, Gallie and Paugam also emphasise the importance of the family model as influencing how individuals deal with unemployment. For instance, the level of family stability may determine a more or less uncertain professional situation. According to Gallie and Paugam, there are multiple configurations within Europe in relation to the family model and its role. The authors distinguish between three models of family residence: the 'extended dependence model', the 'relative autonomy model' and the 'model of advanced autonomy'.[3]

These models have a symmetrical relationship with their welfare regimes. However, Gallie and Paugam (2000, p 17) caution:

> It might be tempting to conclude that there is a continuum between these two poles and to attribute the decisive role in the creation of family residence models to the type of unemployment welfare regime that prevails in each country. But any such conclusion would be over hasty.

Thus, Gallie and Paugam prefer writing about unemployment welfare regimes when considering public authorities' sphere of intervention, and to refer to family models if examining the private sphere. And they use the notion of 'systems of social regulation' when analysing the intersecting influences of public and private institutions.

Perceptions of unemployment in EU member states can also differ according to the level of industrialisation and economic development as well as to sectoral restructuring of the economy. On the basis of the three elements identified – the nature of social protection for the unemployed, the family model and the pattern of economic development – Gallie and Paugam demonstrate how the problem of unemployment is approached in very distinct ways inside the EU territory. Asymmetries between countries in relation to these three areas underlie considerable differences in terms of the constitution or structure and level of unemployment in member states. Therefore, although member states are challenged by common problems and dilemmas, they react very differently to global and domestic dynamics and (new) external pressures that have arisen in the last few years. These differences in responses stem from each member state's specific institutional characteristics.[4] In the context of this diversity, convergence around a single European (social) model and the construction of a uniform European Employment Strategy remain particularly difficult.[5]

Potentialities and implications of a European Employment Strategy

Bearing in mind the diversity of social and political configurations that characterise each member state, we nevertheless point out that the European Commission has established a degree of commonality between states in the area of employment policy, mainly in the late 1990s. According to Milner (2000), trends have emerged in relation to: the implementation of active employment policies; the creation of social partnerships; labour market restructuring in order to increase flexibility; and policies aiming to promote women's formal employment. Some of these strategies involve redistributing competences between several actors and different levels of administration, with the purpose of promoting both social cohesion and economic growth, and creating new jobs.

States' moves towards creating an autonomous economic and political space that combines economic stability with social well-being,[6] point to the fact that European member states share some common values. According to Quintin and Favarel-Dapas (1999), these values can provide the bases for a European social policy. We agree with Robert Geyer (2000) that although the social dimension has lagged behind other aspects of integration (for example the creation of a European common market) some progress is evident in the sphere of social policy, especially in the last two decades of the 20th century. For instance, important employment policy initiatives have been undertaken by member states since 1993 when the European Commission designated the structural character of unemployment as the central element of social policy debates in the EU.[7]

Two decisive landmarks of European employment policy are the Special Jobs Summit of EU Heads of State and government that took place in Luxembourg in 1997, and the inclusion of a new employment section in the Amsterdam Treaty that same year. The main contribution of the 'Luxembourg process' is the elaboration of employment-policy guidelines on which member states draw up National Action Plans for Employment. As Watt (2003, p 2) summarises it, the Amsterdam Treaty stipulates that:

> Employment was a matter of 'common concern' to the member states, and laid the basis for giving the European Union level a role in coordinating member states' labour market policies. Importantly, the Treaty emphasised from the start that European Union involvement with employment was subordinate to the overall coordination of economic strategy via the so-called Broad Economic Policy Guidelines.

These two initiatives launched the European Employment Strategy and are linked to the adoption of the (new) OMC. The Lisbon European Council agreed on the OMC in March 2000. Through its instruments – benchmarking, peer-group pressure, bringing together different policy actors and policy learning – it can be seen as 'a promising institutional mechanism for advancing on all the grey areas of "common concern"' (Ferrera et al, 2000, p 84).

The OMC and the field of employment

We have an optimistic view of the OMC: it exhibits a new form of coordination in the EU, overcoming the impasse in developing

European social policies. Progress in this area is now anchored in priorities defined consensually, with the OMC occupying an intermediary position between European integration and harmonisation, on one hand, and mere cooperation, on the other (Hespanha and Valadas, 2001). Another characteristic of the OMC is its tendency to reproduce the differences that exist between countries, enabling different options for policy strategy (Milner, 2000). The policies that follow from the OMC approach recognise common principles and goals and, at the same time, reinforce national specificities by, for instance, linking to strategies grounded in different priorities. As Robert Geyer (2000) suggests, instead of constituting a threat to national social policies, the EU's new social policy orientations should be seen as encouraging and facilitating diversity.

Apart from the positive contributions that can be attributed to the OMC, authors have identified some limitations. One risk that accompanies this kind of policy mechanism relates to the uncertainty of intervening in domains that have an undeniable social and political importance but where consensus is more difficult to achieve (Hespanha and Valadas, 2001). Eberlein and Kerwer (2002, p 2) point out that:

> As a largely voluntary exercise, [OMC] lacks the bite of real sanctions, especially when it comes to implementing broadly defined targets. Participants might only be 'willing' to learn from others and adopt 'best practice' if there is a credible 'shadow of hierarchy'. Thus, it might simply serve to support the pursuit of symbolic politics, instead of supporting real action.

Considering these (and other) arguments, we think there are some significant questions that need to be clarified, namely:

- Will policies resulting from the deployment of the OMC contribute to the reproduction of inequalities, deepening differences between systems of social protection?
- Will countries where social policies are less equitable and efficient pursue strategies that have less ambitious targets, rather than follow best examples/performances?
- Will the OMC encourage countries with higher social protection standards to reduce costs and even diminish their patterns of universality and generosity?

We currently believe that the answers to these questions might be 'yes'. To support our point of view, we emphasise Streeck's (1995) ideas concerning the new phase of the European governance strategy, marked by a neovoluntarist approach. We point to his comments on the EU's domestic political economy that 'neovoluntarism stands for a type of social policy that tries to do with a minimum of compulsory modification of both market outcomes and national policy choices, presenting itself as an alternative to hard regulation as well as to no regulation at all' (Streeck, 1995, p 424). Thus, we describe an emerging mode of governance at the European level as applying new methodologies and representing an inversion of centralised state practices involved in traditional forms of interventionism undertaken by EU member states (see also Eberlein and Kerwer, 2002, p 3).

Territorial Employment Pacts (TEPs)

Territorial Employment Pacts form a political initiative launched in 1997 that provides a concrete example of the application of these (new) orientations. In the next section, we demonstrate how, closely linked to the implementation of the employment-policy guidelines,[8] TEPs meet criteria and principles associated with the OMC. That is, TEPs involve: the absence of strict regulatory requirements; trials adapting national/international strategies to local circumstances; and a diminished role for the state given its need to work with other participants (for example, social partners and civil society).

We emphasise that TEPs do not constitute a new European initiative. Their origins are evident in previously regulated initiatives (for example, Articles 130A-D of the EU Treaty and the Structural Fund regulations). Territorial Employment Pacts emerged from a series of projects, principles and goals established in: previous European Councils (for example, Florence, June 1996, and Dublin, December 1996), EU Treaties (Treaty of Amsterdam) and various European Commission communications. Territorial Employment Pacts do not modify existing procedures of structural interventions, nor do they demand the creation of new structures or legal instruments. Rather than requiring additional financial resources, TEPs 'were designed to increase the impact of the Structural Funds on regional and local employment' (EC, 1996, p 3).

Moreover, some characteristics of the TEP approach to unemployment – such as partnerships – had already been tested in initiatives developed in other EU policy domains (for example social exclusion). Another feature of TEPs that European member states have tried to promote is the sharing of innovative and best practice (Fundação Europeia para a Melhoria das Condições de Vida e de Trabalho, 1993). An additional key characteristic of TEPs is the important role attributed to policy makers and local citizens in social and economic development projects. Therefore, although TEPs do not represent a new initiative, they seek to integrate new principles that European member states have put into practice since 1990 and to apply them to unemployment problems.

The TEP approach emerged in the context of high unemployment levels in (almost) all European countries, as recognised by the coordinator of a TEP:

> 'The idea of creating Pacts in Europe appeared in a situation of very high unemployment in Europe, with unemployment rates of 12, 15% and basically it consisted of the creation of solutions, developed through local partnerships, which should create employment in the social spheres that would solve structural problems of unemployment. The Pacts were supposed to make local actors discuss these kinds of questions.'[9]

More concretely, European member states expect TEPs to identify origins of unemployment in each region, evaluate possibilities for economic development in each region, prevent unemployment and find new areas of activity into which to incorporate (some) unemployed people. In short, TEPs are expected to 'help to identify not only the local causes of unemployment but also specific solutions and strategies' (EC, 1996, p 5).

TEPs in practice

A key characteristic of TEPs is the mobilisation of local and regional actors, whose contribution may be important to the creation of concrete and innovative employment projects at the local or regional level. In this respect, a former Portuguese central government representative at the regional level emphasises that:

> 'Beside the subject of unemployment the other issue that the European Commission considered very important in the context of the creation of Pacts was the local or territorial dimension ... the perception that the

> questions of employment should not only be approached at the macro-economic level but also through territorial action. This came from other European policies, namely rural development policies like the LEADER programme. In practice, European policies rediscovered a subject ... that had already shown positive results related to local development potentialities, to territorial development, to local productive systems, etc.'[10]

In this statement, our interviewee stresses that through the creation of TEPs, countries are encouraged to explore potentialities of strategies at the territorial level. It is expected that the widespread use of a regional or local partnership will allow governments to:

- identify the difficulties, concerns and future prospects facing each of the territorial players with responsibility in the employment field;
- mobilize all available resources in favour of an integrated strategy which is accepted by all parties concerned, based on their real needs and expressed in a formal commitment – namely a 'Territorial Employment Pact';
- improve the integration and coordination of job-creation measures; and
- put into effect employment schemes and measures which can serve as a model (EC, 1996, p 9).

The designation of 'Pact' itself requires a dialogue between local and regional partners that will be the basis for a concerted plan of action. The European Commission document quoted above also includes various practical and financial commitments, rigorously establishes objectives and quantifiable goals and identifies target groups and specific areas for job creation. Concerning a TEP's partners, it is expected that 'even where the initiative comes from local government, the broadest possible spectrum of other operators must be involved (for instance, industry, professional groups, non-profit-making organisations, educational establishments and universities)' (EC, 1996, p 6). Differences in competences require that national and regional authorities play a role in implementing TEPs and that the institutions of the EU (specifically, the European Commission) 'ensure the general coordination of local initiatives and assess and disseminate results. They will also draw conclusions and prepare general recommendations for future use' (EC, 1996, p 6).

As our research demonstrates, TEPs' emphasis on consolidating a broad and effective partnership between actors is important for implementing strategies to combat unemployment at the local/regional level. More concretely, TEPs require that not only decision makers participate in discussions and definition of strategies, but also people targeted by those decisions, which did not happen previously:

> Earlier, it was rare, even in Member States, for an entrepreneur and a jobless person to sit down at the same table as people from trade unions, the church, local authorities and organizations to try to solve problems not only of labour availability but also the social excluded and ageing, or the young unemployed. (Monkare, 1999)

The involvement of partners of different origins – from both private and public sectors – and the emphasis on mobilising actors at the local level can be seen as positive aspects of TEPs and are closely linked to the OMC. It is particularly significant that the actors will represent different sectors if we consider the heterogeneous nature of unemployment (for example, skill levels, health problems and housing conditions). On the other hand, in order to participate, partners with different institutional cultures (for example, local authorities, business associations, firms and not-for-profit organisations) will often have to confront different methods of intervention and therefore negotiate with one another.

A further positive aspect of TEPs is the creation of plans of action at the local level that are tailored to address specific problems and that adapt national policies or initiatives to suit local needs (Greffe, 1998). We emphasise that TEPs are not meant to harmonise the employment situation across European member states, but are expected to consolidate actions that respond to the multiple territorial configurations of unemployment. Nevertheless, it is clear that ideas and experiences that succeed in a given territory are likely to be exchangeable and adapted in other areas.

TEPs also have limitations, of which the more significant are as follows:

- TEPs' contributions may be modest due to the complexity of employment problems, particularly in the context of economic globalisation (EC, 1997, p 4).
- As happened with previous European initiatives, TEPs can be transformed into a supplementary administrative circuit, making actions involved too burdensome or difficult to manage (EC, 1997, p 4).
- Some impacts of TEPs will not be immediately recognisable, for instance, the (positive) results of strategies to raise workers' skills and competences and thus their employability. Similarly, converting industrial sectors is essential to creating jobs but takes a lot of time.
- Where substantial quantitative goals are absent, it is difficult to objectively quantify TEPs' results.

The success of a TEP depends on partners' involvement and representativeness of a given region, whether the plan of action proposed is realistic and how relevant targets set by the TEP are for resolving local problems (EC, 1997, p 5). Thus it is our opinion that the diverse participants redefine TEPs to accord with: their specific goals and interests; the instruments (technical means, human resources, and so on) they have for achieving their objectives; their organisational models; their understanding of the extent of the problems in the territory under consideration; and the dominant political culture. Objectives and strategies to address problems in a particular territory may therefore vary significantly according to who is playing the principal role in the TEP at a given moment. Furthermore, in countries such as Portugal where there is little experience of partnership work (Valadas, 2003), and which are characterised by 'institutional individualism', TEPs can very easily be undermined as each partner focuses on its own priorities and interests, neglecting the needs of the population. In such circumstances, predominant actors often build strategic alliances with other sources of power (for example national government representatives) so that they can, for instance, obtain the financial support they need to reach a certain goal.

In our research this tendency was clearly evident in the Marinha Grande TEP. Marinha Grande is an industrial municipality located in the district of Leiria on the Região Centro coast of Portugal. It is a very small territory composed of two parishes, Marinha Grande and Vieira de Leiria, and has 34,000 inhabitants. The views of local entrepreneurs played a central role in shaping the strategies pursued by the partners in the TEP. Local entrepreneurs were influential in the first phase of implementing the TEP. Then priorities for action changed and municipal council representatives assumed leadership of the TEP.

According to partners in the Marinha Grande TEP, problems of unemployment in the region can be resolved through furthering economic development. Consequently, they developed initiatives to create a vigorous entrepreneurial environment. As these initiatives required huge amounts of money, a strong financial dependency on the central government emerged. Since the central government did not guarantee the necessary (financial) support, most of the proposed measures failed or were postponed and have not yet been implemented.[11] These observations shift our attention to how nation states continue to regulate and govern local and regional initiatives through selecting and supporting them.

The importance of the local-level approach

The constitution of partnerships, as well as their results and shape, oblige us to carefully analyse the specificities of a region's social, political and economic characteristics, and their broader context. Drawing upon Crozier and Friedberg's (1977) theories, (local) actors will deal with an employment initiative differently depending on their autonomy, how they make use of their (political) power and the strategies they elaborate to sustain their point of view and their interests. In order to register all these variations and territorial possibilities, we emphasise the importance of a local-level analysis, since it can provide important feedback on how supranational or international social policies are reconstructed/adapted by local interventions.

Returning to the example of the Marinha Grande TEP, the involvement and the role played by different actors in implementing the TEP varied significantly, highlighting their pursuit of contrasting priorities and strategies. These differences arise from distinctive political and economic circumstances since, for instance, different central government representatives had dissimilar views of what priorities should be pursued. It is interesting to note that once the political party governing the municipal council obtained the majority of votes in the 1997 elections, its ability to negotiate with the other partners diminished. On the other hand, the low level of recorded unemployment and the extension of the territory covered by the TEP, combined with the presence of an industrial cluster (based on the glass and moulding industry), led to a strategy focused on furthering economic development. Nevertheless, the majority of actors involved did not support this strategy and it was soon replaced with less ambitious goals and priorities[12] (Valadas, 2003, p 267).

Reflections on the impact of the OMC on the Portuguese welfare state

From the example of the Marinha Grande TEP we can make some observations about the interrelations between different levels of power involved in locally implementing a European (supranational) initiative and, more generally, about the impact of these new forms of governance.

One of the key elements of the OMC is partnership working. In Portuguese society, people and organisations have collaborated informally in the past, but it was only after Portuguese integration into the EU that more formal and institutionalised forms of cooperation emerged in social policy domains. Rodrigues and Stoer's (1998, p 10) work on partnerships in Portugal highlights the articulation, from the 1990s onwards, of the official European understanding of partnership and its definition based on local cultures and associative roots. In spite of the importance that is accorded to the construction and development of partnerships in the field of employment, and which is emphasised by Portuguese governmental representatives, important obstacles remain. For instance, there are significant difficulties with constructing and developing relationships based on mutual trust (Glendenning et al, 2002, p 232). Experiences of joint working indicate dissimilar values and goals between representatives of the private and public sectors, as well as between different levels of government. These differences are linked to some of the specificities of the Portuguese welfare state,[13] namely the tendency towards centralisation.

The capabilities attributed to Portuguese local government representatives are insufficiently used because of a lack of both financial and technical resources. Local actors are subsequently forced to engage in informal and personalised relationships with central government representatives in order to obtain the support they need to fulfil their goals, which generates and/or reinforces individualised practices. Actors strategically situated at both national and international levels of intervention played a critical role in the success or failure of measures. In the Marinha Grande TEP, a local entrepreneur's contract with central government representatives determined the choice of the territory, and perception of the strategy as interesting and original. Furthermore, although there is growing engagement with entrepreneurs and other members of the local community, there remain important signs of distrust and significant divergences between local government representatives and entrepreneurs, and between entrepreneurs and worker representatives.

Portugal is an interesting example of how local actors engage in informal mechanisms and practices of networking. There are very distinct experiences of partnership working (Ruivo, 2000), which do not allow the identification of general patterns. Nevertheless, we can see from the Marinha Grande TEP that the state retains its power over the private sector as well as the voluntary and community sectors. Furthermore, the central government delegates responsibility and encourages local actors to innovate and intervene in the short term to resolve problems; however, the state does not provide the necessary technical nor financial support to accomplish these (new) tasks, contributing to a situation of 'false empowerment' (Valadas, 2003, p 264). Because of these tendencies of the state, a substantial transformation of Portuguese welfare governance practices in the near future is highly unlikely.

Conclusions

The historical and institutional characteristics of social protection models essentially remain a matter of national policy. Nevertheless, we recognise that these characteristics are increasingly influenced by decisions and agreements defined at an international level. This is especially the case in EU member states, which have been involved in a slow but continuous process of building European social policies, particularly in the employment domain. New developments, such as high levels of unemployment, the policy constraints of European Monetary Union and the intensification of international competition, have reinforced the importance of initiatives aimed at promoting jobs and combating unemployment.

We share the same (cautious) position of authors such as Pierson (1998), Ferrera et al (2000) and Geyer (2000), that the replacement of national-level regimes by a European social policy regime or European welfare state is unlikely to occur. Instead, we need to consider the diversity of situations and policy outcomes that characterise different European territories. The mechanisms that have been used to construct a European Employment Strategy reinforce these differences, despite dealing with common concerns and programmes of action. The 'soft measures' (such as benchmarking and mainstreaming) adopted under the OMC can be distinguished from older procedures connected to old-style governance (namely regulatory, top-down and uniform procedures) in the sense that the former do not involve imposing too rigid restrictions. On the contrary, such 'soft measures' are seen to facilitate and encourage diversity.

Therefore, although policies to combat unemployment have incorporated an unquestionably European dimension, the role of the nation state remains important since, for instance, it is involved in complex negotiation processes. And given that not all states have the same power nor pursue identical strategies, we agree with Ferrera et al (2000, p 5) that 'policy changes have to be endorsed by elected governments and parliament and continue to be mediated by national political parties, organized interests, and other relevant institutional structures like bureaucracies and systems of interest intermediation'. In this context, an analytical question that should orient future research is how EU social policy interacts differently with distinctive national-level social policy regimes or national-level regime types.

Notes

[1] Data was collected in 2001 and 2002, using document analysis and interviews with key actors involved in implementing the TEP of Marinha Grande, including municipality members, social partners, local entrepreneurs, leaders of local associations, workers from local industries and representatives of the Portuguese state at the regional level.

[2] Sub-protective regimes offer the unemployed less than the minimum level of protection needed for subsistence; a higher level of protection is provided by the liberal/minimal regime and the employment-centred regime; the universalistic regime is the only system that offers comprehensive coverage of the unemployed as well as a higher level of financial compensation and a more ambitious active employment policy (Gallie and Paugam, 2000, p 6).

[3] According to Gallie and Paugam (2000, p 16) 'the extended model characterizes a situation where different generations are brought

together in the same household under the wing of the core generation … offering everyone a minimum of protection'. In the model of advanced autonomy 'the self-realization of the young adult is regarded as inconceivable without acquiring autonomy from the parents' (Gallie and Paugam, 2000, p 17). This means that young adults usually live separately from their parents, although they may remain to some degree financially dependent on their parents. The relative autonomy model describes an intermediary situation between the other two models. The autonomy of the individual is higher than in the extended model and 'individual responsibilities in the household are much more weakly defined' (Gallie and Paugam, 2000, p 16). In this model, parental solidarity is activated when adult children are trying to enter the labour market.

[4] See Ferrera et al (2000, p 52) for an analysis of how different welfare state regimes are adjusting to new external and domestic challenges.

[5] Regarding the barriers to the development of EU social policy, see Leibfried and Pierson (1994).

[6] This idea is one of the characteristics of the 'European social model' whose prospects have been analysed by several authors (for example, Ferrera et al, 2000; Geyer, 2000).

[7] This is the main contribution of the European Commission's *White Paper on growth, competitiveness and employment* (1993).

[8] In 1998 and 1999, the employment-policy guidelines included specific proposals inviting all member states to explore every potential source of employment and implement initiatives that best take advantage of the possibilities offered by the creation of local jobs involving activities unfulfilled by the labour market. The European Commission's (EC, 1999) proposed employment-policy guidelines for 2000 reinforced the role of local interventions.

[9] This statement was obtained in our study of the implementation of the Marinha Grande TEP, one of three TEPs developed in Portugal.

[10] This statement was obtained in the empirical research mentioned in note 9.

[11] Political support was clearly evident in the conception and originality of the proposals. By contrast, required financial support for most initiatives was not immediately guaranteed. A representative of the central government at the regional level explained in our empirical research that the TEPs emerged during a transition between two programming periods of the European Social Fund (1994-99 and 2000-06) and therefore fell into a funding gap.

[12] For instance, the proposal to create a Local Development Company was abandoned. Instead, utilising resources differently or adjusting existing projects was encouraged (for example, professional training and virtual learning designed to attract young people to the moulding industry).

[13] The implementation of a universal welfare state only started to be discussed in Portugal during the political transformations that occurred after 1974. This period coincided with a negative international economic environment and contributed to delays, irregularities and discontinuities in the consolidation of social policies (Mozzicafreddo, 1997, p 41).

References

Castles, F.G. and Mitchell, D. (1990) *Three worlds of welfare capitalism or four?*, Discussion Paper No. 21, October, Canberra: Australian National University, Graduate Programme in Public Policy.

Crozier, M. and Friedberg, E. (1977) *L'acteur et le système: Les contraintes de l'action collective*, Paris: Éditions du Seuil.

Deacon, B., Hulse, M. and Stubbs, P. (1997) *Global social policy: International organizations and the future of welfare*, London: Sage Publications.

Eberlein, B. and Kerwer, D. (2002) 'Theorising the new modes of European Union governance', *European Integration Online Papers (EIoP)*, vol 6, no 5, pp 1-16.

Esping-Andersen, G. (1990) *The three worlds of welfare capitalism*, Cambridge: Polity Press.

EC (European Commission) (1993) *White Paper on growth, competitiveness and employment: The challenges and ways forward into the 21st century*, Brussels: COMPLETAR.

EC (1996) *Guide of the Territorial Employment Pacts for Employment* (online), (available at: http://europa.eu.int).

EC (1997) *Local development and territorial employment pacts: Report of the seminar*, (available at: http://europa.eu.int).

EC (1999) *Guide to Territorial Employment Pacts 2000-2006* (online), (available at: http://europa.eu.int).

Ferrera, M. (1996) 'The southern model of welfare in social Europe', *Journal of European Social Policy*, vol 6, no 1, pp 17-37.

Ferrera, M., Hemerijck, A. and Rhodes, M. (2000) *The future of Social Europe: Recasting work and welfare in the new economy*, Oeiras: Celta Editora.

Fundação Europeia para a Melhoria das Condições de Vida e de Trabalho (1993) *Acção das comunidades locais e política social: Documento de debate*, Luxemburgo: Serviço das Publicações Oficiais das Comunidades Europeias.

Gallie, D. and Paugam, S. (eds) (2000) *Welfare regimes and the experience of unemployment in Europe*, Oxford/New York: Oxford University Press.

Geyer, R. (2000) *Exploring European social policy*, Cambridge: Polity Press.

Glendenning, C., Powell, M. and Rummery, K. (eds) (2002) *Partnerships, New Labour and the governance of welfare*, Bristol: The Policy Press.

Greffe, X. (1998) 'Les partenariats territoriaux pour l'emploi', *Guide de Pratiques*, no 4, pp 1-27.

Hespanha, P. and Valadas, C. (2001) 'Globalização dos problemas sociais, globalização das políticas: o caso da estratégia europeia para o emprego', in P. Hespanha and G. Carapinheiro (eds) *Risco social e incerteza: Pode o estado social recuar mais?*, Porto: Edições Afrontamento, pp 123-75.

Leibfried, S. (1993) 'Towards a European welfare state? On integrating poverty regimes into the European community', in C. Jones (ed) *New perspectives on the welfare state in Europe*, London: Routledge, pp 133-56.

Leibfried, S. and Pierson, P. (1994) 'The prospects for social policy', in A. de Swaan (ed) *Social policy beyond borders: The social question in transnational perspective*, Amsterdam: Amsterdam University Press, pp 15-58.

Milner, S. (2000) 'Employment policies in the European Union and the European Social Model: Towards a new orthodoxy?', paper presented to UACES Conference, Budapest, April.

Monkare, S. (1999) 'Address at the Territorial Employment Pacts dissemination', Local Action for Employment, 7th European Conference and Exhibition, Brussels, 8 November.

Mozzicafreddo, J. (1997) *Estado providência e cidadania em Portugal*, Oeiras: Celta Editora.

Pierson, P. (1998) *Beyond the welfare state: The new political economy of welfare*, Cambridge: Polity Press.

Quintin, O. and Favarel-Dapas, B. (1999) *L'Europe sociale: Enjeux et réalités*, Paris: La Documentation Française.

Rodrigues, F. and Stoer, S. (1998) *Entre parceria e partenariado: Amigos, amigos, negócios à parte,* Oeiras: Celta Editora.

Ruivo, F. (2000) *Poder local e exclusão social: Dois estudos de caso de organização local da luta contra a pobreza*, Coimbra: Quarteto.

Streeck, W. (1995) 'From market making to state building? Reflections on the political economy of European social policy', in S. Leibfried and P. Pierson (eds) *European social policy: Between fragmentation and integration*, Washington, DC: Brookings Institution, pp 389-431.

Valadas, C. (2003) 'Globalização e Europeização das políticas sociais no domínio do emprego: Análise das dinâmicas locais num contexto sócio-económico (pré)determinado: a Marinha Grande', Masters Thesis in Sociology, Faculty of Economics University of Coimbra.

Watt, A. (2003) 'Reform of the European Employment Strategy after five years: a change of course or merely of presentation?', paper presented at the seminar on the Regional and Local Dimension of the European Employment Strategy, Cordoba, 17 October.

ELEVEN

From government fragmentation to local governance: welfare reforms and lost opportunities in Italy

Yuri Kazepov and Angela Genova[1]

This chapter discusses the impact of new forms of local governance emerging in Italy as a result of welfare reforms that took place from 1990 to 2004. Particular attention is devoted to activation policies – policies aimed at combating the social exclusion of people in a condition of economic and social need by empowering or obligating individuals to attain autonomy from welfare dependency. These policies have been chosen because they represent a relatively innovative attempt in Europe to institutionalise new participatory practices involving multiple actors at the local level. Significantly, these policies have produced new governance arrangements in Italian social policy. Furthermore, no welfare reform is taking place in Europe without involving activation as a new approach to solving problems that had allegedly oppressed welfare finances and fostered claimants' passive attitudes. Nonetheless, the meaning of activation is ambiguous, covering quite heterogeneous policies (van Berkel and Hornemann Møller, 2002) and differs across countries.

Despite differences in social and economic policies, there are common features in an overall process of change in most industrialised countries. These include:

- consolidation of unemployment as a structural condition for part of the working-age population;
- increasing budgetary constraints within which welfare policies are developing;
- mainly market-oriented labour market reforms, which seek more flexibility;

- increasing transfer of welfare services to third sector agencies, implying the need for greater coordination and for new procedures to co-define means and goals of social policies with all actors involved;
- progressively more complex patterns of social exclusion, which increasingly exhibit individualised features and therefore require different perspectives and skills, for both understanding the issues at stake and planning adequate interventions; and
- a shift in rhetoric from passive to active measures in social policy debates.

From welfare government to welfare governance

Since the end of the 1970s, these elements have strongly affected the role of the state. The state has lost its centrality and autonomy and its various levels and institutions have become more fragmented and less unified. However, the changes have marginally affected the state's main functions; the state has maintained its power to regulate relationships between citizens, including extracting and redistributing resources between them. The state's power, however, has been radically reorganised, with the emergence of more complex networks among sub-national territorial levels, which have increased and institutionalised the number of actors involved in policy making. Similarly, the political system of the European Union (EU) has been transformed into a system of multi-level network governance (Kohler-Koch, 1999), in which subsidiarity seems the key regulatory principle.

In more differentiated (and fragmented) societies, the traditional method of governing from above is now inadequate for coping with the complexity so that the relationship between state, market and society has been reshaped towards a network model of governance (Loughlin, 2004) characterised by new partnership relations. These interlocked processes develop a wider system of governance that is providing 'new opportunities' and 'limits' to welfare policies. In western countries, a process of rescaling has transformed both government and governance. State power in many areas has moved from the national level down to regional or local sites, or out across local transnational networks (Brenner, 2004).

The shift from government to governance, however, has not involved the replacement of government with governance (Le Galès, 2002; Kazepov, 2004). Instead, the state and its apparatus have changed roles as key actors, alongside other (private) bodies, become more involved in coordinating new processes of governance. This trend has been described as a shift from government to metagovernance (Jessop, 2004).

In the EU, all nation states have been subject to common pressures, which have led to a degree of convergence in regard to an expanded role for governance. Nonetheless, within each EU country, political outcomes have been shaped by the existing modes of government and governance.

In Italy, these changes have combined to form a set of highly fragmented social policies that increasingly produce the perverse effects of inequality and inefficiency. Due to the particular way in which social stratification has developed geographically since the Second World War, people in the same condition of need, but living in different parts of the country, have access to different institutional resources.

Since 1990, Italian policy solutions proposed to counteract the negative effects of fragmentation and to regulate tendencies towards privatisation and individualisation, have foreseen increasing coordination among the different actors involved in local welfare production. New ideas about the relationship between citizens and the state entered the political agenda and began to change the institutional frame and the relationship between public and private spheres. Laws were enacted that introduced governance as a new way of regulating public interest, mainly through networks of actors at the local level, with subsidiary and/or complementary roles. Ongoing reforms in both labour market and social policies also emphasise that the local level is where problems should be solved through coordinated action among stakeholders. Massive legislative change in the 1990s made extensive use of concepts like 'collaboration', 'coordination' and 'networking', even providing ad hoc funding for such purposes. Localisation has occurred mainly through activation measures, which require the mobilisation of different local actors. Activation policies and the forms of governance they involve are becoming ever-more deeply embedded in a complex rescaling process, involving vertical, horizontal and transversal dimensions. The local level is embedded vertically in an increasing number of different institutional levels, from the neighbourhood to the EU, that have growing regulatory power. At the horizontal level, these policies and related governance involve increasingly differentiated actors (public, semi-public, private and third sector), linked together in designing, delivering and evaluating services. Transversally, activation measures attempt to overcome divisions, and create synergies, among areas of intervention (labour market policies, social assistance schemes, and so on).

This chapter discusses the context of the Italian case: its relevant actors, characteristics of welfare reform and the related process of rescaling. Specific attention is given to changes in labour market and social assistance policies occurring since 1990. In particular, it focuses on the relationship between welfare policy reforms, their impact and the emerging new forms of partnership and modes of governance. It is shown that in Italy the institutional design of social policy reforms has often lacked coherence, wide scope and foresight. These limitations have influenced the form and substance of emerging governance patterns and coordination arrangements. Our hypothesis is that each of these patterns is strongly influenced by the interplay between the territorially fragmented socioeconomic context and lack of institutional coherence in a frame of overall path dependence that makes change difficult to implement. This hypothesis ties in with recent typologies that seek to explain differences in modes of governance (Pierre, 1999; Geddes and Le Galès, 2001; Jessop, 2002; DiGaetano and Strom, 2003). Most authors agree that different institutional settings, with their structural contexts and political cultures, are more receptive to some modes of governance than others (DiGaetano and Strom, 2003). Jessop (2002, pp 247-55) goes further, stressing the relatively high degree of coherence between welfare regimes and emerging new forms of partnership and governance. These theoretical perspectives frame our analysis.

The Italian welfare system

The main features of the Italian welfare system as it developed after the Second World War are as follows (Flora, 1986; Ferrera, 1996, 2000; Saraceno, 2002):

- *Strong relationship between labour market participation and social protection*: except for health, provisions depend on the claimants' labour market position or the categories to which they belong (for example, lone parents, blue-collar workers in big or medium-sized firms, older people, and so on).
- *Strong subsidiarity*: the family plays a major role in cultural (church), economic (family businesses) and participatory aspects of social welfare; women have comparatively low employment activity rates

and heavy care responsibilities in a still-strong gender division of labour.

This well-known and synthetic picture is incomplete. To understand the Italian welfare system as the sum of all agencies producing welfare and interacting with one another, additional crucial distinctions from continental European countries need to be observed:

- *Strong north–south divide*: territorial imbalances characterise not only the socioeconomic structure, but also the institutional design of policies, which are often regionally and locally fragmented. The centre-northern regions are highly industrialised, where a diffused industrial sector comprised mainly of small- to medium-sized enterprises strengthens the occupational basis. In contrast, unemployment is high in the southern regions, where widespread informal work goes hand in hand with a subsistence economy. High income inequality is a consequence.
- *Underdeveloped safety net*: fragmented social policies, particularly in social assistance schemes, and a strong emphasis on pensions serve to reinforce inequalities in the redistributive system.
- *Weak and passive form of subsidiarity*: the state does not directly support families to maintain standards of living and overcome conditions of need, but provides direct support only to people in the labour market. The strong gender division of labour implicit in this form of subsidiarity results in very unbalanced household distributions of power.
- *Women and young people as particularly vulnerable groups*: this is especially true in the south, where high unemployment and very low labour market participation results in deprivation, in which female emancipation is unlikely to occur.

These characteristics have led several authors to classify Italy within a south European model of welfare (Leibfried, 1992; Mingione, 1996) and not within the conservative model as Esping-Andersen did (1990, 1999). Their main argument is that, despite evident commonalities with countries where welfare provisions are attached to contributory records, the above characteristics refer to a different regulatory principle (the family and reciprocity networks being crucial and strategic elements). These characteristics have been reproduced within the institutional settings of Italian labour and social policies from the Second World War up to the end of the 1970s. Starting from the 1980s – and most significantly since 1995 –

a deep process of reform took place involving rescaling and institutional competences and responsibilities. Inspired by the subsidiarity principle, reforms have assigned increasing regulatory power to local authorities in delivering social services, in defining eligibility criteria and in designing the overall policy scheme, thereby multiplying the actors involved in these processes.

This shift had the potential to set a process of deep change in motion. The innovativeness of the policies, however, clashed with the path-dependent tendency of existing institutional settings that are crucial to understanding the outcome of the reform processes. Path dependency should not be considered as a mere rhetorical device. Our hypothesis is that institutions that get structured over longer periods of time are deeply rooted and constrain choice, reducing the probability of path changes and preventing an evolutionary tendency. Taken-for-granted routines and practices tend to consolidate the existing institutional settings. They establish 'a system of nested rules, which are increasingly costly to change' (Goodin, 1996, p 23), producing a self-reinforcing effect over time. This view should not bring us to conceive institutions as only conservative. On the contrary, they are also enabling contexts. As Jessop and Nielsen (2003, p 4) put it: 'institutions always need to be re-interpreted and re-negotiated, they can never fully determine action; but nor do they permit any action whatsoever so that life is no more than the product of purely wilful contingency'. This implies that the path-dependent character of institutions has to do with the interplay of actors' opportunities and structural constraints. Paths might be changed, but this possibility has to be framed by the given contextual opportunities (Kazepov, 2004).

From passive to active social assistance schemes

From the post-war period to the end of the 1980s, Italian labour market policies were aimed mainly at protecting the breadwinner, thereby confining the risk of poverty while unemployed to the labour market entry level. In fact, once a person was in the labour market (with a secure regular job) that person was difficult for employers to dismiss. The rigid and fragmented nature of Italy's passive labour policies exacerbated the segmentation of the Italian labour market, increasing the difficulties for young people without work experience in finding work. In 1990, Italian adult males had the lowest unemployment rate in Europe: 1.6% compared with a EU average of 6.1%. This low rate was due to the fact that the vast majority of workless males were not considered to be unemployed because they were entitled to relatively generous measures like the *Cassa Integrazione Guadagni*, a scheme aimed at temporary wage compensation in case of economic crisis. Most former workers of large- and medium-sized manufacturing industries were covered by this measure. Workers who were not covered by the generous, insurance-based measures were covered by a much less generous scheme and only for up to 180 days. This policy environment defined a highly segmented access to social protection.[2]

The main reason for this segmentation and the lack of a coherent design for labour policies resulted from their introduction during political instability and on an emergency and temporary basis. These wait-and-see policies helped to contain significant social tensions and provided a functional equivalent to a non-existent unemployment benefit. As a result, unemployed people who were not covered by insurance and did not find a new job before their entitlement period expired, were left without any institutional help. This group was never very large in the northern regions, but is now increasing due to long-lasting industrial restructuring processes.

From the end of the 1980s this picture started to change. In 1996 Prime Minister Prodi introduced with the agreement of the main five trade unions the key reform to promote active labour policies. This reform opened the Italian labour market to atypical forms of work[3] and significantly reformed public employment services to increase the number of people benefiting from active measures in line with European Employment Strategy guidelines.[4]

Prime Minister Berlusconi signed the most recent reform in 2002. It was permeated by a welfare-to-work approach. Public employment services were reformed further, increasing the importance of private actors and activation measures, and introducing compulsory orientation meetings to define training programmes and job experiences in order to improve competitiveness and social inclusion.

In this new context, traditional passive labour policies have become irrelevant, because almost all new jobs fall under the statute of atypical work with virtually no social protection guarantees attached to them (Fargion, 2004). Furthermore, the new forms of social support have still to be fully implemented. Italian labour policies to the end of the 1990s paid scant attention to the institution of a last safety net. This was due to the fact that the great majority of the population was covered by contributory schemes (that is, families were protected through the position in the labour market of the

[male] breadwinner)[5] while assistance to particular categories of need (for example, the homeless, the poor who cumulate several conditions of need) was still seen as charity and a prerogative of voluntary, mainly Catholic, associations.

Labour policies and income support schemes have developed in an independent and irrational way; totally uncoordinated with each other. The changes in labour market policies since 1990 have significantly affected the redistributive power within the family, and consequently social assistance reform has become a crucial necessity. However, since 1977 policies targeted at people in a condition of economic and social need were the responsibility of the regional and local authorities. The lack of a national framework law left regions and municipalities in a legislative *vacuum* for more than 20 years (Negri and Saraceno, 1996; Kazepov, 2000). Only in November 2000 was a national framework law for social assistance finally approved. Until then, many regions had approved regional framework laws, although some did not. However, regions did not coordinate their efforts, so that there were different access criteria to benefits and services in different regions. Municipalities brought a further level of complexity by designing either specific rules for specific categories, often interpreting the framework law loosely and maintaining high discretion in the distribution of benefits. One main consequence of this complex morphology has been the consolidation of a differentiated system of social citizenship, whereby citizens are entitled to different sets of rights, related not so much to their condition of need, but to the specific eligibility rules and to the specific way in which social services are organised in the place where they live, exacerbated further by patronage arrangements. Moreover, in a context of budget constraints, claimants are categorised in target groups like minors, single mothers or older people.

These differences are seldom justified by specific local socioeconomic features, and in most cases are the result of political discretion. Discretionary power is supposed to prevent public services from a potential economic breakdown rather than to enable specific conditions of need to be addressed more adequately. As a result, a problematic lack of certainty in terms of the entitlements of people in need has occurred.

At the end of the 1990s, the rising vulnerability in the labour market stimulated social and political debate concerning activation measures and a new minimum income measure. As a result, the *Reddito Minimo di Inserimento* (RMI), the first national means-tested minimum income payment was tested for four years in order to overcome local differences in welfare services.

The changing scenario and new forms of governance

During the 1970s and 1980s the labour market and social assistance policies became increasingly inadequate in alleviating need in a society undergoing deep transformations. On the contrary, they reproduced high levels of inequality. This scenario began to change rapidly during the 1990s when reforms began to make labour market regulations more flexible, and labour policies and services more decentralised. These reforms were partly a result of European requirements (for example, the Maastricht Treaty and the European Monetary Union), although they were introduced considerably later than in most European countries. Access to income maintenance for the unemployed was widened by extending eligibility to new categories previously excluded, but duration and generosity were tightened. Consequently the previously well-protected family breadwinners exposed to mass industrial dismissals began to face conditions of vulnerability within more flexible market relations.

The new framework law (328/2000) on social assistance and social services tried to address this situation of increased vulnerability and fragmentation by defining some general eligibility criteria. According to this law the state has the responsibility for defining the 'essential levels for social interventions' (*Livelli assistenziali essenziali – LIVEAS*) and to structure social policies by providing guidelines to regions and municipalities.

The process of territorial reorganisation implied by this law is embedded in a wider trend of changing the institutional relationship between state, regions and local authorities. The 2001 revision of the Italian constitution entailed a new role for municipalities which became, according to the principle of subsidiarity, the main actors of social policies within a context in which regions have gained the legislative power over most policy areas (health, education and means-tested income maintenance, social assistance). The devolution process of administrative responsibilities, planned at the constitutional level in 2001, has still to be fully defined in the details and implemented. In early 2005, the definition of regional competences was under discussion in the Parliament, but it is not difficult to foresee an increasing regional differentiation maintaining and even reinforcing existing inequalities.

The subsidiarity principle underlying this process stresses the local community as the most suitable context to face local needs. Law 285/1997, containing 'Provisions for the promotion of the rights and opportunities of children and adolescents', represented one of the first and most innovative examples of this trend. Considerable financial resources were made available to local communities, and have enabled a widespread network of services to be set up throughout the whole country with the objective of improving the living conditions of children and adolescents. The law has represented an instrument for changing the system of Italian social and educational policies. It has proved to be innovative in various aspects, first of all calling for institutions, civil society and the third sector to become involved in a shared and responsible approach to planning and managing actions.

This approach has been also subsumed by law 328/2000 confirming the common European path towards a multi-level governance process. The emphasis on the local dimension, however, seems to put citizenship rights in Italy again in the hands of local discretion. Local social policies are defined in *Piani di Zona* (area plans), that is, concerted planning documents agreed by the actors of the *Ambito* (the area), which includes one larger municipality or a group of small municipalities and the relevant stakeholders representing the territorial unit for social policies.

Most Italian regions (but not all) have been involved in defining *Piani di Zona*; however, the results have been quite varied due to differences in the quality of interaction among actors and the contents and consequences of area plans (Gori, 2004). The main welfare policy challenge is to increase the role of area plans, moving from a locally fragmented (even though) concerted planning document towards a concerted and integrated system of social services within the *Ambito*. The implementation and operation of the new national framework law is made more complex by the 2001 constitutional reform that attributed welfare competences to the regions, and generated big and long-lasting transition problems in a regulative context where differences persist and are legitimated from the institutional point of view. The nation state no longer has the power to provide guidelines. On the contrary, regions are now fully autonomous on all welfare issues except for defining the basic level of welfare provisions. Nonetheless, in 2005, after five years, the state has still not defined the *LIVEAS*, leaving space for a high degree of discretion at the local level (municipalities, provinces, regions).

In this context, one of the most innovative policies, the RMI (a minimum income scheme with active and empowering tools), has been withdrawn and substituted with the *Reddito di Ultima Istanza* (RUI, last-level income support), which has still to be implemented. The problem lies in the fact that, after the constitutional reform, the RUI became a regional responsibility, with no institutionalised activation measure attached to it. Lacking *LIVEAS* and targeted funding, the RUI lost its appeal and did not become a priority for the regions. Even though rich regions also did not implement it, the poorer ones will remain trapped in a self-reinforcing vicious circle (Gori, 2004).

Some critical issues in the transformation trend

As mentioned before, Italian welfare reforms converged in identifying the local dimension as the locus of action. This trend brought about some major problems, related to the unsynchronised character of the ongoing reforms and to their territorial articulation. The problem of unsynchronised change results from the fact that, since 1991, there has been a big coverage gap, which has been overcome only through institutional flexibility and emergency legislation. As we have seen, access to unemployment benefits has widened to cover more categories of workers, but the period of benefit eligibility has shortened, and no national minimum income scheme is in place. Therefore, when an unemployed person's unemployment benefit expires, they do not have a safety net to rely on.

The continuous approval of amendments and extensions to unemployment benefits is a clear example of the existing mismatch in covering emerging social risks. This trend has greatly affected the risk of becoming poor in Italy. In fact, the status passage implicit in the shift from the generous temporary lay-offs to the mobility lists and then eventually to the ordinary unemployment benefit does not automatically entitle claimants to means-tested social assistance once the former benefits are over, at least not in all cities and not for all groups at risk. The consequent institutional vulnerability necessarily implies a higher dependence on the family. But socio-demographic changes[6] also tend to weaken the family's support capacity by increasing the risks of poverty for particularly vulnerable groups, such as children and/or young people within single-parent families or within households with an unemployed breadwinner, or single non-self-sufficient older person.

The second main problem results from the local impact of the ongoing processes of decentralisation and privatisation of employment services. First, the most active municipalities – which are mainly the ones of the centre-north where unemployment rates are low – will develop efficient services with clearly articulated and participative partnership agreements, while the most disadvantaged municipalities (in the south) – which have greater need for adequate activation policies – will not succeed in building up an efficient set of activation programmes, nor will they develop new partnership agreements or networks, thus exacerbating the north–south divide. Second, private placement services are likely to concentrate in the most dynamic regions, mainly the big cities and only on the qualified workers.

The public will thus have to take care of the most marginal cases, concentrated in poorer regions, thereby leading to a self-reinforcing tendency to failure. In other words, instead of enabling better interventions targeted on the specific contextual problem, too much flexibility at the local level could reproduce existing inequalities. Local needs have to be considered, but living conditions should not be too divergent. Signs of a perpetuation of the north–south divide are already evident.

Activation reforms and the lost opportunities for local governance

The experience of the RMI testing demonstrates the negative consequences of the unsynchronised character of welfare reforms upon governance arrangements and their resulting territorial articulations. The Italian RMI is addressed to people who are not able to financially maintain themselves and their families and who eventually suffer psychological, physical and social disadvantages. It seeks to be the last safety net by covering areas of need poorly protected by other measures. When introduced, the RMI sought to reduce discretion, which was characteristic of access to social assistance provisions. This may not seem a relevant task, compared to other European countries, but in southern Europe the RMI had path-breaking potential. It consists of a monetary benefit granted to people with an income below a given threshold, together with different personalised in-kind forms of support and activation. In order to maintain eligibility, beneficiaries are asked to undertake specific obligations, outlined in personalised contracts (for example, accepting adequate job opportunities and completing compulsory schooling). Means-testing rules were consistently applied throughout Italy in the municipalities involved in the test.

The activation measures and the attached in-kind support were aimed at helping individuals overcome social marginality by preventing the drift towards dependency and improving quality of life mainly through work and ad hoc social inclusion projects. In terms of governance, this policy has institutionalised the participation of several actors and different resources have been mobilised, resulting in the need for strong coordination among policies and actors.

The testing phase of the RMI showed that solutions varied widely: from clearly articulated forms of pervasive government that coordinates different pre-existing publicly run social services, to co-defined goals with third sector agencies and associations institutionalised in long-term partnership agreements with consistent flows of different kinds of resources. Within these two extremes lots of mixes were possible, but one element has always been crucial: inter-institutional collaboration at the various levels had to be agreed and legitimised by the respective hierarchies. For instance, the National Insurance Board (INPS) had to allow social services to check data on income at the local level in order to verify eligibility of claimants; public employment services have to be able to develop one-stop-shops with local social service providers without too many bureaucratic obstacles; and so on.

The actors of local governance arrangements

The implementation of activation measures – often provided through partnership agreements with third sector associations – is one of the new terrains in which the local dimension of governance is particularly evident. Here actors have begun to interact in new ways, aiming partly at common goals, building up networks and trying to find new and innovative solutions by sharing visions and commitments. In fact, different public services (social, psychiatric, training, families) have often worked together on multi-problematic cases. The new governance arrangements has meant not only coordination among different sectors within the one municipal administration, but has also involved other parties.

The new regulative framework of welfare policies (328/2000) institutionalised the 'mixity' of the Italian welfare system (Ascoli and Ranci, 2002), thereby recognising and legitimising the important role played by non-profit organisations in welfare services. Consequently, the increasing externalisation of the delivery of many social policies has produced a plurality of actors involved in policy implementation, each with different interests, goals and priorities. Besides the actors traditionally involved in dealing with unemployment and social exclusion issues at the local level (namely municipal social services and local public employment services) numerous other actors with different institutional roles are now to be found, such as volunteers' associations, social cooperatives and non-profit and for-profit firms. In addition, within each institutional structure there is a diversity of roles, capacities and profiles (psychologists, teachers, mediators, social workers, professional trainers and counsellors). Among these actors, here we concentrate on one who is providing social work under new conditions, which we consider particularly emblematic of the changes occurring in the street-level everyday development of activation policies.

This new form of social worker plays an increasingly important role because they contribute to defining and carrying out the specific policy measures. However, they are not social workers in the technical sense, as they most often do not have a degree in social work and are seldom employees of public structures. Rather, they work in cooperative firms or are contracted by the municipality. Generally, they do not have a specific professional profile with a clearly defined career and are less protected in their job contract than in the past. They are tutors or cultural mediators and their responsibility is to define a recipient's activation programme, to supervise its implementation and to mediate between the different social actors taking part in the process (for example, recipients, social workers from the municipality, psychologists, employers, colleagues and professional teachers).

The contracting-out process (Ascoli and Ranci, 2002) has redistributed responsibility for service provision, which used to be exclusively public (state or municipal). Today, new providers who are often third sector agencies have primary responsibility, while local authorities, who are ultimately responsible for the provision, play only a secondary role. This means that each of the two parties involved can blame the others in case of shortages, delays or failures in provision (Freedland, 1998). In this way, weak relations between professionals, the municipality and the agencies providing social services threaten the process of building up new forms of governance. This also creates confusion in terms of their accountability. The big challenge lies in the need to change the mentality of actors (Bifulco and Vitale, 2004) by limiting the use of discretion, which has been so diffused in previous decades when administrative and social work responsibilities were mixed. This challenge intersects with the increasing plurality of actors involved in the delivery of provisions, in-kind services and activation programmes, giving a different meaning to discretion. For example, third sector actors are less likely to limit access than traditional social workers, even though they face budget constraints that limit both their working time and the options they have in designing activation projects. The plurality of actors demands coordination and clear guidelines about the use of discretion in order to avoid reproducing inequalities.

Within this frame, beneficiaries are the other actor of activation policies. They are the (relatively passive) target of the policy, not active subjects, or bearers of rights and competences. They are considered to have acquired new rights, but their capacities have to be built. They need to develop their capability for voice (Sen, 1992, 1999; Bonvin and Farvaque, 2006: forthcoming). They are generally not involved in the development and evaluation of programmes. Even though activation plans are defined and agreed upon by all parties and are increasingly negotiated, there is a strict hierarchical asymmetry between the claimant, the social worker and the people implementing the activation plan. This is due to many reasons, not least the fact that these programmes have so far mostly selected extreme cases with cumulative deprivation, highly lacking in motivation and unaware of their own resources. For these reasons they aim at making these 'objects of intervention' new 'competent subjects'. In practice, this approach is still to be fully implemented as, for instance, claimants do not have institutionalised feedback mechanisms. Yet, most beneficiaries perceive the activation programme as a coherent path they undertake, and this is a sign of how coordination and governance processes impact on their experience as well. Claimants become clearly aware of the lack of coordination when links between the different phases and organisations are not as clear as they could and should be. The number of innovative cases addressing this issue is growing, but they remain an exception.

Beneficiaries' capability for voice is a long way from being implemented. In fact, such an achievement requires the deep involvement of claimants in the definition of all phases from the design of the activation measure to its implementation.

New forms of governance and underlying processes

As we have seen, context plays a major role in structuring the forms of local governance. Our analysis shows that in Italy these forms are changing extensively even though they maintain a strong path-dependent character. The socioeconomic structure, within which cities are embedded, as well as the welfare system, influence the process of change locally.

In order to analyse how processes produce new forms of governance in the development of socioeconomic activation schemes targeted to people in economic and social need, case studies have been conducted in 12 Italian cities.[7]

Despite the heterogeneity of the socioeconomic contexts and the different activation measures developed at the local level, some important common elements emerge from the case studies.

Within all cases the (implicit) rhetoric of governance is always framed positively:

- The measures are more effective when actors share the main goals and the choice of the means to be used, when they agree on the division of labour and resource allocation. If this coordination exists, it fosters a holistic view of the problem.
- Checking eligibility and means testing, which are important in avoiding fraud and inequalities, are more effective in contexts where different bodies collaborate actively in providing information and support as needed.
- Problem solving seems to be the most popular function of governance coordination arrangements. The various public and non-profit actors emphasise that, when the vision is implicitly shared, it helps overcome many problems.

For social workers employed within the public administration, the emerging forms of governance are most often seen as forms of coordination that mainly imply the exchange of information, whereas shared views are often taken for granted, as if all agree on what the problems are and on the possible solutions. This is a simplistic view and few social workers and social services officials seem to be aware of the fact that the new forms of governance change the overall delivery of social welfare provisions. They experiment in their daily work with the advantages of good coordination practices, in terms of the efficacy of interventions, of coherency among the various activation phases and of smooth communication flows. Nevertheless, they also know that there are several obstacles to be overcome, including the difficulties resulting from the different goals, languages and links of the different institutions involved.

The different roles played by the actors involved, as well as their different governing relations and rationalities, contribute to define different political objectives and, in so doing, outline different modes of governance. DiGaetano and Strom (2003) classify modes of governance into five ideal types (Geddes and Le Galès, 2001; Jessop, 2002; Kazepov, 2004).

The *clientelistic* mode is characterised by individual and personalised relationships among politicians and clients or favoured interests, who interact pragmatically to reach selective benefits. The *corporatist* mode pursues programmatic aims by promoting negotiation and compromise among public and private actors, and building consensus among exclusionary ruling coalitions of powerful economic and/or community interests. The *managerial* mode of governance is marked by formal, bureaucratic and contractual relations between government officials and private sector interests (Pierre, 1999), leading to authoritative decisions. In the *pluralist* mode, government is the arena of competition among private interests, in which it brokers, bargains and manages conflicts. The *populist* mode of governance is characterised by the mobilisation of popular support through politicians and community movement leaders pursuing symbolic political objectives.

In Italy, the traditional territorial differences interact with the different modes of governance and give rise to a wide variety of activation measures and services, thereby perpetuating fragmentation in welfare policies. The strong territorial fragmentation in Italy means that there are examples of all these modes of governance in the different regions, and also within single regions. A clear divide seems, however, to emerge. Northern regions adopt a more managerial and pluralist mode of governance, with some populist enclaves. Central regions follow more corporatist and negotiated modes of governance, while southern regions present a mix of clientelistic and populist modes, with some – either corporatist or pluralist – enclaves.

Conclusions

The increasing number of actors participating in the design and delivery of local social policies (*Piani di Zona*, area plans) opens up opportunities for new forms of local governance. Although, considering both the overall context within which the process of social policy reform occurs and our case studies, it clearly emerges that, even where new coordination initiatives were well established, the development of new governance arrangements is still at an early stage if not totally absent (Pesaresi, 2003). In particular, linking social policy innovation and governance to promote local economic growth and competitiveness is poorly addressed in Italy. One can observe some feeble attempts but they have little chance to really influence and change the status quo, especially in the most deprived areas where this approach is most needed.

The problem results from the fact that activation policies often have to make up for other policies, especially in Italy's fragmented and particularistic welfare system. This issue is crucial and points to a broader problem of coordination between administratively managed benefits and insertion schemes, and also between these schemes and structural economic policies. Structural public policies and investments – which are public competition goods (Le Galès and Voelzkow, 2001) – must focus on this goal, to foster institutional capacities that decrease territorial inequality. If no synergy for local development can be created, the divide between contexts with different socioeconomic opportunities and institutional structures will increase. Some good practices occur in areas where effective coordination among different kinds of measures and resources has been attempted (for example, area contracts, law 285 on children's support, RMI, EU Urban programmes and the European Social Fund). In this sense, local economic growth and social inclusion and cohesion are not contradictory goals, but interdependent.[8]

However, the shift in recent decades in both political rhetoric and scientific literature towards the local and urban causes of social exclusion may be misleading. The local focus may hide some of the national and supranational mechanisms producing social exclusion, thereby allowing policy makers to foster mainly cosmetic interventions at the local level, rather than produce more effective reforms in fiscal policy, for instance, in achieving a more just distribution (Castel, 1991; Pahl, 2001).

A solution that promises greater social inclusion by simply decentralising governance through partnership and participation in all sectors of the populations both mystifies and underestimates the goal of social justice as just redistribution (Fainstein, 2001). From this perspective, governance should be a means, not an end, in establishing a virtuous cycle between growth and inclusion. Yet, the impacts of governance patterns on the relationship between these two goals are not predictable in every context, especially in Italy's fragmented welfare state. The future challenge is to identify practices that balance social justice (enabling social inclusion) and economic growth through competitiveness, by addressing the two issues directly in their mutual relations, and combining a local participative perspective with a more just and redistributive one. Presently, the rescaling process of Italian labour market and social assistance policies does not go in this direction, but reinforces inequality by not backing up new labour market flexibility with measures that adequately tackle the increasing risk of social exclusion. The lack of nationally defined basic standards (*Livelli assistenziali essenziali*) lets different modes of local governance emerge according to the institutional milieu of the local municipalities and the resources available to them instead of existing needs.

Notes

[1] Many thanks go to Stefania Sabatinelli, who contributed to an earlier version of this chapter and some of the projects on which it is based. Eduardo Barberis should also be gratefully mentioned here. He provided extensive comments on an earlier version of the chapter.

[2] Until the late 1980s, the ordinary unemployment benefit corresponded to the ridiculously low amount of around €0.4 per day per person and was granted only to people who had worked a given number of days before unemployment. Now the benefit corresponds to 40% of the last wage.

[3] The new atypical forms of work have been regulated by the so-called *Riforma Biagi*, law 30 of 2003.

[4] In 1997, responsibility for active labour policies shifted from the central state to regions and provinces. Regional commissions are in charge of planning and auditing labour policies; while provinces deal with managing job placement services (Decree 469 of 1997).

[5] Adult males had and still have one of the lowest unemployment rates in Europe while young people have one of the highest ones. The latter were supposed to be in care of the former (passive subsidiarity) and therefore there seemed to be no need for a minimum safety net.

[6] Italy is undergoing major socio-demographic changes: (a) a drop in the fertility rate (1.2 children per woman); (b) a decrease of family median size (45.2% of couples has only one child); (c) an increase of divorces and separations (the latter have increased by 100% since 1990, although still limited in absolute terms); and (d) an ageing of the population, due to growth of life expectancy (75 years for men and 83 for women).

[7] The case studies were carried out within two research projects between 2000 and 2004. The first project was funded by the European Foundation in Dublin, under the title 'Integrated approaches to active welfare and employment policies' (Kazepov and Sabatinelli, 2000). It involved Bolzano, Cologno Monzese and Naples. The second project (2003-05) was funded by the Italian Minister for University and Research and analyses 'The new forms of governance in Italian social assistance schemes'. It involved Turin, Milan, Bologna, Florence, Ancona, Rome, Naples, Bari and Cosenza.

[8] Nevertheless, especially in the southern regions, these initiatives often encounter severe problems related to organised crime in the distribution of public resources.

References

Ascoli, U. and Ranci, C. (eds) (2002) *Dilemmas of the welfare mix: The new structure of welfare in an era of privatization*, New York: Kluwer Academic Press.

Bifulco, L. and Vitale, T. (2004) 'Contracting of social policies in local welfare: a change in position of the recipients?', paper for the II Espanet Conference, Oxford, 9-11 September.

Bonvin, J.-M. and Farvaque, N. (2006: forthcoming) 'Capability for work and capability for voice', in S. Deneulin, M. Nebel and N. Sagovsky (eds) *Capability and justice: Towards structural transformation*, New York: Kluwer Academic Press.

Brenner, N. (2004) *New state spaces: Urban governance and the rescaling of statehood*, Oxford: Oxford University Press.

Castel, R. (1991) 'De l'indigence à l'exclusion, la désaffiliation: précarité du travail et vulnérabilité relationnelle', in J. Denzelot (ed) *Face a l'exclusion, le modele francais*, Paris: Editions Esprit.

Censis (2003) *37 rapporto censis*, Milan: Franco Angeli.

DiGaetano, A. and Strom, E. (2003) 'Comparative urban governance: an integrated approach', *Urban Affairs Review*, vol 38, no 3, pp 356-95.

Esping-Andersen, G. (1990) *The three worlds of welfare capitalism*, Cambridge: Polity Press.

Esping-Andersen, G. (1999) *Social foundations of post-industrial economies*, Oxford: Oxford University Press.

Fainstein, S. (2001) 'Competitiveness, cohesion and governance: their implications for social justice', *International Journal of Urban and Regional Research*, vol 25, no 4, pp 884-8.

Fargion, V. (2004) 'From the Southern to the Northern question: territorial and social politics in Italy', in N. McEwen and L. Moreno (eds) *The territorial politics of welfare*, London: Routledge, pp 127-47.

Ferrera, M. (1996) 'The southern model of welfare in Social Europe', *Journal of European Social Policies*, vol 6, no 1, pp 17-37.

Ferrera, M. (2000) 'Reforms guided by consensus: the welfare state in the Italian transition', in M. Ferrera and M. Rhodes (eds) *Recasting the European welfare state*, London: Frank Cass, pp 187-208.

Flora, P. (ed) (1986) *Growth to limits: The western European welfare state since World War II*, New York/Berlin: De Gruyter.

Freedland, M. (1998) 'Law, public services and citizenship – new domains, new regimes?', in M. Freedland and S. Sciarra (eds) *Public services and citizenship in European law*, Oxford: Oxford University Press, pp 1-34.

Geddes, M. and Le Galès, P. (2001) 'Local partnerships, welfare regimes and local governance: a process of regime restructuring?', in M. Geddes and J. Benington (eds) *Local partnerships and social exclusion in the EU*, London: Routledge, pp 220-41.

Goodin, R. (1996) *The theory of institutional design*, Cambridge: Cambridge University Press.

Gori, C. (ed) (2004) *La riforma dei servizi sociali in Italia: L'attuazione della legge 328 e le sfide future*, Roma: Carocci.

Jessop, B. (2002) *The future of capitalist state*, Cambridge: Polity Press.

Jessop, B. (2004) *The European Union and recent transformation in statehood* (online), Department of Sociology, Lancaster University, available at: www.comp.lancs.ac.uk/sociology/papers/jessop-eu-transformations-statehood.pdf

Jessop, B. and Nielsen, K. (2003) *Institutions and rules: Research Papers: Network institutional theory*, No. 11/03, Roskilde: Institut for Samfundsvidenskab og Erhvervsøkonomi, Roskilde, Denmark.

Kazepov, Y. (2000) *Italia, Europa: Il Rmi tra sperimentazione e generalizzazione: Prospettive sociali e sanitarie anno XXX*, No. 20/22, Milan: Irs, Milano.

Kazepov, Y. (ed) (2004) *Cities of Europe: Changing contexts, local arrangements and the challenge to urban cohesion*, Oxford: Blackwell.

Kazepov, Y. and Sabatinelli, S. (2000) *The missing link: Fragmentation and coordination in social policies in Italy*, Report for the European Foundation for the Improvement of Living and Working Conditions, Dublin.

Kohler-Koch, B. (1999) 'The evolution and transformation of European Governance', in B. Kohler-Koch and R. Eising (eds) *The transformation of governance in the European Union*, London: Routledge, pp 14-35.

Le Galès, P. (2002) *European cities: Social conflict and governance*, Oxford: Oxford University Press.

Le Galès, P. and Voelzkow, H. (2001) 'The governance of local economies in Europe', in C. Crouch, P. Le Galès, C. Trigilia and H. Voelzkow (eds) *Local industrial systems in Europe: rise or demise?*, Oxford: Oxford University Press, pp 1-24.

Leibfried, S. (1992) 'Towards a European welfare state? On integrating poverty regimes into the European community', in Z. Ferge and J.E. Kolberg (eds) *Social policy in a Changing Europe*, Boulder, CO: Westview Press, pp 245-79.

Loughlin, L. (2004) 'The "transformation" of governance: new directions in policy and politics', *Australian Journal of Politics and History*, vol 50, no 1, pp 8-22.

Mingione, E. (ed) (1996) *Urban poverty and the underclass*, Oxford: Blackwell.

Negri, N. and Saraceno, C. (1996) *Le politiche contro la povertà in Italia*, Bologna: Il Mulino.

Pahl, R. (2001) 'Market success and social cohesion', *International Journal of Urban and Regional Research*, vol 25, no 4, pp 879-83.

Pesaresi, F. (2003) 'La governance dei piani sociali di zona', *Prospettive Sociali e Sanitarie*, vol 20, pp 1-7.

Pierre, J. (1999) 'Models of urban governance: the institutional dimension of urban politics', *Urban Affairs Review*, vol 34, no 3, pp 372-96.

Rebeggiani (with D. Bubbico) (1999) 'Politiche attive del lavoro e struttura dellíoccupazione giovanile nel Mezzogiorno', paper presented at Consiglio Nazionale delle Ricerdil (CNR), Rome, 28-29 January.

Saraceno, C. (ed) (2002) *Social assistance dynamics in Europe. National and local poverty regimes*, Bristol: The Policy Press.

Sen, A.K. (1992) *Inequality reexamined*, Oxford: Oxford University Press.

Sen, A.K. (1999) *Development as freedom*, Oxford: Oxford University Press.

van Berkel, R. and Hornemann Møller, I. (eds) (2002) *Active social policies in the EU: Inclusion through participation?*, Bristol: The Policy Press.

TWELVE

Reforming welfare governance: reflections

Paul Henman and Menno Fenger

The implementation and ongoing administration of policies is long regarded as a key factor in the success or failure of public policies. Furthermore, many studies (for example, Mashaw, 1983; Lipsky, 1980; Clarke et al, 2000; Clarke and Newman, 1997) have demonstrated that the way in which public policy is administered significantly contributes to the nature and effects of the welfare state, particularly as they pertain to citizen–state relations. It is therefore surprising that in the proliferation of comparative welfare state studies, the practical and implementational side of welfare has received relatively less attention.

The chapters in this book have provided a first, general overview of the contribution a comparative practical approach of welfare reform might offer to contemporary welfare state studies. They show the effects of the implementation of both 'governance' and 'New Public Management' (NPM) principles, which have highly influenced welfare administration since the 1990s, in reconfiguring the nature and experience of welfare claimants, welfare staff and welfare agencies. By focusing on the changing institutional participants of welfare administration and practices of administering and managing welfare delivery, the authors in this volume have gone beyond the more traditional approach in welfare state research that focuses on welfare reform policies, causes and consequences. In our view, it is these implementational and practical aspects of welfare reform that are necessary to understand the full nature and effects of welfare reform.

In this final chapter, we focus first on the overall lessons that might be learnt from the chapters in this book. Following the structure of the book, we begin by focusing on the changing *participants* in welfare administration, followed by an analysis of the impact of welfare reform on the street-level *practices* in welfare agencies and a discussion of the spaces of welfare administration *processes* as they increasingly move beyond their traditional base of the nation state. This section also focuses on the interrelatedness of the separate elements of our 'triple P' framework. Analysing the participants, practices and processes from an integrative perspective makes clear that three different logics of welfare administration might be distinguished. These logics shape the implementation of welfare reform in a way that is comparable to the way in which Esping-Andersen's (1990) welfare regimes shape the development of welfare policies. The second section recalls the governance–governmentality framework that was developed in Chapter Two, and examines the observations from the book's chapters from this perspective. This illustrates the value of governance and governmentality frameworks for understanding the nature and effects of both the administration of welfare reform and the reform of welfare administration. Finally, we reflect on the implications of the approach that stood central in the book for the future of welfare state research. Unlike Kasza (2002), we do not reject the idea of general comparative welfare state research, but we do support his call for more in-depth, policy-specific research. From our perspective, this research should thereby take in mind the crucial role of implementation and ongoing administration in the delivery of welfare services.

Welfare administration: changing participants, processes and practices

This book aims to identify and analyse issues of implementation that are connected with the processes of welfare reform found throughout the developed world. In this section we highlight some general lessons on the changing participants, practices and processes from the contributions in this book.

Participants

The landscape of actors involved in welfare administration has changed dramatically since the 1990s. New actors have entered the stage; familiar actors have changed their appearance or disappeared from the stage. The most prominent feature of the chapters in this book is the changing role of non-governmental organisations (NGOs) in the administration of welfare. In the past, the role of NGOs in welfare has varied considerably in welfare states, from the active involvement of social partners in the form of trades unions and church-based agencies in continental welfare states to the marginalisation of NGOs in state-dominated welfare provision in liberal welfare states. Furthermore, NGOs vary in terms of their institutional set-up, from private, for-profit organisations, to not-for-profit secular or faith-based charities.

The contributions from White, Fenger and Barnes in this book (Part One: Chapters Three to Five) make clear that through welfare reform processes, NGOs are subject to two opposite forces. On the one hand, their involvement in welfare administration aims to increase the link between civil society and welfare administration. White (Chapter Three) argues that the formalisation of state–third sector relations represents a strategy for rebuilding the capacity of the welfare state in the wake of the neo-liberal attack of the 1980s and 1990s. On the other hand, the performance of NGOs, particularly their efficiency and effectiveness, has obtained increasing attention from governments. This has become especially pronounced as NGOs are increasingly used as the organisational means through which government-funded benefits and services are provided. Previously independent and self-funded NGOs are incorporated in governmental activities. The relation between governments and NGOs shifts from subsidising and cooperation to contracting. This implies that the neo-liberal market incentives affect the role and functioning of NGOs (compare: Smith and Lipsky, 1993). In particular, the chapter by Barnes (Chapter Five) demonstrates the way in which the enrolment of NGOs into government welfare provision has transformed NGOs from voluntary-based and care-focused organisations to more streamlined organisations run along more business and professional lines. This transformation of NGOs from charities to professional organisations is not isolated to the domain of welfare administration, but it clearly manifests itself in this domain, as the chapters by Barnes and Ramia (Chapters Five and Nine) illustrate. Competitive government funding concurrently reconfigures client–NGO relationships. Welfare services that were distributed on a rationality of need, are increasingly replaced with a logic of deservingness based on likely results and client outcomes. Clients with entrenched and hard-to-address problems are marginalised in preference to clients with better prospects. The chapters of Handler, Howard and Wright (Part Two: Chapters Six to Eight) repeat these observations in their studies of workfare in the US, Australia and the UK respectively.

Fenger (Chapter Four) illustrates the wide variety of NGO involvement in welfare administration across countries. Although NGOs are undeniably becoming more important in contemporary welfare states their role varies from contract partners in welfare states that are moving in a neo-liberal, NPM direction to networking partners in countries that seek to undo some of the effects of the neo-liberal reforms (compare: Considine and Lewis, 2003).

Practices

The way in which welfare reform affects street-level workers is a crucial topic when focusing on the practical side of welfare administration. Whereas some authors claim that the era of information and communication technology (ICT) and managerialism has limited discretionary powers of street-level workers (compare: Bovens and Zouridis, 2002; Evans and Harris, 2004), the chapters of Handler, Howard and Wright in this volume (Chapters Six to Eight) illustrate the continuing significance of street-level workers' roles in welfare administration. Partially following Sandfort (2000), three types of street-level implementation might be distinguished. First, the 'traditional bureaucratic' type, which has been designed to minimise discretion and variation, increase efficiency and centralise control. Second, the NPM type, which focuses on outcomes or performance instead of procedures, and uses quasi-market mechanisms to control street-level bureaucrats. Finally, the 'governance' type of implementation, which views the street-level bureaucrat as a builder of harmonic relations with a wide variety of actors, including clients and potential employers.

The chapters in Part Two on the street-level side of welfare administration illustrate without exception the trilemma in which street-level bureaucrats are caught in the welfare reform era. They are supposed to act on behalf of state or private agencies, serve the interests of potential employers of their unemployed clients and take care of the interests of their clients at the same time. The chapters also reveal a concurrent tension for staff in eligibility testing for benefits, versus the new onus on employment services and activation requirements. These triple loyalties might be regarded as an additional trigger for the routines that street-level workers developed and that are, for instance, described in Lipsky's seminal work (Lipsky, 1980). So despite attempts to control street-level processes by either using new ICTs to reinforce bureaucratic control mechanisms or creating new quasi-market control mechanisms, the increasingly multiple loyalties of street-level workers might account for the limited effects of these strategies. The era of welfare reform definitely has not simplified the work of street-level bureaucrats or abolished their discretionary powers. Rather, the nature of administrative discretion is recast (Dearman, 2005).

Processes

Until the last decade of the 20th century, the concept of the welfare state was intangibly connected with the nation state. However, Castells (2000) argued that in the 'information age', economic, social and cultural processes go beyond the borders of the nation state.[1] According to him, the nation state lost its place as a central focal point for all kinds of processes, and was being replaced simultaneously by both the international and the local level. He argued that growing international interdependencies force policy makers to focus on the international level, whereas at the same time the specific consequences of these international interdependencies manifest themselves at the local level. For instance, a multinational's decision to relocate a production unit from Europe to East Asia is a decision that illustrates the international level of operation of most multinationals, but at the same time the consequences of the closure of this unit are manifested at the local level, in the town in which the unit was situated.

The chapters of Ramia, Valadas, and Kazepov and Genova (Part Three: Chapters Nine to Eleven) clearly show that this tendency of simultaneous upscaling and downscaling of governance issues also might be found in the field of welfare policies. The emergence of international NGOs and their involvement in processes of welfare administration on the one hand, and the slow but steady development of social policies at the European level on the other (see Hemerijck, 2002; de la Porte and Nanz, 2004), are clear examples in this volume of the growing international scale in which welfare policies are developed, administered and implemented. At the same time, the chapters of Handler, Valadas, and Kazepov and Genova (Chapters Six, Ten and Eleven) underline the importance of decentralisation in welfare administration. Welfare reform has replaced the traditional bureaucracy that formed the base of welfare administration in almost all countries with either neo-liberal managerial forms of administration or with consensual, 'governance' forms. Both types have in common that they are now much more sensitive to the context in which they operate than the traditional bureaucracy was. So in addition to the trend of simultaneous internationalisation and localisation that Castells has identified, the introduction of either neo-liberal or 'governance' welfare reforms requires a reinforcement of the role of local-level organisations in welfare administration.

The localisation of welfare administration cannot be interpreted as a simple decentralisation of governance or managerial power. As is well documented in the literature examining NPM, such decentralisation processes are, somewhat paradoxically, often accompanied with a reinforcing centralisation. Central governmental powers accede day-to-day decision making and management processes to tighter definition and continual monitoring of performance objectives. Local agency operations can become more independent – and often are through outsourcing and marketisation – although tightly controlled in agency objectives and funding. This double-shift is particularly evident in the chapters by Barnes and Howard (Chapters Five and Seven).

The localisation of welfare administration might also reinforce regional differences in prosperity. On the one hand, localisation of welfare administration provides increased sensitivity and flexibility to local circumstances (see Valadas's chapter, Chapter Ten), but on the other hand it may also mean a localisation of risk that resembles Beck's notion of the individualisation of risk (compare: Beck, 1992). Whereas the wealthy and privileged regions can maintain more generous welfare benefits and services for their citizens, benefits and services in poorer regions are minimal because they cannot afford a more sophisticated level. These increasing regional differences ultimately are reflected in the participants and practices in welfare administration at the local level.

Towards three models of welfare administration

From the discussion of the insights of the three parts of this book, we can distillate three 'ideal types' of welfare administration: a bureaucratic type, an NPM type and a governance type. Table 12.1 summarises the key elements of each of these types.

The traditional bureaucratic model of welfare administration relies on state agencies as the central actors. These state agencies preferably operate on the national level, thereby safeguarding equity and equality in both programmes and implementation. These values are safeguarded by an extensive set of rules of procedures to which street-level bureaucrats have to comply. Although this type of welfare administration is nowadays often regarded as an endangered species, it has proved to be remarkably persistent over time.[2]

Over the last three decades the NPM model of welfare

Table 12.1: Three models of welfare administration

	Participants	Practices	Processes
Bureaucratic	State agencies	Street-level bureaucrats apply procedures and rules	Nation state remains central actor
New Public Management	Private agencies and NGOs as contract partners	Street-level bureaucrats work to performance targets	Coordinating and controlling role for nation state
Governance	Networks of government, private agencies, NGOs and other actors	Street-level bureaucrats work with diverging interests	Simultaneous move to supranational and local level

administration has challenged the dominance of the bureaucratic model. It brings with it a different set of actors, including private or privatised agencies, or forces familiar actors such as NGOs into a different managerial role. It also leads to a different role for the nation state in processes of welfare administration. Instead of implementing policies, in this model the state is concerned with controlling and coordinating the contractual relations with different partners. Street-level bureaucrats are much more concerned with the compliance with performance targets than with the application of rules and procedures. This arrangement reinforces mechanisms of creaming and the construction of a moral image of 'deserving' and 'undeserving' clients.

Finally, sustainable network relations between a wide variety of public, private and non-profit actors characterise the governance model of welfare administration. In this model the street-level bureaucrat evolves into a case manager, whose main concern is to coordinate and mediate between the different actors that have relations with their clients. In this governance approach, the nation state loses its key position in the welfare administration to both the local and supranational level.

This rough distinction of three ideal-typical welfare administration models highlights the interconnectedness that exists between the analyses in our framework. In the following section, we further elaborate on the values of the framework that has been developed and applied in this volume.

Governance and governmentality

Although the *governance* of welfare has been a central organising focus of this book, Chapter Two of this collection argued that a Foucault-inspired *governmentality* framework provided a more critical and insightful analytic of contemporary welfare governance than the widely used governance framework. In this section we return to this perspective to ask what the observations of the book's chapters, which are summarised in the preceding section, might contribute to a governmentality analysis of contemporary welfare administration.

Political rationalities

Peter Miller and Nikolas Rose (1990) characterise governmentality as involving both 'political rationalities' and 'technologies of government'. In terms of this framework, the chapters of this book did not give significant direct attention to the 'political rationalities' of welfare administration. However, it was clear that their accounts of welfare administration are largely influenced by, if not embedded within, 'neo-liberal' discourses. As has been well analysed by governmentality scholars, neo-liberal discourses seek to minimise the activity of the state by 'governing at a distance' using market mechanisms of competition, incentives, expert advice, performance targets and so on (Miller, 1992; Rose, 1993; Dean, 1999, Ch. 8). These practices were evident throughout the chapters. New Public Management is entirely consistent with this broader rationality. However, the reality of contemporary welfare states is that neo-liberal rationalities coexist with other political rationalities – namely, neo-paternalism, communitarianism and consumerism – albeit sometimes in conflict, sometimes symbiotically. However, we must also be mindful that while liberalism is widely regarded as upholding the liberty of the free individual, liberalism also has a history of illiberal or authoritarian practices (Valverde, 1996; Hindess, 2001; Dean, 2002a). Liberty, it seems, is only appropriate for those who are capable of governing themselves. This mix of rationalities – rather than the unassailable dominance of neo-liberalism – and the complexity and tensions of working within them was particularly evident in the chapters by Howard (in relation to the exercise of professional discretion), Wright (in terms of the constitution of claimants as independent sovereign individuals) and Barnes (in terms of the competing demands of 'meeting needs' versus 'producing outcomes'). In short, despite widespread characterisation of contemporary welfare states as 'neo-liberal', the picture drawn from welfare administration at the street level is much more complex, contested and in flux.

In this complex political environment it is clear that the ascendancy of market imagery has been significantly complemented (or perhaps overshadowed) by a rationality of 'partnerships'. This is clearly evident in a majority of the chapters in this book. However, the nature of these partnerships varies from contractual purchaser–provider or outsourcing relationships to mutual collaborations among equals.

While neo-liberal political rationalities have sought to valorise non-state forms of governance, another political rationality implicit in various chapters was the valorisation of the local. Again this can be seen as resulting from a mix of neo-liberal and consumerist rationalities. The local becomes the place that is more flexible, more responsive and, therefore, more capable of providing individualised services (compare: Rose, 1996). This is clearly evident in Kazepov and Genova's chapter (Chapter Eleven) on the shifting out of activation policies to localities in Italy (and Europe more broadly). However, the findings of Kazepov and Genova echo Dean's (2002b) caution that the nature of political rationalities (and, indeed, their practices and effects) can not be read off from the stated aims and rationales provided by political actors. In this case, Kazepov and Genova highlight the likely exacerbation and solidification of regional inequalities resulting from the nature of localised activation policies in Italy.

Concomitant with a valorisation of the local is the rationality of 'risk' with its associated technology of 'targeting'. The rationality of risk has been well analysed using a governmentality framework (for example, O'Malley, 1996; Weir, 1996; Henman, 2004). Such authors have observed that welfare state policy has involved an individualisation of risk, whereby the former predilection for collectivised, insurantial risk has been displaced by 'prudential citizens' who are expected to take private actions to guard themselves against risks (compare: Kemshall, 2002). In this book, the deployment of risk discourses was not especially evident in relation to welfare clients. However, risk discourses can be seen as underlying practices by welfare staff. For example, 'creaming' the best unemployed persons for job placement while marginalising harder-to-place clients demonstrated risk calculations in managing welfare administration and performance targets (see the chapters by Barnes, Howard and Wright – Five, Seven and Eight). Howard's chapter also examines rationalities of risk in relation to managing benefit processing and decision making.

Finally, it is clear that rationalities of 'responsibility' and 'obligation' (for example, 'no rights without responsibilities') also underpinned much of the welfare reforms examined in Part Two of this book.

Technologies of government

Compared with 'political rationalities', 'technologies of government' were a more direct focus of chapters in this book. In particular, technologies of partnership and the mechanisms by which these are constituted were the specific object of examination in all the chapters of Parts One and Three. White's chapter (Chapter Eight), in particular, provides an insightful investigation of the specific governmental technology of partnership frameworks. Her analysis is particularly fruitful in demonstrating the governmental aspects of this technology in 'naming and framing' a new governmental space (that is, partnerships with NGOs).

In a similar manner, the chapter by Valadas (Chapter Ten) examines the European Union's (EU's) governmental technology of the Open Method of Coordination (OMC). Indeed, the OMC is both an intellectual technology (or rationale) and a policy instrument by which the EU can seek to introduce European-wide social policies that, at the same time, recognise regional and national variations and manifestations.

The OMC is an illustration of the proliferating governmental technologies of advanced liberalism that concurrently devolve and centralise power. They are the technologies through which governments can 'govern at a distance' or, in the words of the governance literature, 'steer, but not row'. Other technologies include the now widespread use of performance indicators and performance targets (see the chapters in Part Two). As Rose (1999) has argued, by simultaneously providing a space in which subjects can act but designating the particular ends and the levels of intensity, such technologies 'govern through our freedom'. Such practices constitute subjects – welfare staff, professionals, managers, agencies and claimants – in particular ways.

Subjects and subjectivities

Thus, a governmentality analysis of welfare reform also gives analytical attention to the way in which subjects and subjectivities are made. A number of chapters in this book demonstrated how contemporary practices of welfare administration operate to constitute different subjects and forms of subjectivity. In Chapter Eight, Wright examines the competing discourses and practices that shape welfare claimants. While consumerist and NPM rationalities have shifted to label claimants as 'customers', Wright demonstrates that the administrative technologies in play contest and destabilise this characterisation: unlike customers, claimants have little or no choice about welfare providers and the nature of the welfare contract they have with the state, and arguably they have little choice about where to obtain the financial resources with which to live. Furthermore, the elements of compulsion and poor-quality services also work to differently constitute welfare subjects. Wright also observes practices of resistance by welfare subjects seeking to subvert the subjectivities that governments and welfare professionals try and construct for them. Such street-level research provides a much-needed depth to governmental relations not evident in other governmentality analyses that emphasise the construction of welfare subjects of entrepreneurial individuals (Dean, 1995).

The chapters of this book also demonstrate that the subjects and subjectivities of welfare staff are being reconstituted by reforms in welfare policy and practice. The chapters by Barnes and Ramia (Five and Nine) clearly show how staff in NGOs have been reconstituted from voluntary to managerial/professional. In doing so, the rationale for their activity is radically altered, as too the pace of their work and the way in which they relate with their clients. Just as welfare clients have increasingly been constituted as entrepreneurial self-governing individuals responsible for their actions, so too are welfare staff, professionals and managers. Within this context, Howard and Wright (Chapters Seven and Eight) observe the conflicting demands, rationalities and objectives that welfare staff must manage in order to account for themselves, their actions and performance.

Another key area in the reconstitution of welfare staff is their shift from working within an organisation to network working. The development of partnerships between the state and NGOs, which is evident in much of this book, involves a new form of working; one in which the focus of external relationships and their ongoing management becomes a central focus of welfare staff. This is particularly evident in the chapter by Kazepov and Genova (Chapter Eleven) in their observation of the emergence of a new form of social worker, one whose role is to manage and coordinate the various welfare bodies required to support a client's activation activities.

As the above section has shown, this book has contributed considerable material towards a governmentality analysis and understanding of welfare state reform. We turn now to consider the directions for future research we would like to see.

The future of welfare state research

As the chapters of this book have shown, there are considerable insights to be learnt from studying the ways in which welfare policy reform is implemented and then administered over time. Such studies add significant depth to the numerous studies of welfare reform that focus on formal and substantive policy change. Most obviously, the work in the public administration discipline that examines transformations in state operations – in particular, research into NPM (or new managerialism) and the use of markets and partnerships in state governance – can be usefully joined with welfare policy research to understand the 'underside' of public policy. In doing so, these two bodies of research cover the two sides of the coin of welfare state activity: policy and administration. It is notable, however, that these two bodies of work have remained largely separate, and both tend to cast their analytical focus on formal changes in government, be it formal welfare policy or formal policy on public service administration.

As a consequence, both bodies of work tend to gloss over the more mundane organisational practices and procedures in welfare agencies that a distinguished history of street-level studies have shown to be extremely important in providing a more complete understanding of the operation and effect of the welfare state, especially as it relates to the experience of welfare claimants. Such detailed studies of the micro-processes of welfare bring to light the capillaries of power that form the very substance of the welfare state. It is these dynamics to which this book has given particular attention and which we believe is a highly fruitful, yet understudied area of research.

Policy co-production and street-level research

We therefore see studies of what we might call 'the production of policy' beyond formal policy decision making as a key direction in welfare state research. In this book, clear examples of such work include the street-level studies of Barnes, Handler, Howard and Wright, whose work builds on the path-breaking work of Handler and Hollingsworth (1971), Lipsky (1980), Mashaw (1983) and others. Given that governments have increasingly focused their policy attention on the construction and delivery of welfare services – as is particularly evident in the shift from welfare to workfare – it is surprising that more work of this sort has not been undertaken (exceptions include Brodkin, 2000; Lennon and Corbett, 2003; Handler, 2004; Herd et al, 2005; Saunders, 2005). We see several reasons for this.

First, street-level studies require significant time and financial resources to support researchers in the field to undertake ethnographic and interview studies. Policy research that takes a more macro-level view can be more readily obtained from published statistical research and published government documents on formal government policy. In contrast, street-level or micro-policy research requires detailed observation on the ground. Second, street-level studies require access to organisations, which may be difficult to obtain, particularly in a context whereby formerly independent NGOs are increasingly involved in the co-production and co-delivery of welfare policy and are now more sensitive to critical analysis due to government funding implications. Finally, we believe that our disciplinary frameworks for understanding policy have not served us well in conceptualising and analysing the nature and effects of welfare policy.

Reconceptualising policy production

Thus, a second key area for research is the reconceptualisation of policy production. Chapter Two by Henman examined the way in which policy and administration have been traditionally conceptualised as distinct and separate domains. In that chapter, the governmentality framework was advanced as a way in which to bridge this divide in conceptualising and analysing welfare reform.

We suggest that further conceptual and theoretical work needs to be done in advancing frameworks that understand policy production as a process that not only involves formal decision making by politicians, but also incorporates policy implementation and administration processes. We believe that a focus on policy production, as conceptualised in this manner, will greatly advance policy studies and our understanding of the nature and effects of welfare reform. Such conceptual work needs critical attention.

Dynamics of policy production

A focus on policy production in this broader sense sensitises the researcher to a range of dynamics that are traditionally overlooked in policy analysis focusing on formal policy. In particular, it points to practices of bureaucratic disentitlement (Lipsky, 1984) and the differing logics of bureaucratic justice (Mashaw, 1983).

Lipsky's classic work demonstrated the ways in which welfare claimants or potential claimants become effectively disentitled from welfare benefits and services, not by formal policy, but by administrative processes. The work in this book and other studies of workfare have shown the ways in which contemporary welfare practices disentitle (potential) claimants (for example, Herd et al, 2005). Practices include the continual emphasis on compliance and surveillance, difficult claims procedures, onerous ongoing activities to maintain compliance, stigmatisation, poor advertising/ communication of services and ambiguous accountability mechanisms.

To these processes, we might expect to observe an increasing disentitlement flowing from the greater use of complex quasi-market, purchaser–provider and partnership arrangements, particularly in a context of ongoing rapid policy and organisational change. While such arrangements are sometimes advocated for enhancing 'joined-up', one-stop-shop services in which claimants receive individualised service delivery, more often than not the result is a fragmentation of services in which potential and current claimants (who, on average, have lower educational, literacy and numeracy levels) become confused by the administrative processes and requirements. This is further exacerbated by the increasing speed of policy change and the greater level of complexity and targeting of policy made increasingly feasible by advanced information technologies (Henman, 1999). As a consequence, potential and actual claimants might be expected to have increasingly less knowledge of welfare benefits and services, to be less able to identify what they might be entitled to and less certain of the processes both for applying for those benefits and for exercising their appeal rights. These dynamics would clearly result in greater levels of bureaucratic disentitlement, the extent and changes of which are in great need of further research. Indeed, the development of a 'complexity index' – in which complexity levels could be measured alongside take-up, overpayment and appeal rates – would provide a significant development in this domain. Measures of public confusion about the welfare system would also be most welcome.

The issue of policy discretion

The related area of welfare appeals processes is also in need of urgent research attention. Just as bureaucratic processes may be observed to have effectively disentitled welfare claimants, so too it is important to examine whether there have been any changes in appeal processes that may undermine eligibility and receipt. For instance, in the name of efficiency, governments may have shifted some appeals from external umpires to internal reviews. Furthermore, the increasing use of non-governmental agencies to deliver government-funded services might be expected to reduce rights to appeal, and to destabilise the locus of accountability. What have been the recent changes in these domains, and how have they affected and redefined citizenship rights and levels of take-up? Moreover, what have been the changes in the forms of procedural justice operating in welfare systems? In this regard, Adler and Henman (2001, 2005a) recently examined the effects of computerisation in national social security systems on models of procedural justice. They discovered that computerisation tended to reduce the professional mode of procedural justice, while enhancing bureaucratic, managerial and market modes.

Chapter Seven by Howard highlights the way that there appears to be no clear trajectory in the operation of discretionary judgement to frontline welfare staff (compare: Sandfort, 2000; Bovens and Zouridis, 2002; Evans and Harris, 2004). On the one hand, new discourses of managerial autonomy and decentralisation coupled with consumerist discourses of individualised and flexible service delivery might suggest that discretionary judgement of street-level service providers might be maintained, or even broadened, under welfare reform. On the other hand, technological innovation in the form of computerised automation of decision-making processes, the goal of achieving legal clarity and accountability requirements for government-contracted welfare providers seem to press for reducing frontline discretion. Longer-term trajectories and the identification of cross-national patterns would be a highly fruitful direction of inquiry. In particular, such changes have clear implications for the nature of welfare work and the meaning of professional practice and professional autonomy (Dearman, 2005). Indeed, as was observed in the chapters of Barnes, Handler, Howard and Wright (Chapters Five to Eight), the increasing scope and depth of the use of performance statistics to monitor welfare staff (both individually and collectively) is constituting complex working environments in which professionals encounter difficult moral and ethical dilemmas in negotiating and managing the multitude and often conflicting requirements of government (and their own employers). These dynamics have significant implications for client service and social citizenship – such as the re-emergence of the deserving and undeserving poor (see Chapter Five by Barnes). We certainly need to get a much greater understanding of these complex dynamics in defining the lived experience of welfare workers and welfare claimants.

Information and communication technologies are now critical to the operation of the welfare state. Along with state and non-state agencies, welfare workers and claimants, ICTs are an essential partner in the co-production of welfare. The role of ICTs in the production of policy has not traditionally received much research attention. However, the advent of the Internet and the creation of 'e-government' have begun to stir some interest. Future research should advance our appreciation of the role of ICTs in welfare state processes. Understanding the way in which new ICTs help to reconfigure welfare administration, welfare practice and even welfare policy and political governance seems critical as ICTs further inextricably implicate themselves in our lives.

Research to date suggests that advanced ICTs have reinforced various political rationalities in generating greater levels of surveillance, increased targeting of 'at-risk' groups, heightened administrative and policy complexity, reduced frontline discretion and realised a 'new conditionality' (Henman, 1999, 2004, 2005a, 2005b, 2006: forthcoming; Bovens and Zouridis, 2002; McDonald et al, 2003). It is, however, important to avoid technology determinism, instead understanding the ways in which the interaction of technological innovation and social, policy and political contexts may lead to differing usages of ICTs for different ends. Indeed, Adler and Henman (2005b) identified that although computerisation in social security has tended to focus on financial objectives – such as cutting costs, increasing productivity and detecting fraud – there is evidence that some of the variations in the uses to which ICTs are put result from the nature of the welfare state regime in which computerisation takes place.

Comparative studies

It is clear that much can be learned from international comparative studies of welfare administration. The chapters in this book offer important initial insights. They also provide the basis for more systematic and in-depth comparative studies. In reference to the models of welfare administration outlined earlier in this chapter, welfare state research would benefit from identifying general shifts in the nature of welfare administration, understanding the links between welfare state policy regimes and welfare administration models, and assessing the extent to which there is any convergence or divergence between different states in their mode of welfare administration. We hope that comparative research of the administration of the welfare state can develop into an important academic enterprise in the same way that comparative studies of welfare state policies and expenditure have done in the past 20 years.

However, we are acutely aware of the dangers in deploying abstract models and categorisations, for they tend of overlook the heterogeneity within each welfare state. This may be particularly relevant in a context where localisation of welfare administration is likely to give rise to a range of administrative approaches within the one welfare state. Accordingly, we echo Kasza's caution in relation to research of welfare state regimes:

> Nonetheless, comparisons limited to one policy area such as health, pensions, or unemployment would reduce the variables in play in terms of the number and variety of policymakers, the principles underlying policy, and the mechanics of welfare provision. At the least, policy-specific research is a more promising avenue to explore for the purpose of devising explanatory comparative frameworks than is the global concept of welfare regimes, which simply cannot work without exaggerating the internal coherence of national welfare systems. (Kasza, 2002, p 284)

Practical versus formal citizenship

Drawing on research domains outlined above, we see studies of welfare administration providing a more nuanced understanding of contemporary social citizenship. It is now widely regarded that the shift from welfare to workfare designates a transformation of social citizenship based on rights to one on obligations (for example, Dwyer, 2004). Such a characterisation clearly follows from an analysis of welfare policy. However, does an analysis of the way in which welfare is administered tend to similarly reflect and thereby reinforce this view of contemporary social citizenship? Indeed, the apparent values of policy and practice may diverge. For example, new obligations on welfare clients may be accompanied with greatly expanded welfare services that empower and facilitate welfare subjects. Alternatively, workfare administration may operate coercively and punitively, in which little support is provided in helping welfare subjects make the transition to work. Studies of welfare policies tend to overlook these important complexities and street-level realities, which are essential in defining the lived experience of welfare subjects.

There are other complications in understanding contemporary reconfigurations of social citizenship. For example, developments in NPM and consumerism arguably puts greater emphasis on service delivery that is of good quality, responsive, flexible and individualised than previous bureaucratic modes of operation (for example, Yeatman, forthcoming). Understanding how these developments mesh with and operate alongside more traditional and less sensitive approaches is worthy of significant research effort.

Concurrently, technological developments are also greatly increasing the surveillance capacities of welfare states. Such practices play an important element in constituting the nature of social citizenship – particularly when increased surveillance is applied differentially through society. In this regard, we need to be conscious of the shift from human surveillance – in which welfare workers visited suspect claimants and worksites – to 'dataveillance' – in which our activities are monitored through our electronic data traces. What this means for social citizenship in general, and the nature of welfare citizenship in particular, is still unclear.[3]

Clearly there remains a highly fertile and largely understudied field relating to the implementation and ongoing administration of welfare policy. We hope that our small contribution has stimulated further study in this area. We excitedly look forward to seeing many more intellectual contributions in this dynamic domain.

Notes

[1] For a similar argument, see also Hindess (1998) and Jessop (1994).

[2] For a contemporary defence of bureaucracy, see du Gay (2000).

[3] See Fitzpatick (2000), Hudson (2003) and Hudson and Dornan (2003) for a debate about social citizenship in an electronic age.

References

Adler, M. and Henman, P. (2001) 'e-justice: a comparative study of computerization and procedural justice in social security', *International Review of Law, Computers & Technology*, vol 15, no 2, pp 195-212.

Adler, M. and Henman, P. (2005a) *Computerisation and e-government in social security: a comparative international study*, E-Government Research Report Series, Washington, DC: IBM Center for the Business of Government.

Adler, M. and Henman, P. (2005b) 'Computerising the welfare state: an international comparison of computerisation in social security', *Information, Communication and Society*, vol 8, no 3, pp 315-42.

Beck, U. (1992) *Risk society: Towards a new modernity*, London: Sage Publications.

Bovens, M. and Zouridis, S. (2002) 'From street-level to system-level bureaucracies: how information and communication technology is transforming administrative discretion and constitutional control', *Public Administration Review*, vol 62, no 2, pp 174-84.

Brodkin, E.Z. (2000) *Investigating policy's 'practical' meaning: Street-level research on welfare policy* (online), Working Paper No. 162, Chicago, IL: Joint Center for Poverty Research, available at:www.jcpr.org/

Castells, M. (2000) *The rise of the network* society (2nd edition), Oxford: Blackwell.

Clarke, J., Gewirtz, S. and McLaughlin, E. (eds) (2000) *New managerialism, new welfare?*, London: Sage Publications.

Clarke, J. and Newman, J. (1997) *The managerial state*, London: Sage Publications.

Considine, M. and Lewis, J.M. (2003) 'Networks and interactivity: making sense of front-line governance in the United Kingdom, the Netherlands and Australia', *Journal of European Public Policy*, vol 10, no 1, pp 46-58.

de la Porte, C. and Nanz, P. (2004) 'OMC – a deliberative-democratic mode of governance? The cases of employment and pensions', *Journal of European Public Policy*, vol 11, no 2, pp 267-88.

Dean, M. (1995) 'Governing the unemployed self in the active society', *Economy and Society*, vol 24, no 4, pp 559-83.

Dean, M. (1999) *Governmentality*, London: Sage Publications.

Dean, M. (2002a) 'Liberal government and authoritarianism', *Economy and Society*, vol 31, no 1, pp 37-61.

Dean, M. (2002b) 'Powers of life and death beyond governmentality', *Cultural Values*, vol 6, no 1-2, pp 119-38.

Dearman, P.R. (2005) 'Computerised information systems and professional autonomy: the record of social work', unpublished PhD thesis, Monash University, Victoria, Australia.

du Gay, P. (2000) *In praise of bureaucracy*, London: Sage Publications.

Dwyer, P. (2004) *Welfare rights and responsibilities: Contesting social citizenship*, Bristol: The Policy Press.

Esping-Andersen, G. (1990) *The three worlds of welfare capitalism*, Cambridge: Polity Press.

Evans, T. and Harris, J. (2004) 'Street-level bureaucracy, social work and the (exaggerated) death of discretion', *The British Journal of Social Work*, vol 34, no 6, pp 871-96.

Fitzpatrick, T. (2000) 'Critical cyberpolicy: network technologies, massless citizens, virtual rights', *Critical Social Policy*, vol 20, no 3, pp 375-407.

Handler, J. (2004) *Social citizenship and workfare in the United States and Western Europe: The paradox of inclusion*, Cambridge: Cambridge University Press.

Handler, J.F. and Hollingsworth, E.J. (1971) *The 'deserving poor': A study of welfare administration*, Chicago, IL: Markham.

Hemerijck, A. (2002) 'The self-transformation of the European social model(s)', in G. Esping-Andersen (ed) *Why we need a new welfare state*, Oxford: Oxford University Press, pp 173-213.

Henman, P. (1999) 'The bane and benefits of computers in Australia's Department of Social Security', *International Journal of Sociology and Social Policy*, vol 19, no 1-2, pp 101-29.

Henman, P. (2004) 'Targeted!: population segmentation, electronic surveillance and governing the unemployed in Australia', *International Sociology*, vol 19, no 2, pp 173-91.

Henman, P. (2005a) 'E-government, targeting and data profiling: policy and ethical issues of differential treatment', *Journal of E-government*, vol 2, no 1, pp 79-98.

Henman, P. (2005b) 'E-government, public policy and the growth of conditionality', paper presented at the European Conference on E-Government '05, University of Antwerp, Antwerp, Belgium, 16-17 June.

Henman, P. (forthcoming) 'Segmentation and conditionality: technological reconfigurations in social policy and social citizenship', in C. McDonald and G. Marston (ed) *Reframing social policy: A governmental approach*, Cheltenham: Edward Elgar.

Herd, D., Mitchell, A. and Lightman, E. (2005) 'Rituals of degradation: administration as policy in the Ontario Works Programme', *Social Policy and Administration*, vol 39, no 1, pp 65-79.

Hindess, B. (1998) 'Neo-liberalism and the national economy', in M. Dean and B. Hindess (eds) *Governing Australia*, Melbourne: Cambridge University Press, pp 210-26.

Hindess, B. (2001) 'The Liberal government of unfreedom', *Alternatives*, vol 26, no 2, pp 93-111.

Hudson, J. (2003) 'e-galitarianism? Social policy, the information society and the Third Way', *Critical Social Policy*, vol 23, no 2, pp 276-98.

Hudson, J. and Dornan, P. (2003) 'Welfare governance in the surveillance society', *Social Policy and Administration*, vol 37, no 5, pp 468-82.

Jessop, B. (1994) 'The transition to post-Fordism and the Schumpetarian workfare state', in R. Burrows and B. Loader (eds) *Towards a post-Fordist welfare state*, London: Routledge, pp 13-37.

Kasza, G.J. (2002) 'The illusion of welfare "regimes"', *Journal of Social Policy*, vol 31, no 2, pp 271-87.

Kemshall, H. (2002) *Risk, social policy and welfare*, Buckingham: Open University Press.

Lennon, M.C. and Corbett, T. (ed) (2003) *Policy into action: Implementation research and welfare reform*, Washington, DC: Urban Institute Press.

Lipsky, M. (1980) *Street-level bureaucracy*, New York, NY: Russell Sage Foundation.

Lipsky, M. (1984) 'Bureaucratic disentitlement in social welfare programs', *Social Service Review*, vol 58, pp 3-27.

McDonald, C., Marson, G. and Buckley, A. (2003) 'Risk technology in Australia: the role of the Job Seeker Classification Index in employment services', *Critical Social Policy*, vol 23, no 4, pp 498-525.

Mashaw, J.L. (1983) *Bureaucratic justice: Managing social security disability claims*, New Haven, CT: Yale University Press.

Miller, P. (1992) 'Accounting and objectivity: the invention of calculating selves and calculable spaces', *Annals of Scholarship*, vol 9, no 1/2, pp 61-86.

Miller, P. and Rose, N. (1990) 'Governing economic life', *Economy and Society*, vol 19, no 1, pp 1-31.

O'Malley, P. (1996) 'Risk and responsibility', in A. Barry, T. Osborne and N. Rose (ed) *Foucault and political reason*, London: UCL Press, pp 189-207.

Rose, N. (1993) 'Government, authority and expertise in advanced liberalism', *Economy and Society*, vol 22, no 3, pp 283-99.

Rose, N. (1996) 'Death of the social? Re-figuring the territory of government', *Economy and Society*, vol 25, no 3, pp 327-56.

Rose, N. (1999) *Powers of freedom*, Cambridge: Cambridge University Press.

Sandfort, J.R. (2000) 'Moving beyond discretion and outcomes: examining public management from the front lines of the welfare system', *Journal of Public Administration Research and Theory*, vol 10, no 4, pp 729-57.

Saunders, P. (ed) (2005) *Welfare to work in practice*, Aldershot: Ashgate.

Smith, S.R. and Lipsky, M. (1993) *Nonprofits for hire: The welfare state in the age of contracting*, Cambridge, MA: Harvard University Press.

Valverde, M. (1996) ' "Despotism" and ethical liberal governance', *Economy and Society*, vol 25, no 3, pp 357-72.

Weir, L. (1996) 'Recent developments in the government of pregnancy', *Economy and Society*, vol 25, no 3, pp 372-92.

Yeatman, A. (forthcoming) *The politics of individuality*, London: Routledge.

Index

T

U

V

W